AF386599

Tamuna Sirbiladze

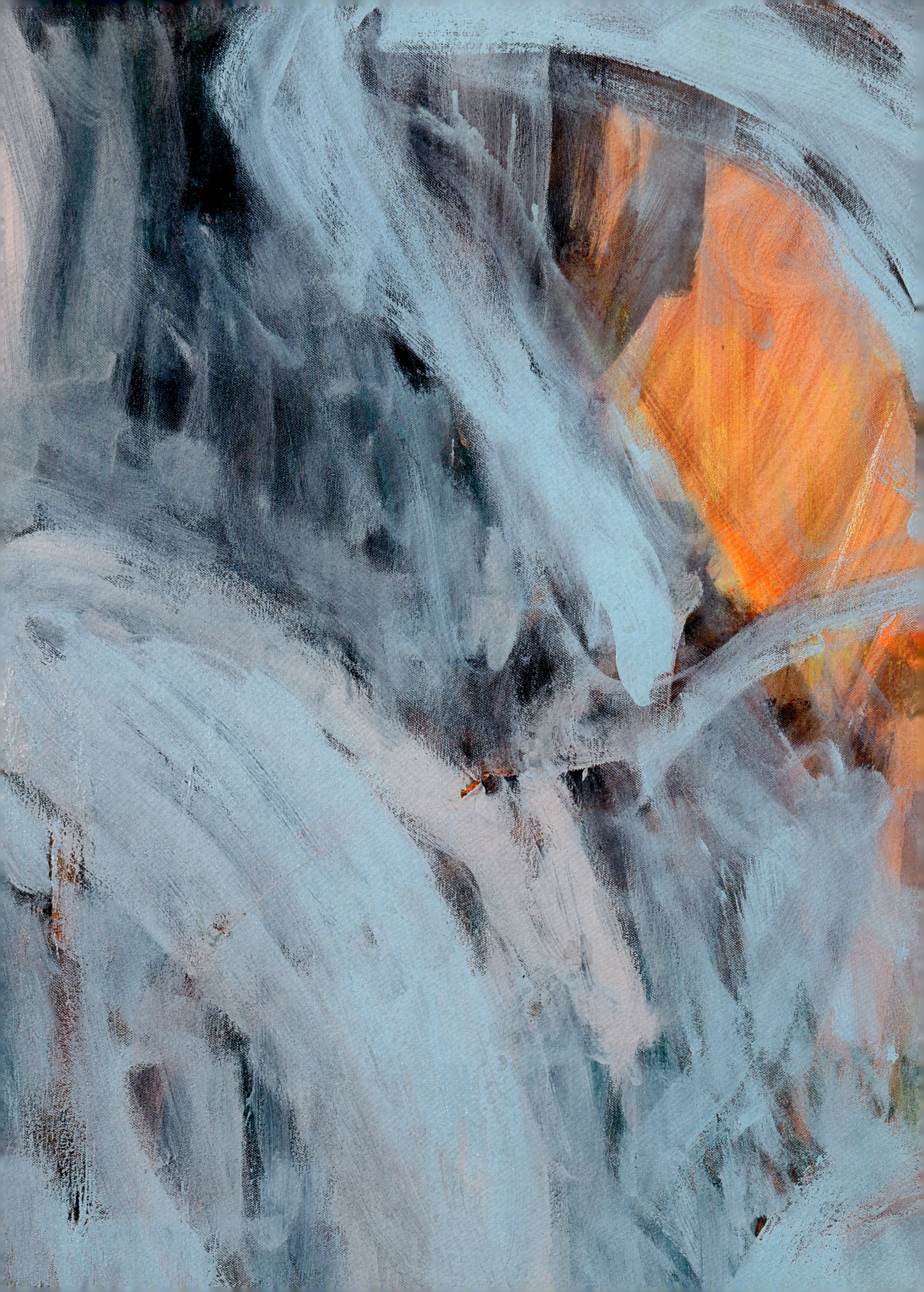

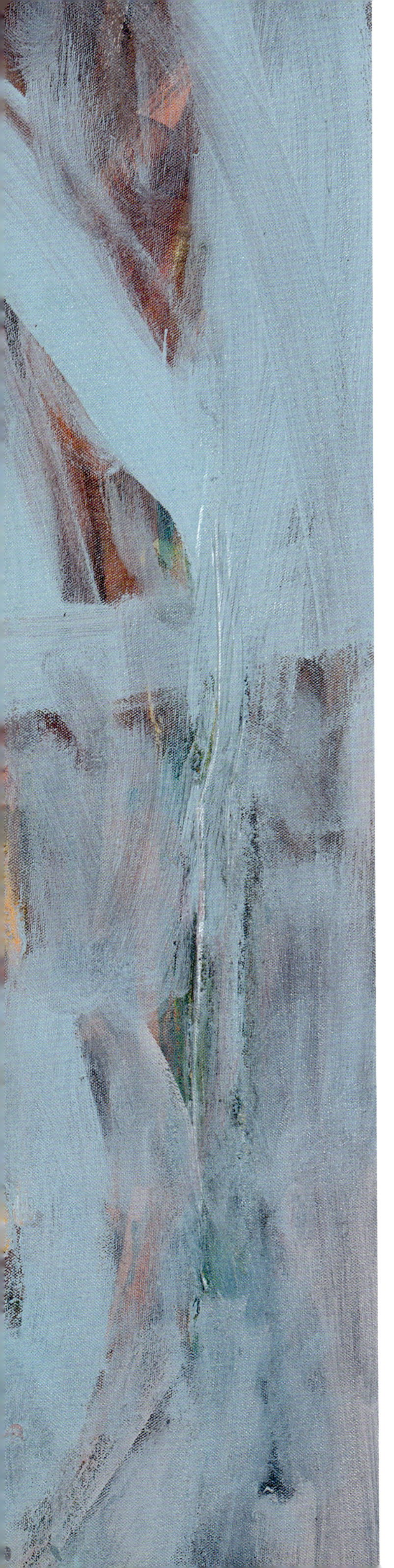

Tamuna Sirbiladze

David Zwirner Books

Kill all your darlings
Max Henry

In one form or another every painter's output is autobiographical. A necessary combination of physical stamina and mental acuity marks the progression of change. Embedded within the material results are the emotive rhythms of one's daily cycle. Expressed with cool analytic detachment or evidenced by sorrow and rage, these actions are a progression of weeks, months, and years accrued into an oeuvre. We get to know someone through her art, or rather, that articulate *otherness* that's unique to individual artistic temperament.

Tamuna Sirbiladze kept up a rigorous studio schedule; the paintings accumulated. She usually had several large, medium, and small formats going at once, without missing a beat. Everything came in bunches; her wacky color combos found their own logic, patterns developed. You couldn't categorize Tamuna as singularly abstract, though. Her interlocking shapes often embed anthropomorphic forms—surreal bodies, heads, eyes, as in *Andre's Breton* (2015; p. 24)—or incorporate still life objects, like the pomegranates in *They Made It Because of the Time* (2015; p. 34); all totally her own quirks. The 2015 exhibition *"good enough" is never good enough* was her first show at James Fuentes, New York. Some of the oil stick and pastel paintings were large-scale banners placed flat on the wall, others on the requisite stretcher. This choice selection of pictures was well edited and announced a seasoned artist.

Overcoming the limitations of the stretcher while working within its parameters is a considerable task facing the contemporary painter. Undaunted, Tamuna tackled it with an insouciant attitude towards rigid formalism. She leaned groups of paintings on the wall that you could sort through like posters on a rack. Her site-specific interventions dispensed with conventional painting installations, whether made directly on walls overlaid with standard raw-canvas works or in cube structures adorned with staccato mark-making. In a 2012 solo show, *Naked Ground*, at Galerie Lisa Ruyter, she took command of the space by installing floor-to-ceiling canvases among the rooms. A couple of canvases totally covered the big windows while still allowing natural light to seep through.

For Tamuna, painting was continually morphing, sometimes aggressive agit-prop, unpolished for the mere sake of aesthetic pleasure. Her method of installation emphasized a site-specific (if idiosyncratic) overall approach to exhibition-making. Painting was its center, expanding and contracting when presented flat on a wall, or as a three-dimensional shelter/refuge utilized as scaffolding to incorporate other artists' works on and around it. This was her way to defy the bourgeois conventions of painting display. Hence the "cube" paintings hint at a dilemma about the consumerist white cube by offering us a box within the standard rectilinear gallery; truthfully, she wasn't against the market so much as she was against catering to its trends and easy sell.

In the studio, Tamuna was often full of surprises, some of which I couldn't quite reconcile as she experimented with numerous forms. Many were delightful oddities that seemed to be one-offs she couldn't help but produce, perhaps alleviating the intensity of finishing a new series with deadlines for shows fast approaching. Among my personal favorites is the enigmatic *White Columns* (2011; p. 64–65), a sizable (two-by-three-meter) horizontal picture. The two vertical columns of said title appear like stacked, asymmetrical vessels about to topple. Composed of neutral gray, off-white, and pastel shades of pink and yellow, the background's rough patchwork of tonal variation emits the stillness found in a Giorgio Morandi still life. Here she captured the silence of a noble room/space set in an undated time-vacuum.

The artist who hits her stride in the studio is by will creating a potent symbol of her existence. It's evident when the work gets exhibited posthumously, and gives credence to the hypothesis about the aura of the art object. Abstract gestures enhanced Tamuna's improvisatory expression while elements of representation and the figure gave her grounding. From her early formative days in Tbilisi, classical underpinnings and the Byzantine remain "hidden" in her work. A figurative series she titled *V Collection* (2012) contains details of iconic paintings she loved and appropriated from the collection of the Kunsthistorisches Museum Wien. A salon hang of several small to mid-size canvases adorned the walls. Caravaggio, Giotto, Raphael, Velázquez: the titans of the canon were her muses and accomplices in cropped paintings that each retain a corresponding resonance with the original. Raphael's *Portrait of Cardinal Alessandro Farnese* has an especially compelling presence, with its bold and shadowy red garment, skullcap, and ground. This is a man who ascended to the papal throne after the fall of Rome in 1527— during tumultuous times. He looks askance, as if he's about to reprimand a subordinate. The eyes project the intrigue of the persona in this distillation, which destroys Raphael's portrait of the cardinal whilst remaining true to its essence of power and intrigue.

"In writing, you must kill all your darlings," said the American author and Nobel Laureate William Faulkner. This quote most certainly applies to the painter's trade that encompassed Tamuna's very productive last few years. A close-up of Caravaggio's cardsharp picture makes for a good example in assessing the creator-destroyer myth of all painters. The chiaroscuro of the baroque master is employed but conjured out of more rudimentary details. The moral of the enduring story is altered from one of urban deception to a metaphor on the fate of the cardholder. The naïveté of the sitter becomes Tamuna's own pure folktale as told through the jagged lines, traditional color, and ungainly (akin to outsider art) anatomical composition.

In the breadth of life and art, Tamuna Sirbiladze played her personal cards well. She "killed" all her darlings in direct pursuit of that cognitive life force between chance and penultimate fate. Those who encountered her understood she was a force of personality, and heroically stoic to the end. With these thoughts in mind, I'll conclude with the wise words of the Aztec King Cacamatzin:

> Who in the end is spared from leaving, despite his gold and all his jade
> Is everyone not bound to go there
> Am I a shield of turquoise, a stone set in mosaic
> Will I ever walk this earth again
> Will they shroud me in fine mantels
> Here on earth I think of those who ruled before me
> As the place of sounding drums draws near.

When it comes to the point, what I'm doing now is almost something like revenge…

Benedikt Ledebur in conversation with Tamuna Sirbiladze

BL   Let's begin by talking about what won't be seen in the book, that is, about your video works and in what context they stand to your other works. When did you begin shooting videos?

TS   When I was given a camera, that was 2001. I had actually never thought about film. When I was sixteen I already had quite clear ideas about what art interested me, and it was neither film nor video. For me film meant a means of entertainment. I liked the heavy, black films, like Pasolini and Godard. I went to the cinema in Tbilisi, Georgia, that showed these special, quality cinematographic films, like the Filmmuseum here in Vienna. It was called the Domkino.

BL   When you came to Vienna, did experimental films also interest you—for example, what Kubelka did, or the films documenting the Aktionists, Kurt Kren's films, etc.?

TS   What I saw impressed me very much as actions, also shocked me, but it didn't suggest film to me as a medium for my own artistic work. It was really like I said—it was only when I got the camera that I also began to explore these possibilities. Firstly, I started to film something or other totally mechanically, everything that interested me, that was happening around me. At the time I was traveling a lot and then I filmed everything, for example the view from the taxi of the skyscrapers in New York or whatever. Of course, that still had no artistic value, but I trained myself as an observer. If you want to make art you don't need a lot of technical support at the outset. At the time, pencil and paper was enough for me, with film or video it's somewhat different.

BL   How did video then develop for you as a means of artistic presentation? What do you show in the videos that can now be seen in your exhibitions? I don't yet know them. Could we watch something, and do you want to show videos at the exhibition at the Wittgenstein house?

TS   No, I won't show anything—I mean at the Wittgenstein house; for you, yes—because I prefer to show my latest pictures at the *Ficker* exhibition. My film works are not really video works, they are the expanded footnotes to my work processes and my work situation. I use the videos as documentation and I mostly work with film when I don't have my studio available.

[*We watch two videos. In the first one—the subject is the visit of the American president to Tbilisi—the picture is divided. On one side we see folklore dances on a stage in the street taking place in the president's honor; on the other side we see how the politicians, Bush and Saakashvili, move—the ritual of greeting; rhythmic (Bush) and unrhythmic (Saakashvili) clapping along with the dances; how they allow themselves to be photographed with the dancers, shaking hands and so on. The second video shows a public event in Rome, an experimental duet improvising on a keyboard and a drum set to Tamuna's picture* Benedetta al Mare *that schematically shows a half-naked swimming woman from above, her head at the lower edge of the picture.*]

BL   With the videos you have the feeling that it's about more than only a documentary, which with regard to "objective presentation" would also be just as debatable. With the first one, because of the juxtaposition of dancing and political dancing, there's the temptation to assume something like a political statement. With the second, because of the length of the video but also because of the way it's filmed, with very quick camera movements and changes of focus, it immediately comes to mind that the impression of being unprocessed and of arbitrary camerawork is consciously being evoked, so a particular aesthetic is preferred.

TS   That's right. In the second video the camera almost follows the rhythm of the music. I really try to leave the raw material itself unprocessed. I do edit and select but I don't rework the material. I try to show only the impression of the subject matter itself, as it presents itself in the camera setting. What I don't like at all with videos is special effects made thanks to high-tech post-processing, for example three-dimensional effects, distortions, oversizing, all those King Kong jokes aimed at a mass public, the synthetic makeup intended to make the films more impressive. Then people are more interested in how it's made than in the subject matter itself. I'm interested in what the subject matter means to me in itself.

BL   What you're saying here about your criteria when you're filming also seems to have something to say about your decisions while painting. It's noticeable in your pictures that you don't look for perspective effects. On the contrary, it often seems you want to emphasize the two-dimensionality of the canvas through the apparition-like nature of your figures. And the lines, for example in the worked-in geometrical patterns that could serve to lead into a perspective, serve you much more to isolate the pattern in the picture space. They rather have the effect of foreign bodies. Of course, the "raw material" that you look for when painting must lie somewhere else. Where is it located? Do you want to suggest a kind of spontaneity?

TS   What now shows itself in my pictures are figures from my imagination which, as such, I want to leave as unworked as possible. Naturally, they are not pure visions or fantasy figures, but nourish themselves from external impressions that have established themselves in me. So they almost stand before my eyes before I paint them.

BL   As imaginary pictures that are difficult to locate? Like your lines that border the figures, they also have something abstract. On the other hand, your washy coloring has something picturesque, emphasizing the fluidity that appears to symbolize the characteristics of imaginary pictures rather than portray them as realistic. Do you see your pictures as representations?

TS   They do have a basis. They are founded on basic concepts or prior decisions, like it always is with naked or half-naked women's bodies—mostly they have something else on, like socks. In China people who still have their socks on are not regarded as naked. In some cultures the legs are most taboo. For a long time I was only interested in abstract painting, in color theories, in the structure of paint on canvas, in "expressive" brushstrokes and so on. They were almost experiments, the quest for a "transcendental" color. I believe in these things. But at some point it became routine, I got into a kind of circular motion that bored me. At the age of twenty I could still connect feelings with pure color and it satisfied me. Then eventually the result couldn't satisfy me anymore, even when it was technically successful and fulfilled my original criteria. Later I didn't even manage the technical side of things; two years after my arrival in Vienna I completely stopped painting and began, for example, as we talked about, with filming.

BL   Beforehand, in the studio, you showed me a couple of older pictures, with writing, with words in the picture. Did you make these pictures after you turned away from abstract expressionism?

TS   Yes, at that time I was looking for something for my art, and I also played around with the computer a lot. I came across the Google search engine. Then I simply put in words like "housewife" or "sublime," and when you clicked on the "images" button you got pictures about these words or about their meaning. I then painted new pictures from various elements of these pictures. Sometimes the search words were the titles of my pictures, sometimes only the search words appeared on white canvas, for example "sublime" with a painted-red frame.

BL   Was that a series? How long did you do that for?

TS   About forty pictures over two years. Then I photographed the pictures and put them on my website. They still exist there, my gift back to the internet.

BL   Let's talk about your current pictures. You've already said that you mainly paint women's bodies, in intimate or private activities such as washing on the toilet. Situations in which they are not normally portrayed; sometimes the situation also appears unpleasant, dislocated, like the picture where the woman figure is standing on a washbasin with one leg pointing upwards. The red paint running from the tap brings up the association with blood. Or what about the bright figure in front of a dark background with a yellow spot in the upper part of the picture?

TS   That's a light bulb. For me these women figures are all very light and joyful, full of zest for life and fun. Maybe women understand me better there than men, as it seems to me just now. When it's a question of women, men easily project their ideas or desires onto something that's presented in a different way. Art is anyway generally dominated by men, and to be an artist as a woman always means tough competition. I also thought this with my prior decision to mainly depict women's bodies in my pictures. A lot of artists insist on putting men on their canvases, they ignore the figure of the opposite sex. I'm not criticizing that, it's simply a fact. But when it comes to the point, what I'm doing now is almost something like revenge. I don't think that I'm already so important that it has an effect, but it's an answer to the completely male history of art. I really once searched for women figures in contemporary artists' work and didn't find a single one. Apparently only the male world exists for these men!

BL   Competition itself is often seen as such a male principle that our society forces women to submit to if they want to count for something. You raise two issues that we can follow up on: the depiction of women in art and women as artists. My disposition to see something full of suffering in representational portrayal can, if anything, probably be explained by my Catholic origin, which is of course also heavily burdened in relation to the role of women. How do you relate to other women artists? For example, what do Cindy Sherman or Valie Export, who have taken on the role of women in art as a subject, mean to you?

TS   They have nothing to do with my art. It's almost a tragedy—for me men as artists were always more important and more interesting, not least because I wanted to fight against their influence. A reverse effect often happens, feminists talk so much about men that men gain in importance again because of it.

BL   Let's talk more about women. Women as artists have been the exception in art history. In the Renaissance, when strong, socially influential women were courted and there were women patrons and art collectors, as a woman painter only Sofonisba Anguissola comes to mind. Besides her self-portraits she mainly painted women. And think of the depictions of women in biblical scenes—Susanna at the bath. But not only woman as erotic object of male desire, but also idealized as Venus or in the many pictures of the Virgin Mary. So maybe you're right about the lack of depictions of women in comparison to men in today's art scene. Instead, there are now more female artists who often experiment with self-portrayal.

TS   Either they portray themselves, like Elke Krystufek, or they portray themselves indirectly, like Tracey Emin—who even if they don't show themselves, always circle around themselves. Then Emin shows her bed with all her private things, dirty sheets, like she's the victim of men. She became a kind of pop star or celebrity because she only told about herself and her misfortune, her difficult childhood, and so on. That's also a way to become famous. I want to depict women but in a more general way, not fixated on myself and also not only on women. What I am now showing at the Wittgenstein house is a series, a kind of research project, but I don't want myself to become the counterpart of those artists for whom only the male world exists. As far as the depictions of women you mentioned before are concerned, think of what situations they are mostly pictured in. In Vermeer they are only allowed to open letters, they probably can't read at all; or in Daumier they are allowed to yawn while they're doing the ironing. Or in Millet, the poor, bent-over women with two or three dirty children. In these cases there are no men to be seen, of course. Toulouse-Lautrec then depicts them as courtesans. Degas shows them at least in the better position of ballet dancers. They are all objects of the desiring, male gaze. With female philosophers it will be about the same as with female artists, but Wittgenstein at least built the house in which we're exhibiting for his sister.

BL   Perhaps you would now like to go into more detail about what earlier you called your "prior decisions"? We can combine it with you talking about one or more of your pictures. There's this picture where a woman is depicted in profile and from a red container in the upper right-hand corner a red hose leads to her behind.

TS   That's a very nice pink enema. And this picture also has perspectival depth, which, as you remarked, isn't there in the other pictures.

BL   Is there a special reason for you choosing to depict an enema?

TS   No special one. On the one hand the point is that something is being washed out, something comes in from outside and something comes out again. Naturally that is also intended to say something allegorical. And I try to transform the bathroom in my house in the picture.

BL   With the shortened perspective, the space appears to collapse in on itself. Most of your pictures have a title. This one too?

TS   It's simply called *Klistier* [*Enema*]. It will soon be shown at the Albertina in the Mozart exhibition, along with another picture that's called *Kotzen* [*Puking*].

BL   But puking can't now also be considered a pleasurable situation!

TS   It can, it's totally funny, meant comically. The title already has something of a joke about it.

BL   Good. Being sick can be the consequence of a successful evening when too much was drunk. There's another picture, I think it's called *Picknick mit Drogen* [*Picnic with Drugs*]. What drugs?

TS   Happy-makers and antidepressants. The picnic takes place in bed between pillows, so once again it's something that normally happens outside and has been moved inside.

BL   So what look like domino pieces are in fact tablet packages. And a mouse-like animal is coming across the bedspread. What's that?

TS   It's a fart, the result of the happy-makers. But careful, if we go on talking like this, people will think we're stoned. What kind of animal did you think? A snake?

BL   A mouse.

TS   But then what's that long thing there?

BL   Its tail.

TS   It's aliens that I depict, or a cross between aliens and people. Freaks, in fact. And they can also have a tail. But I like the fact that people can interpret things into my pictures. As an artist I don't want to control what the representation will be seen as. Beforehand you spoke about this watercolor effect. The pictures are also very airy, they have no weight in their presentation, they're not concrete, heavy material. The pictures can be seen in the attitude of "bad painting," but only as one aspect. At the same time, the colors are very light, with an impressionistic cheerfulness. Anyway, my pictures should be flexible.

This conversation took place on January 13, 2006.

Oil sticks

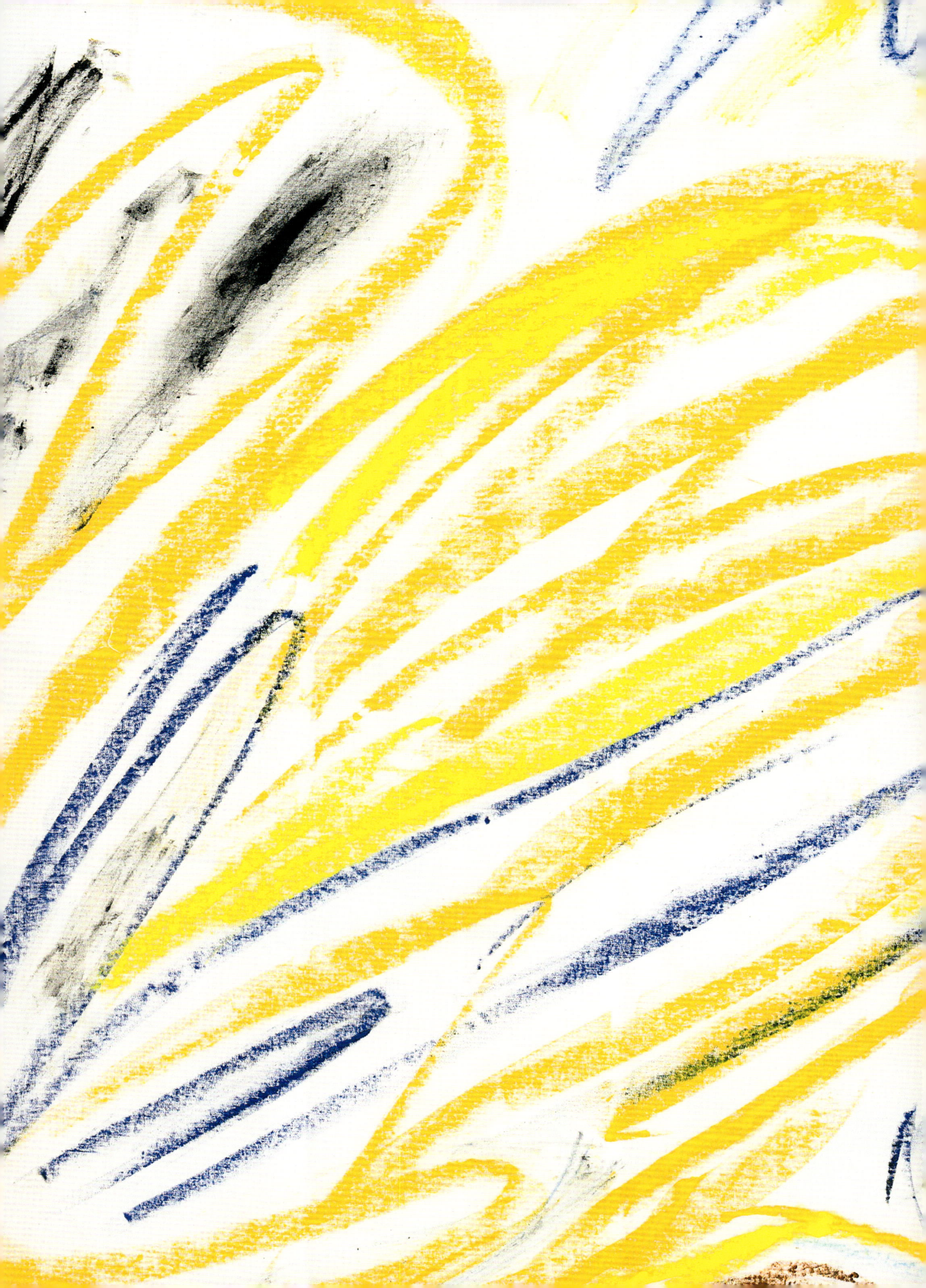

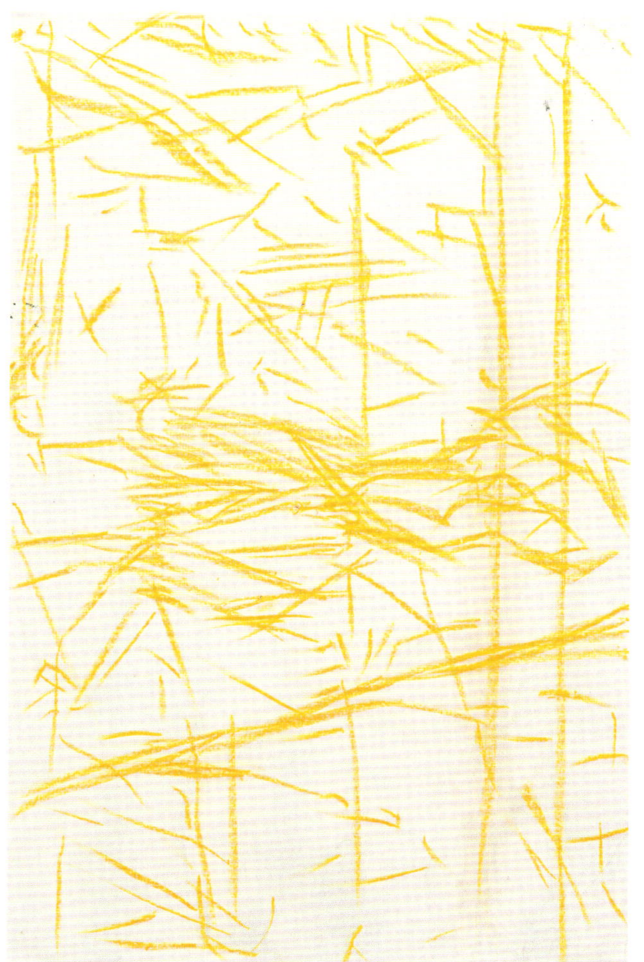 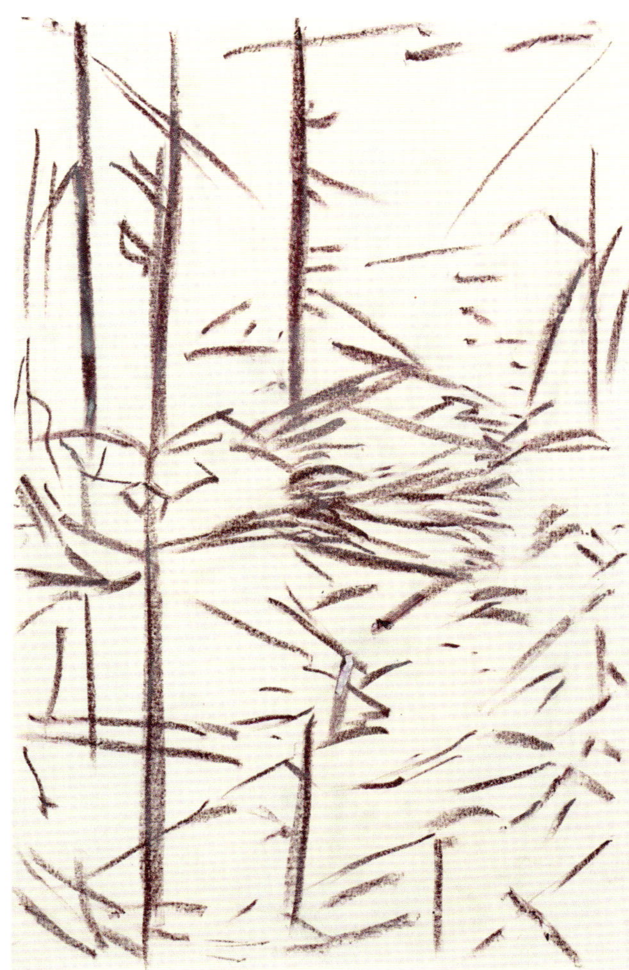

Fold, 2015
oil stick on canvas, 59 × 39 ⅜ inches | 150 × 100 cm

Violett Wrinkle of Deleuze, 2015
oil stick on canvas, 59 × 39 ⅜ inches | 150 × 100 cm

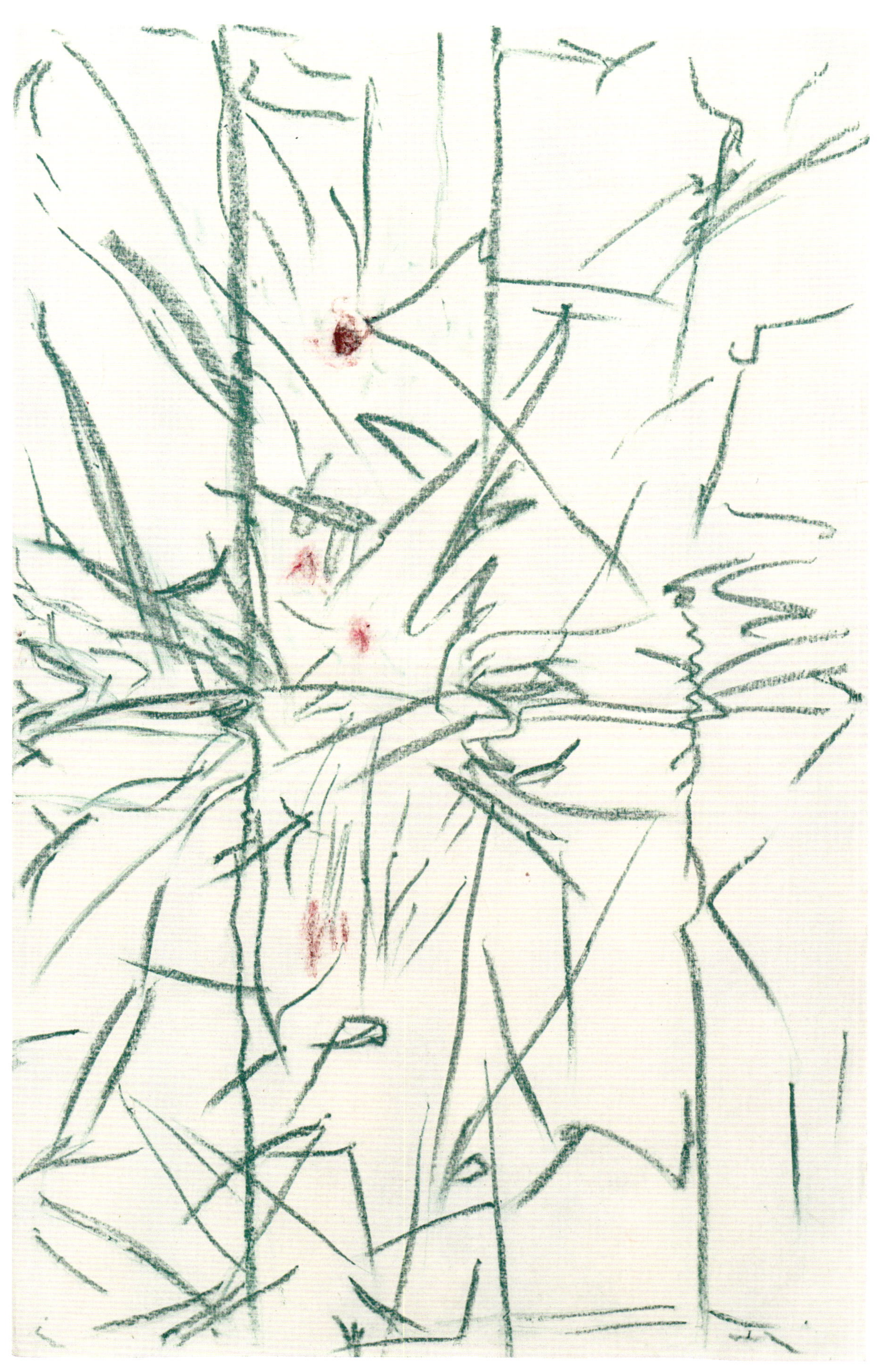

Greengrass, 2015
oil stick on canvas, 59 ⅞ × 38 ⅝ inches | 152 × 98 cm

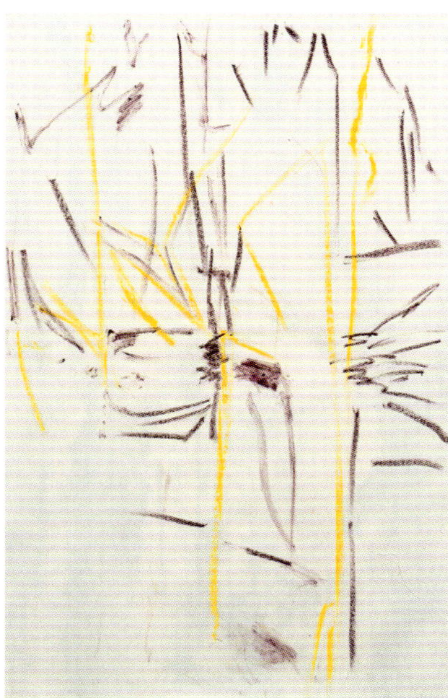

Fold, 2015
oil stick on canvas, 59 × 39 ⅜ inches | 150 × 100 cm

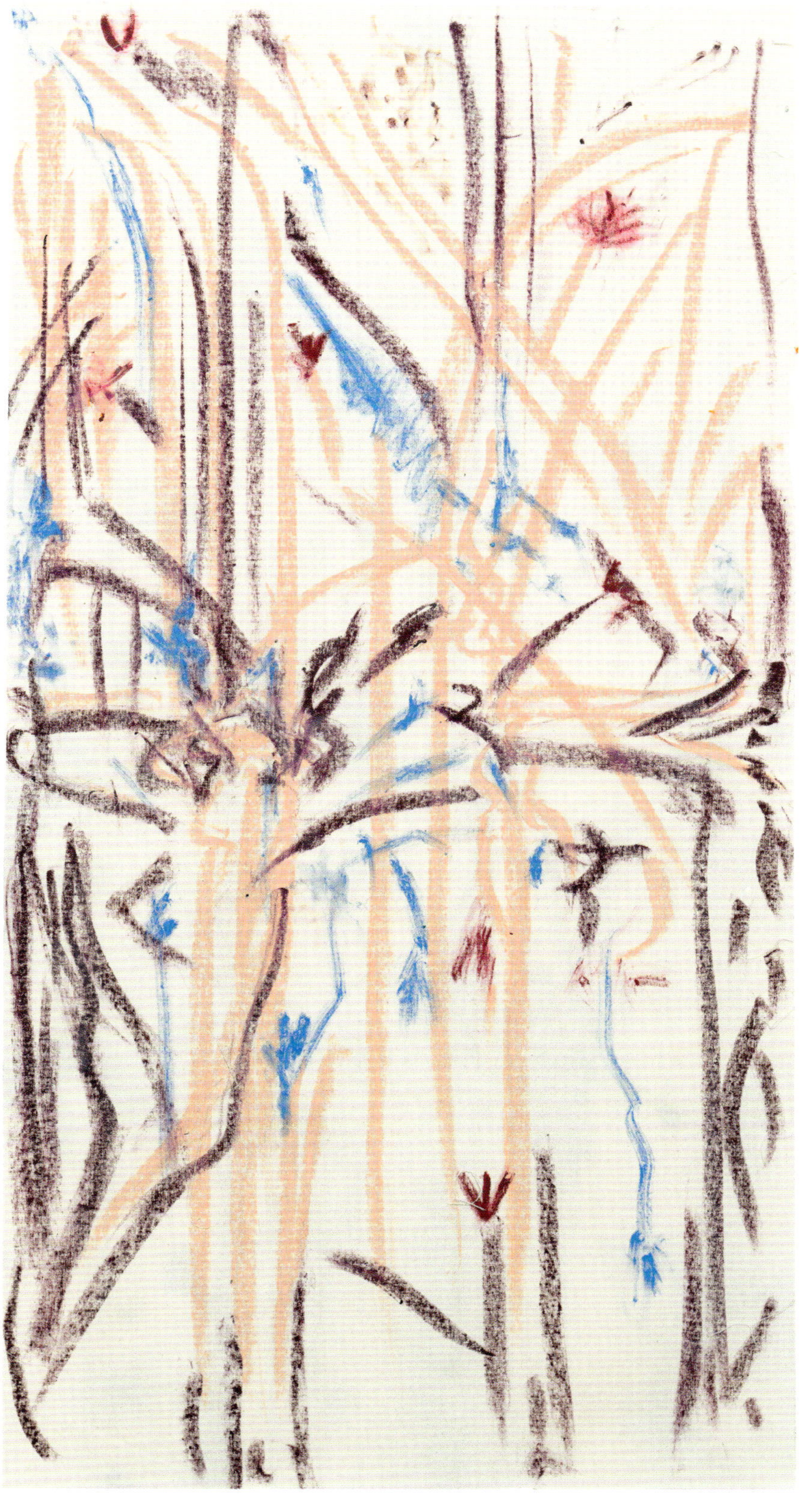

Fold, 2015
oil stick on canvas, 58 ¼ × 31 ⅛ inches | 148 × 79 cm

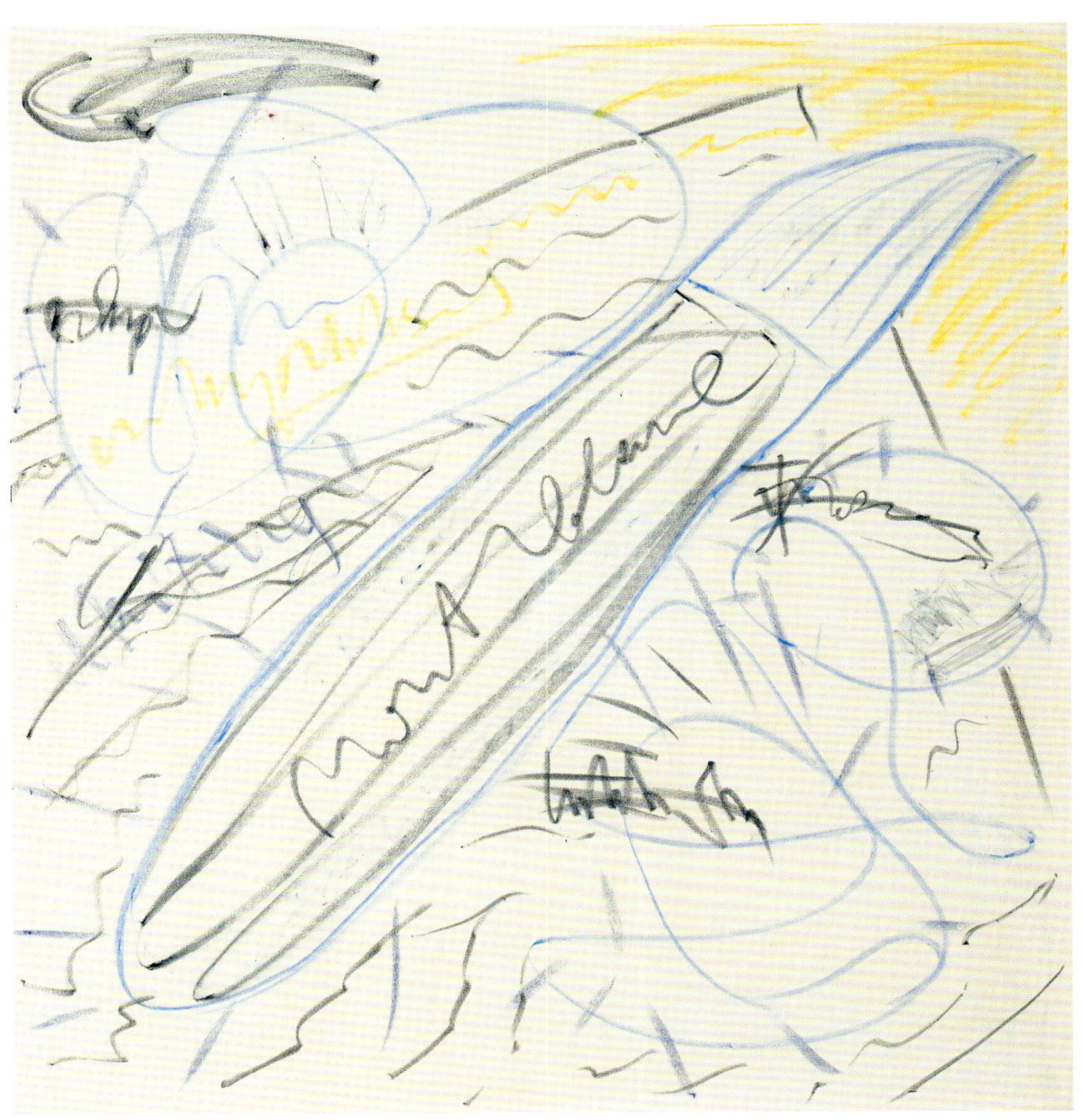

Montblanc, 2015
oil stick on canvas, 78 ¾ × 78 ¾ inches | 200 × 200 cm

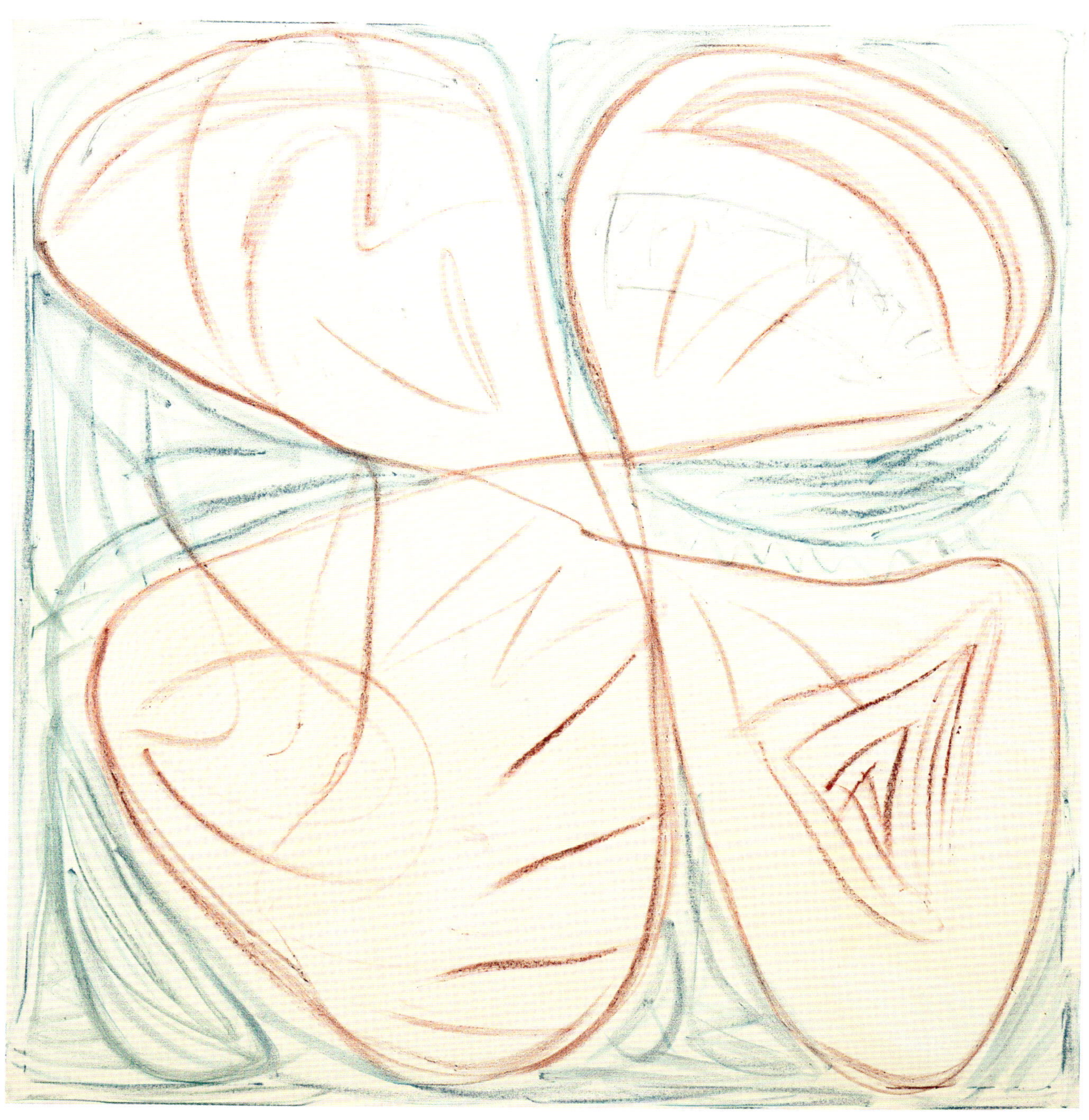

Four-leave Clover, 2015
oil stick on canvas, 78 ¾ × 78 ¾ inches | 200 × 200 cm

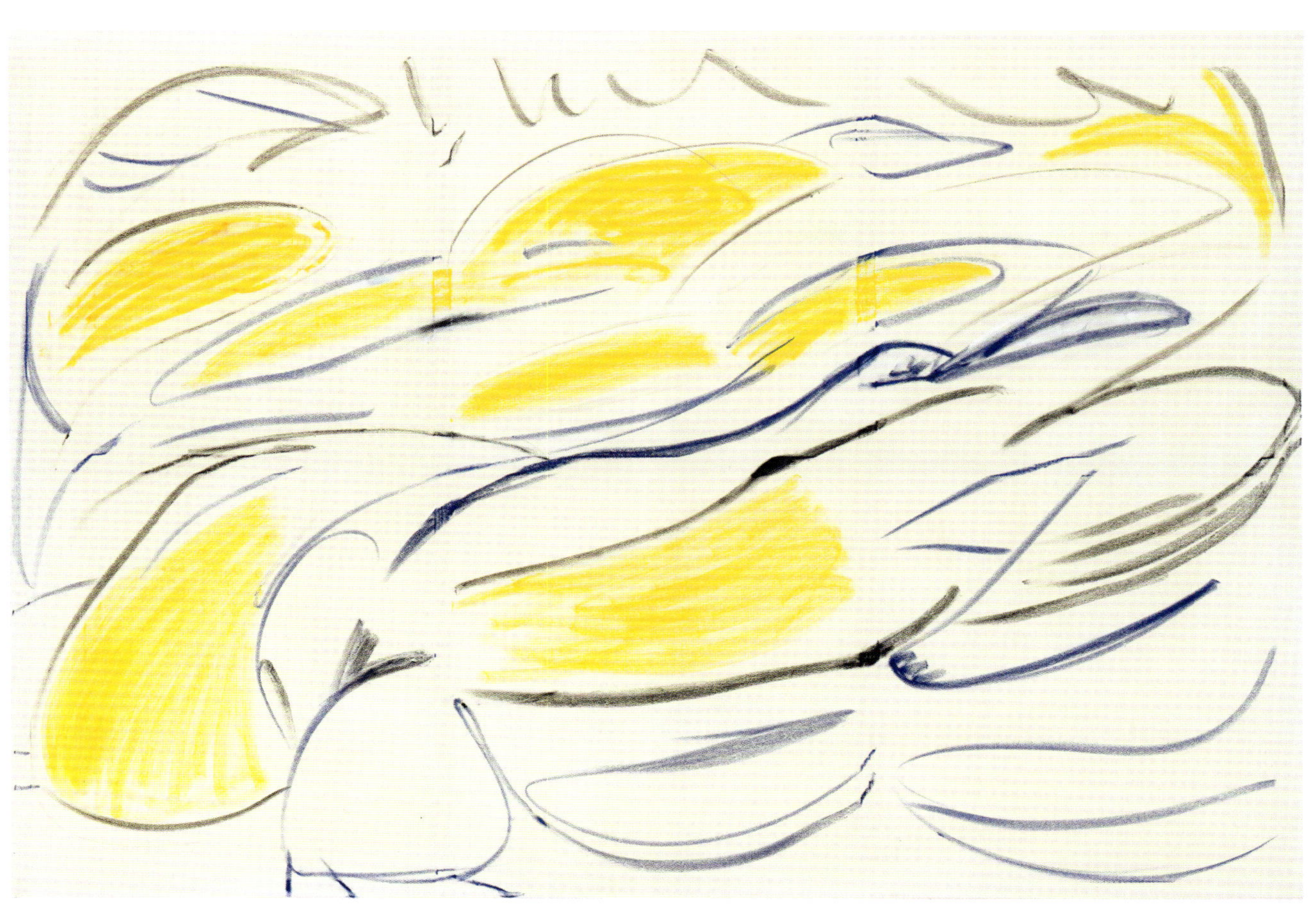

Breaking the Waves, 2015
oil stick and pastel on canvas, 76 ¾ × 114 ⅛ inches | 195 × 290 cm

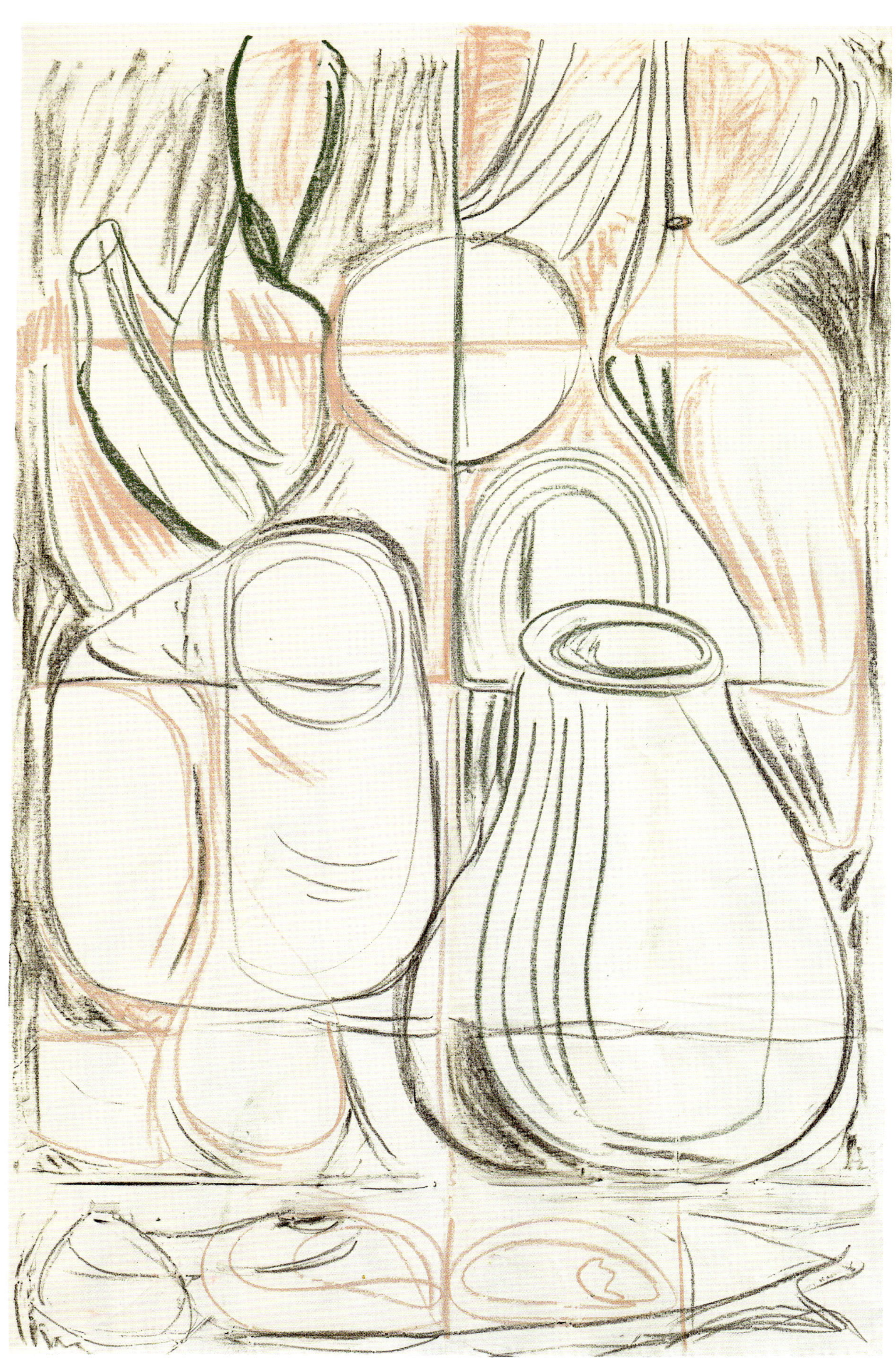

Still Alive, 2011
oil stick on canvas, 118 ⅛ × 78 ¾ inches | 300 × 200 cm

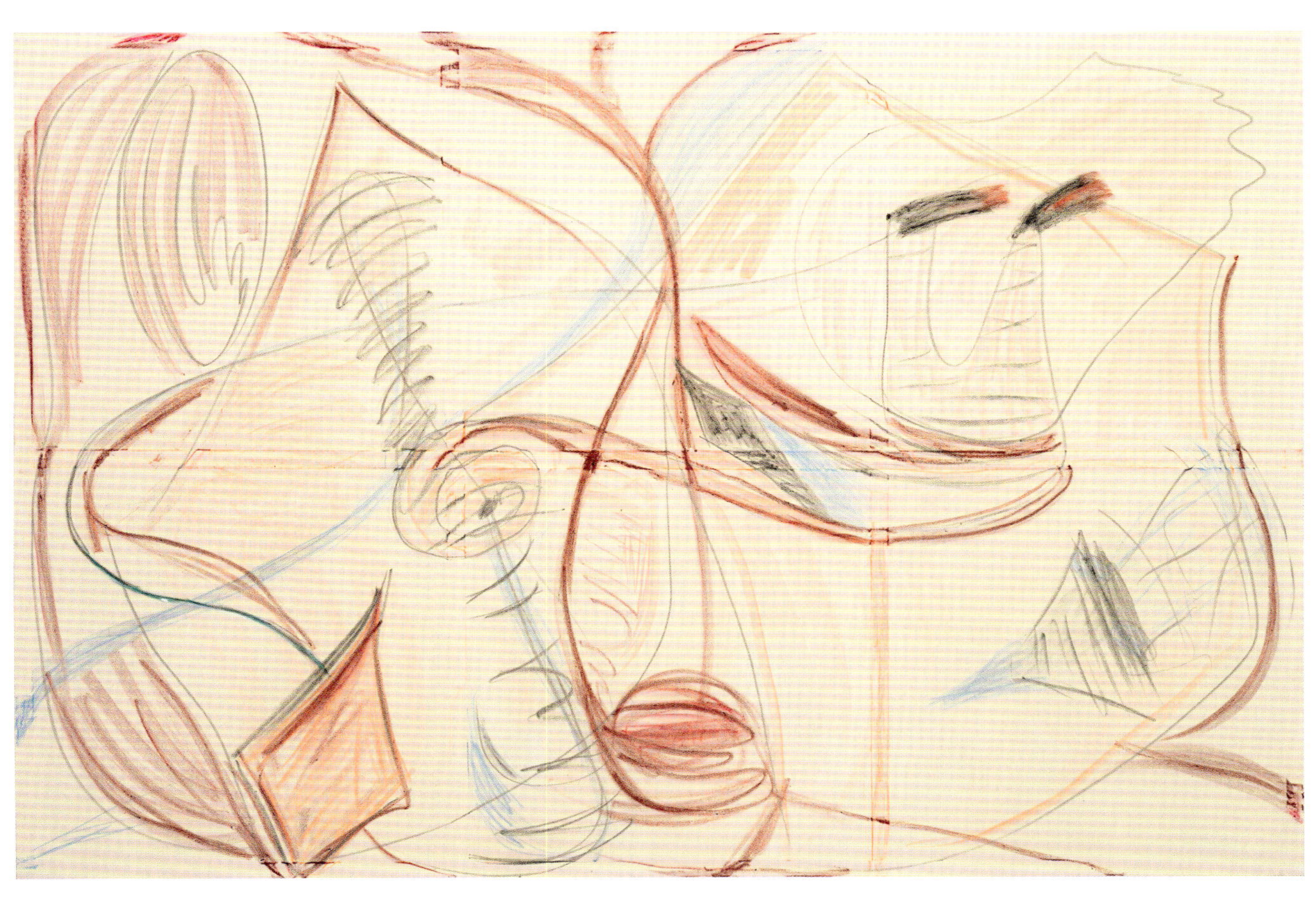

Sound of Silence, 2015
oil stick and pastel on raw canvas, 78 ¾ × 118 ⅛ inches | 200 × 300 cm

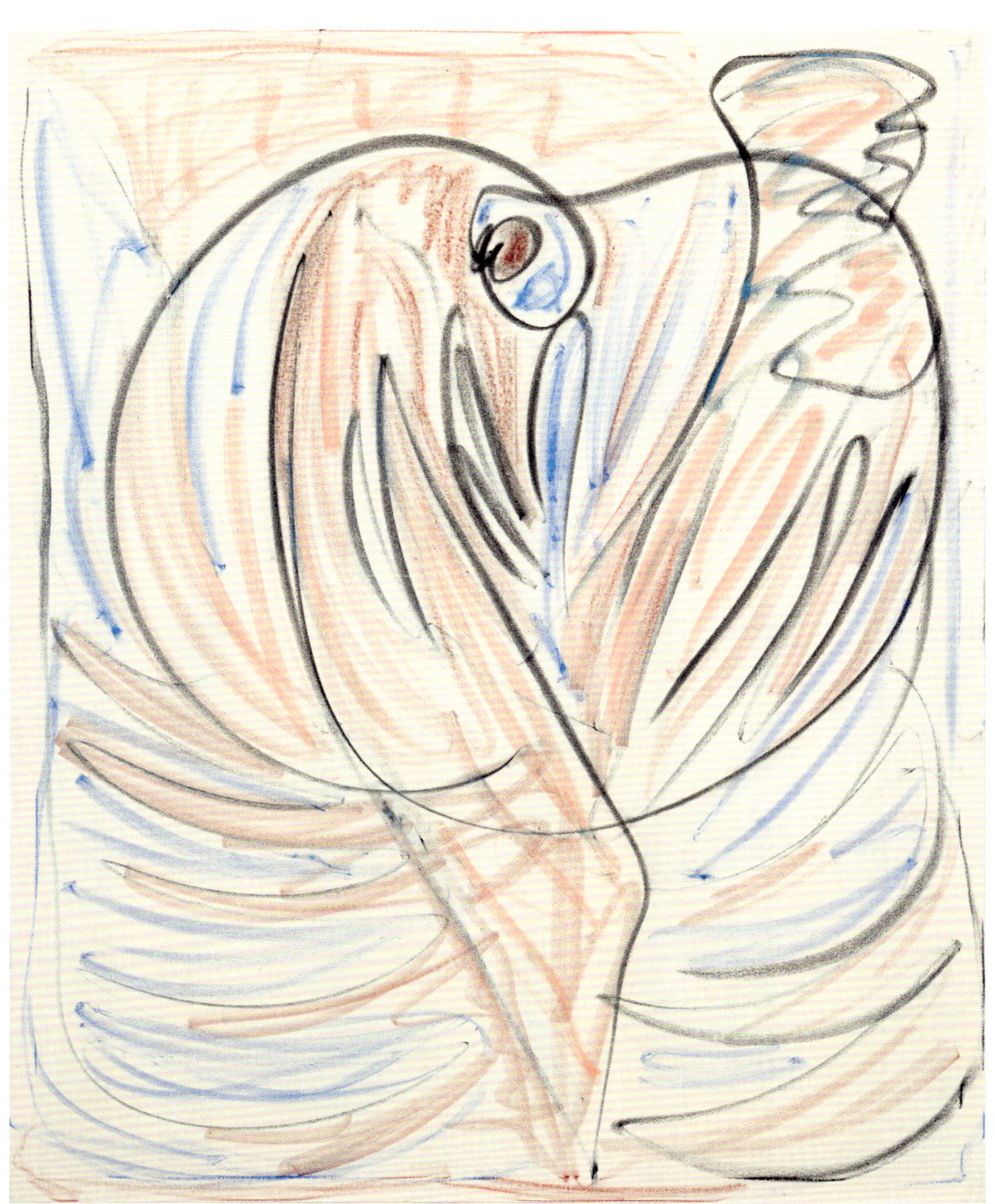

13 December Sunday, 2015
oil stick on canvas, 72 ⅞ × 61 inches | 185 × 155 cm

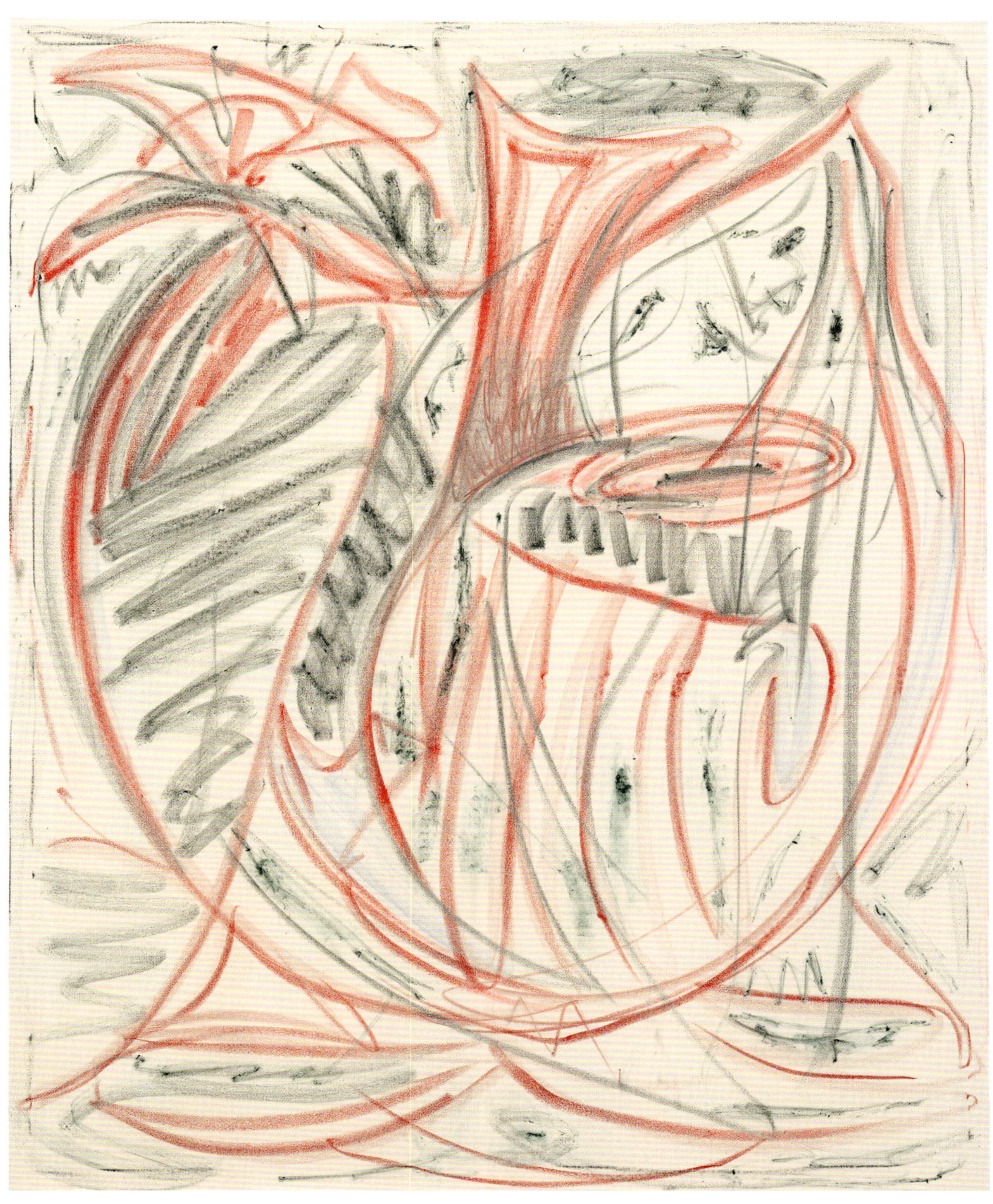

Eve's Apple, 2015
oil stick on canvas, 72 ⅞ × 61 inches | 185 × 155 cm

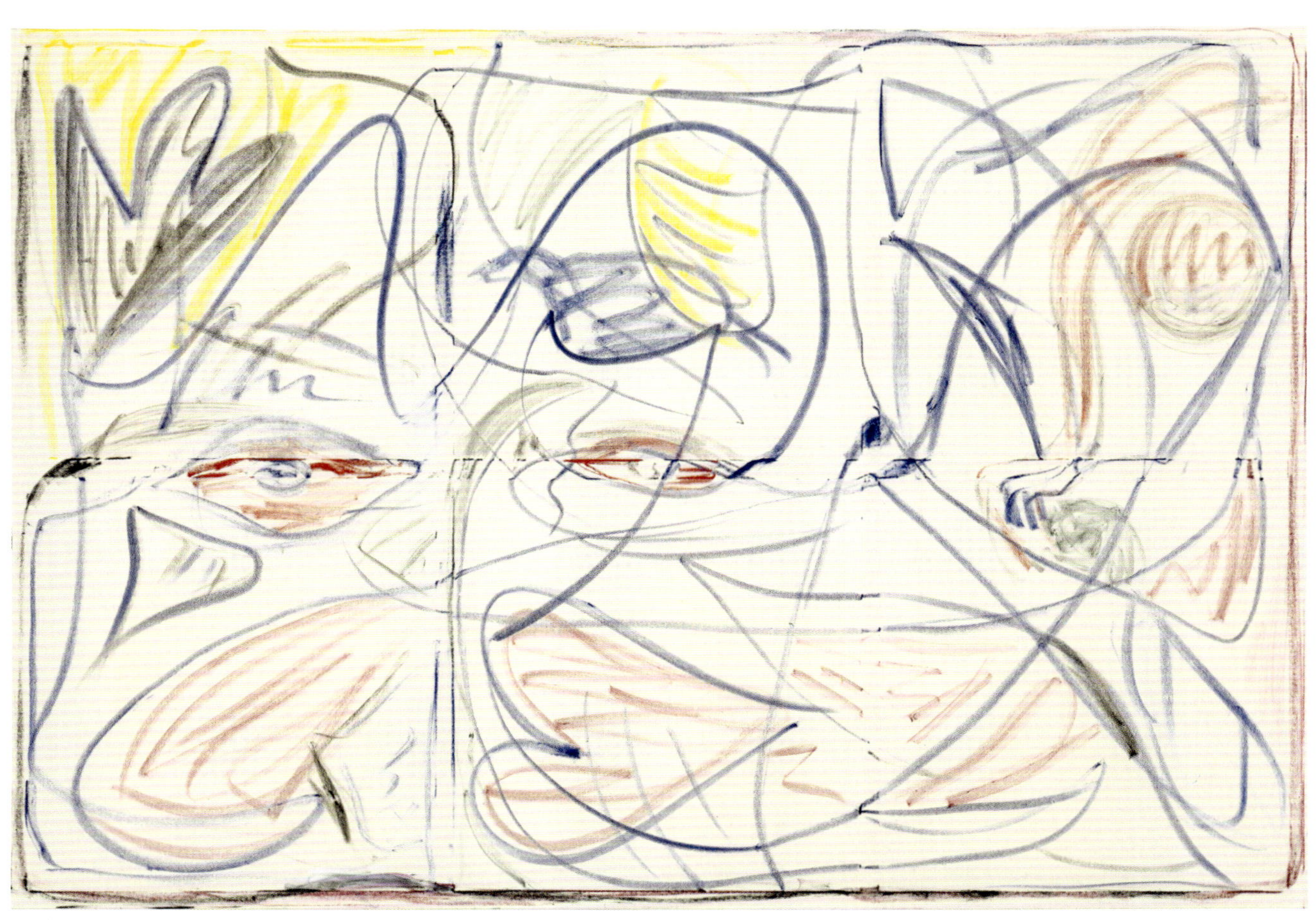

Andre's Breton, 2015
oil stick and pastel on canvas, 76 ¾ × 114 ⅛ inches | 195 × 290 cm

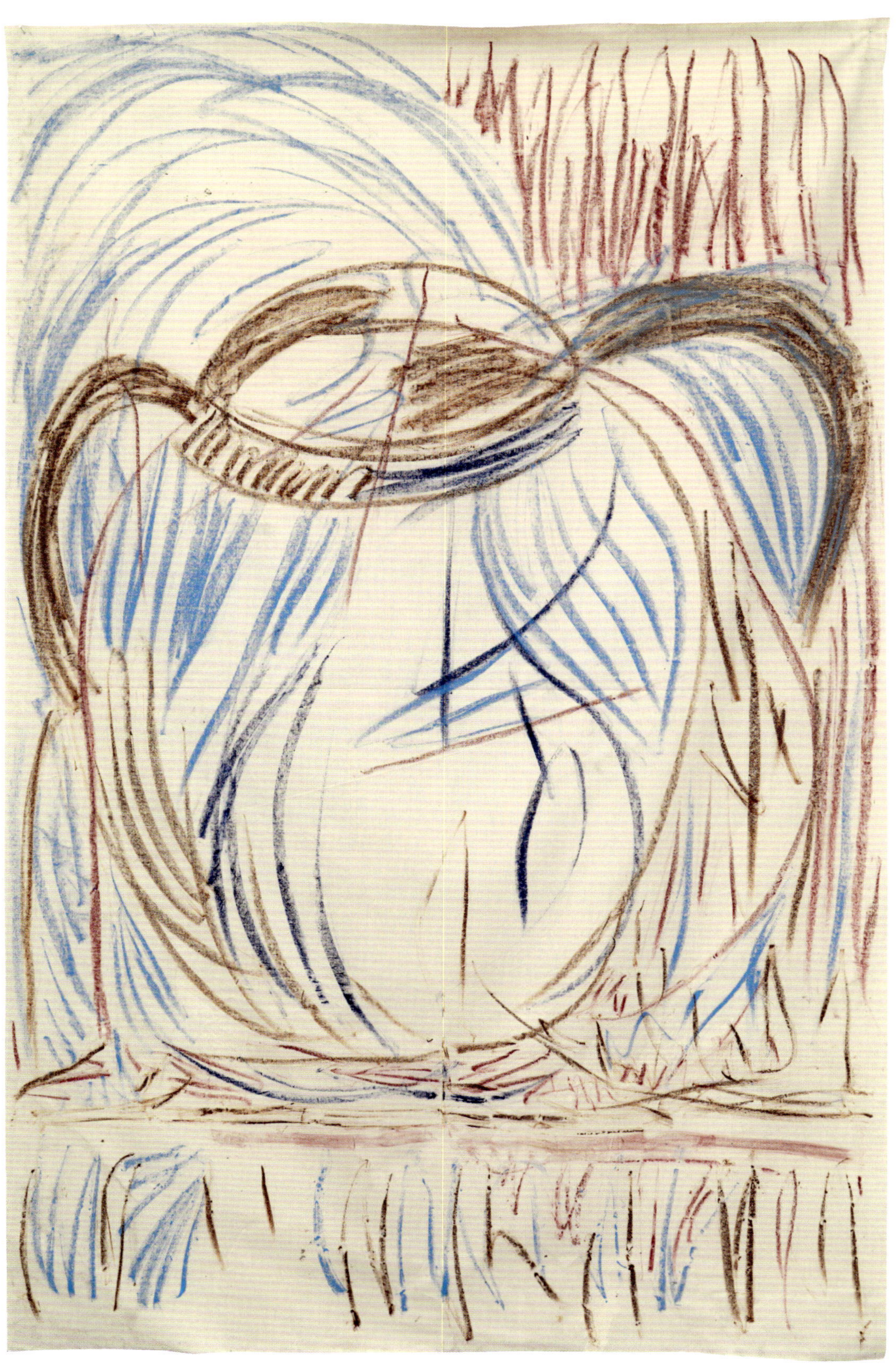

Don't Fool Yourself, 2012
oil stick on canvas, 118 ⅛ × 78 ¾ inches | 300 × 200 cm

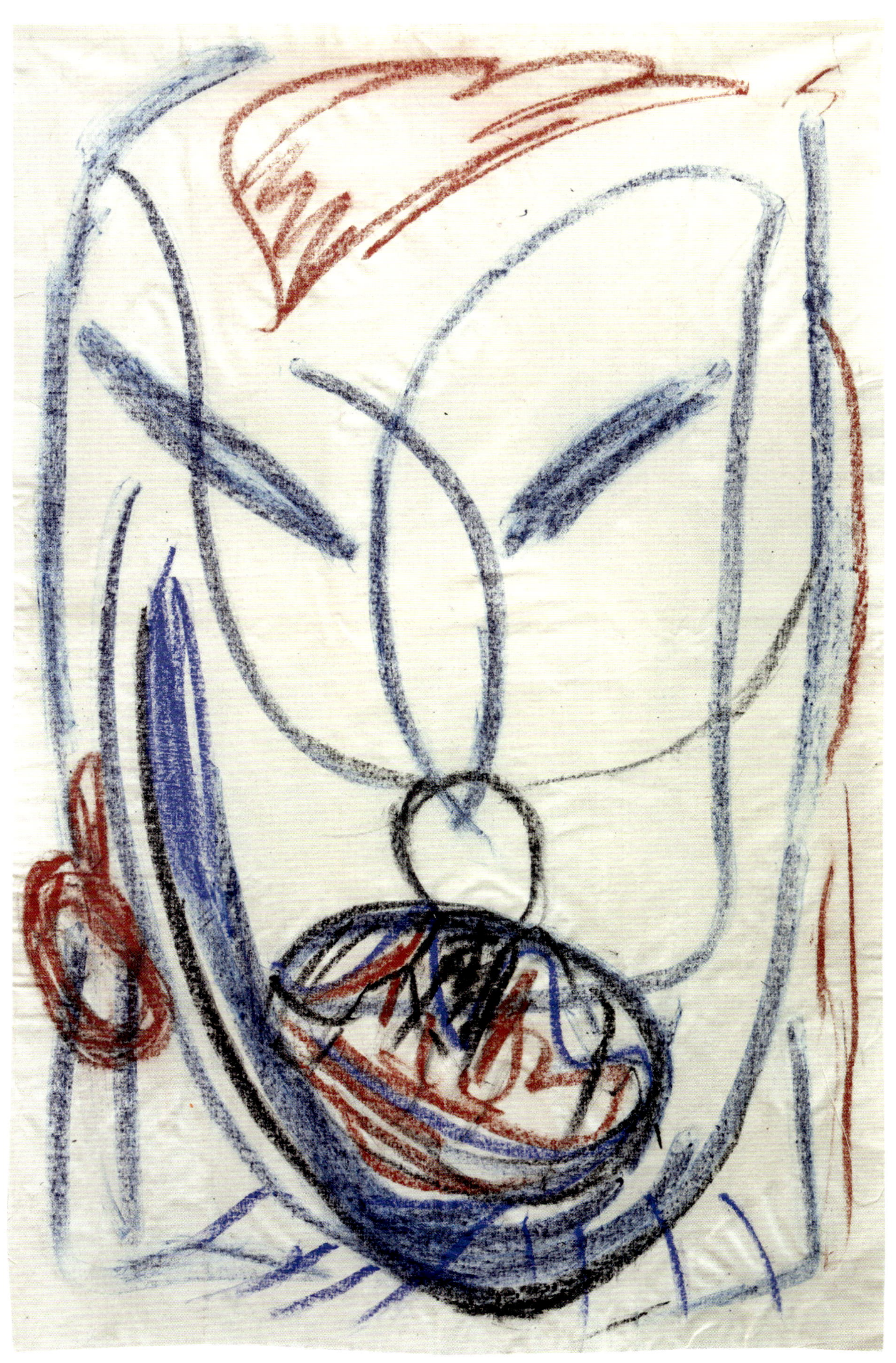

Untitled, 2015
oil stick on raw, unstretched canvas, 59 × 38 ¼ inches | 150 × 97 cm

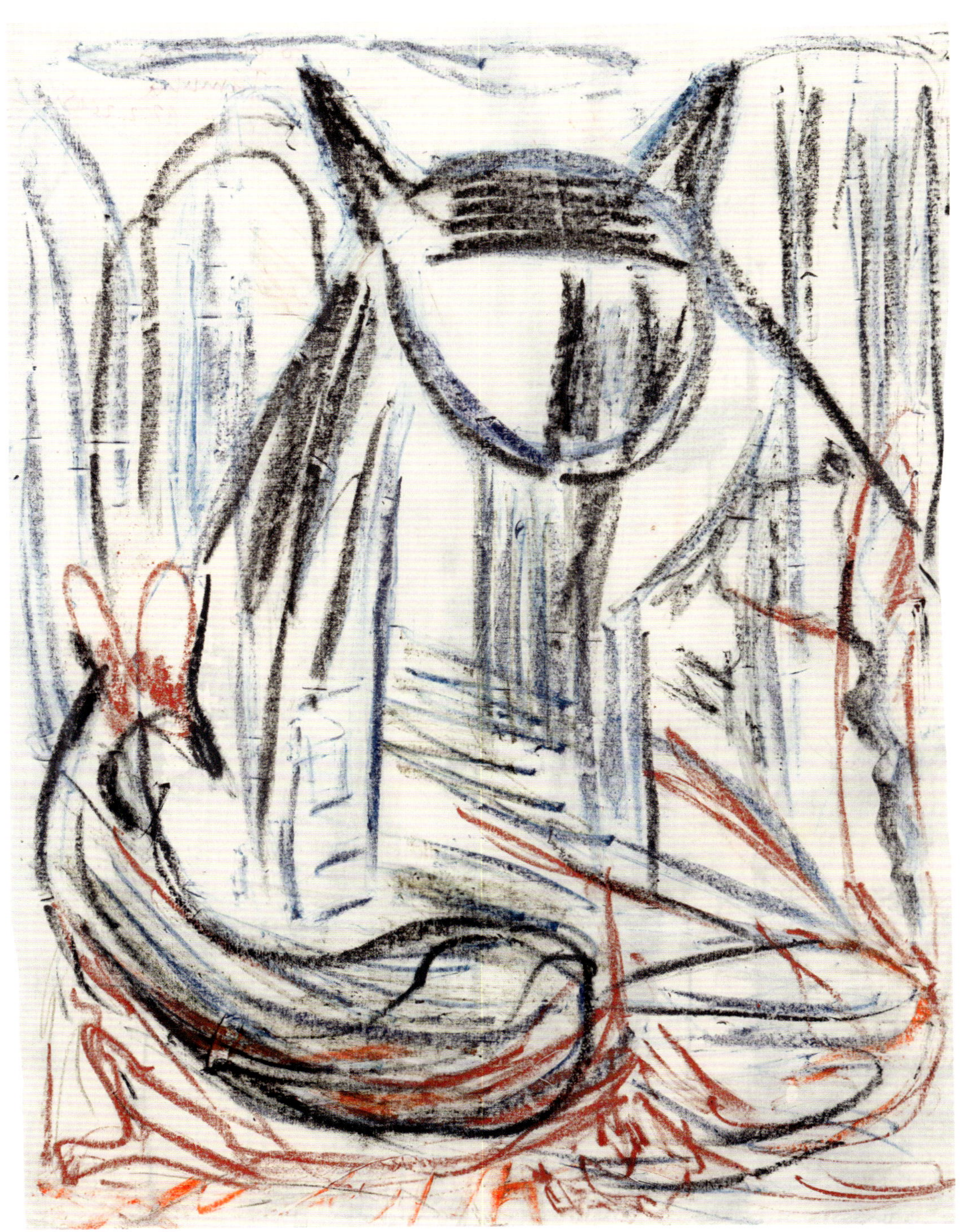

Madonna with a Bambi, 2012
mixed media on canvas, 58 ¼ × 45 ⅝ inches | 148 × 116 cm

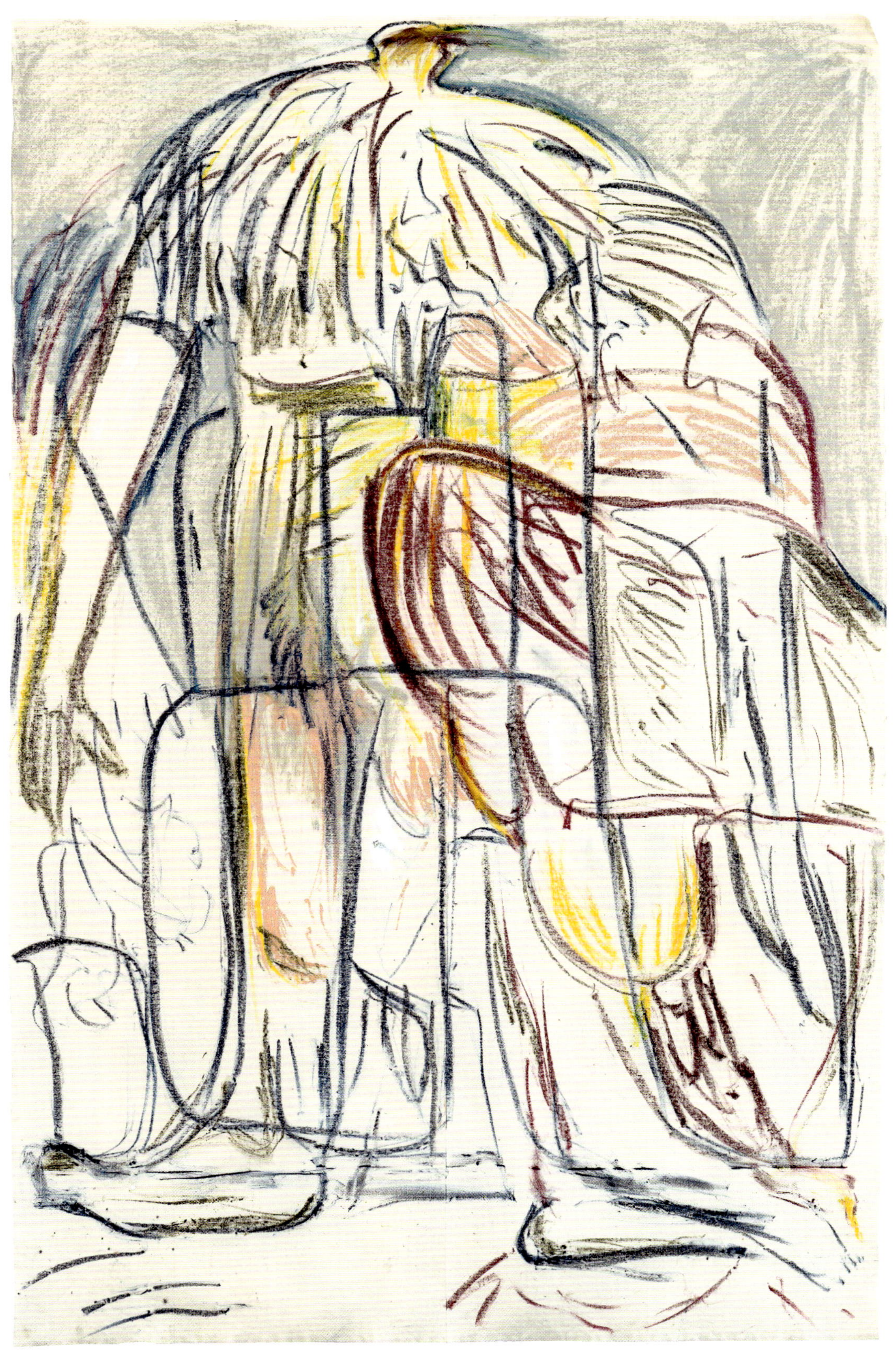

End-of-Days Fantasy, 2011
oil stick on canvas, 118 ⅛ × 78 ¾ inches | 300 × 200 cm

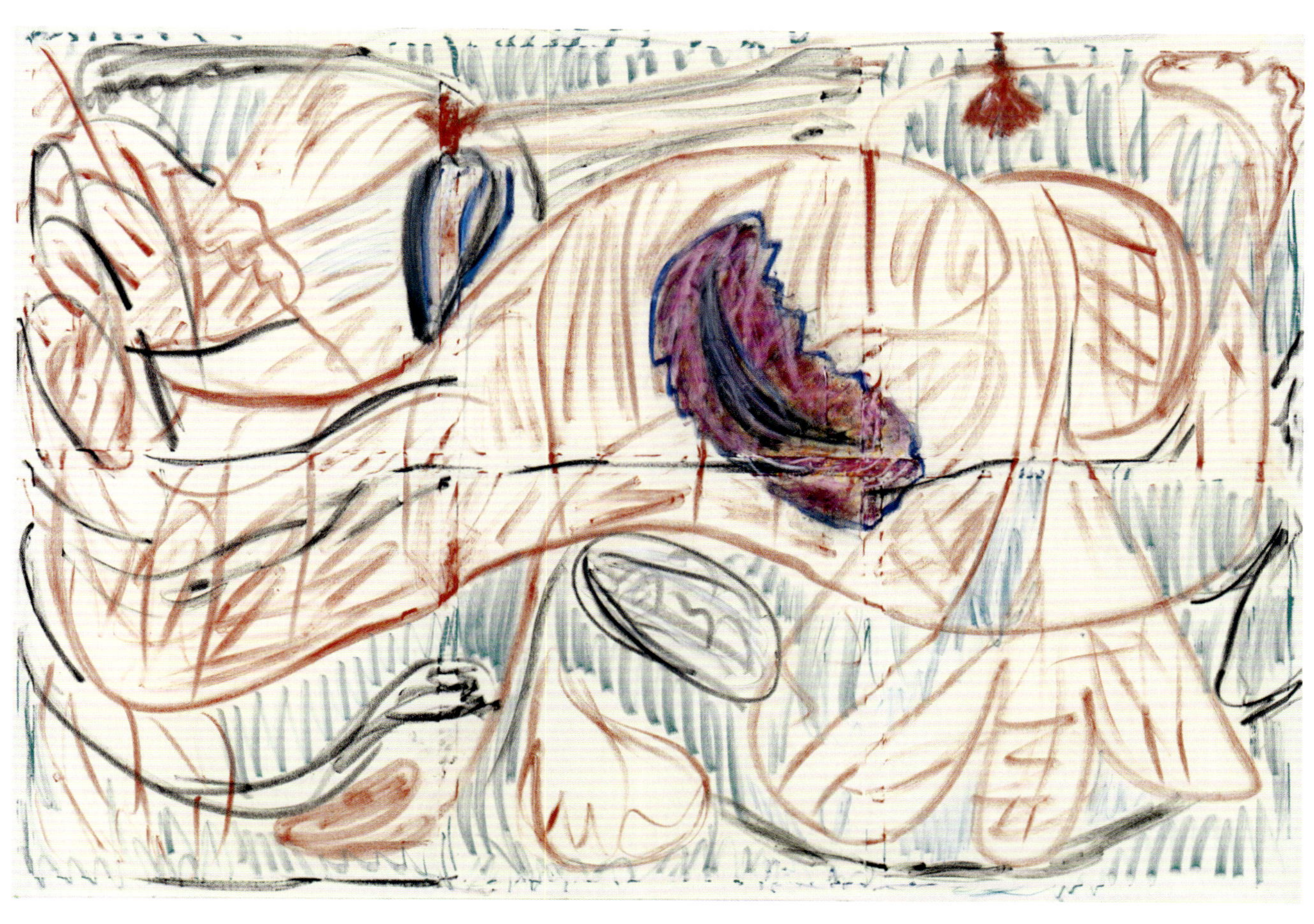

In Which It Is Whether They Went With It, 2015
oil stick on canvas, 76 ¾ × 114 ⅛ inches | 195 × 290 cm

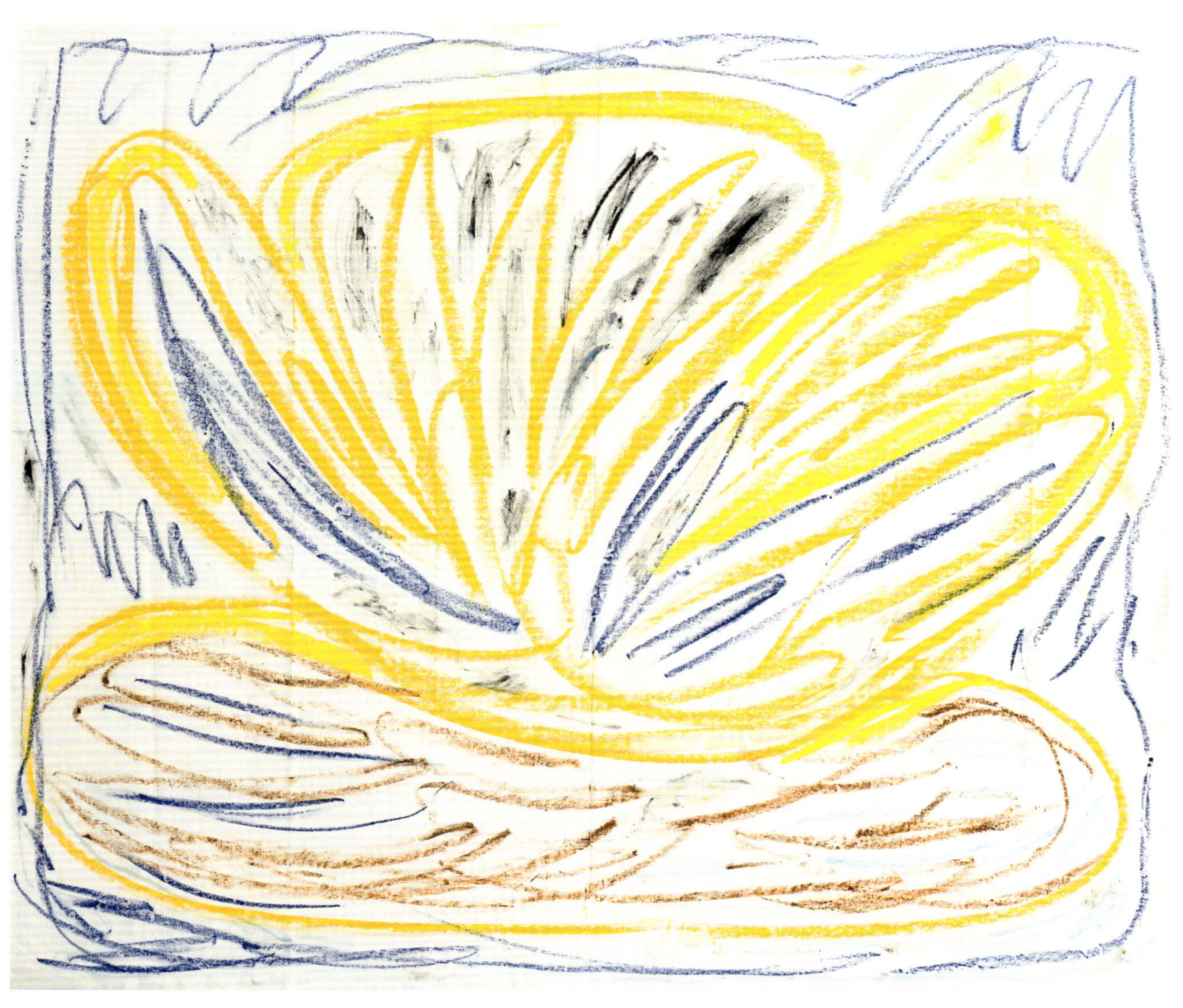

Lotus, 2015
mixed media on canvas, 65 ¾ × 78 inches | 167 × 198 cm

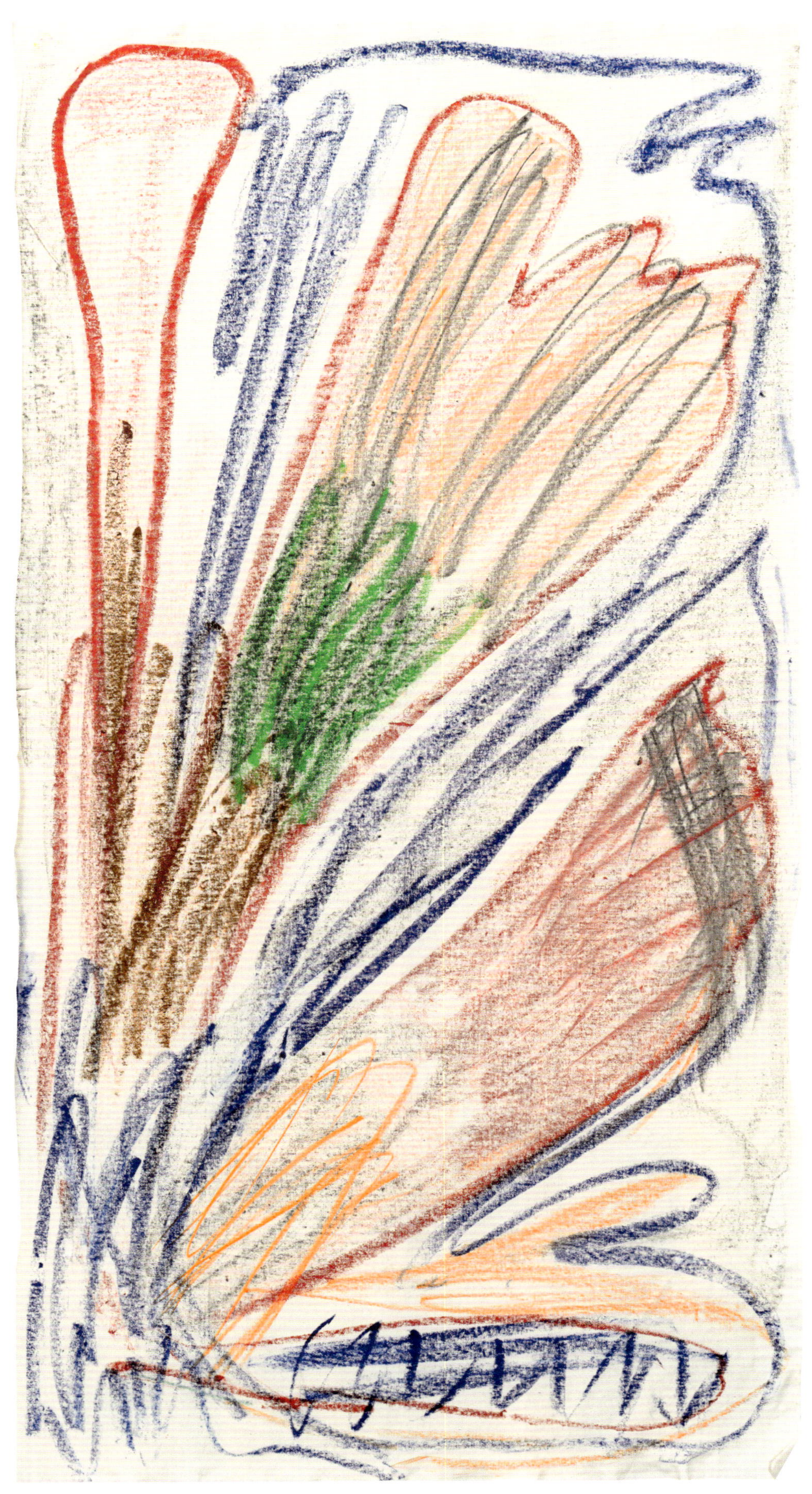

Plant, 2015
mixed media on canvas, 65 × 35 ⅞ inches | 165 × 91 cm

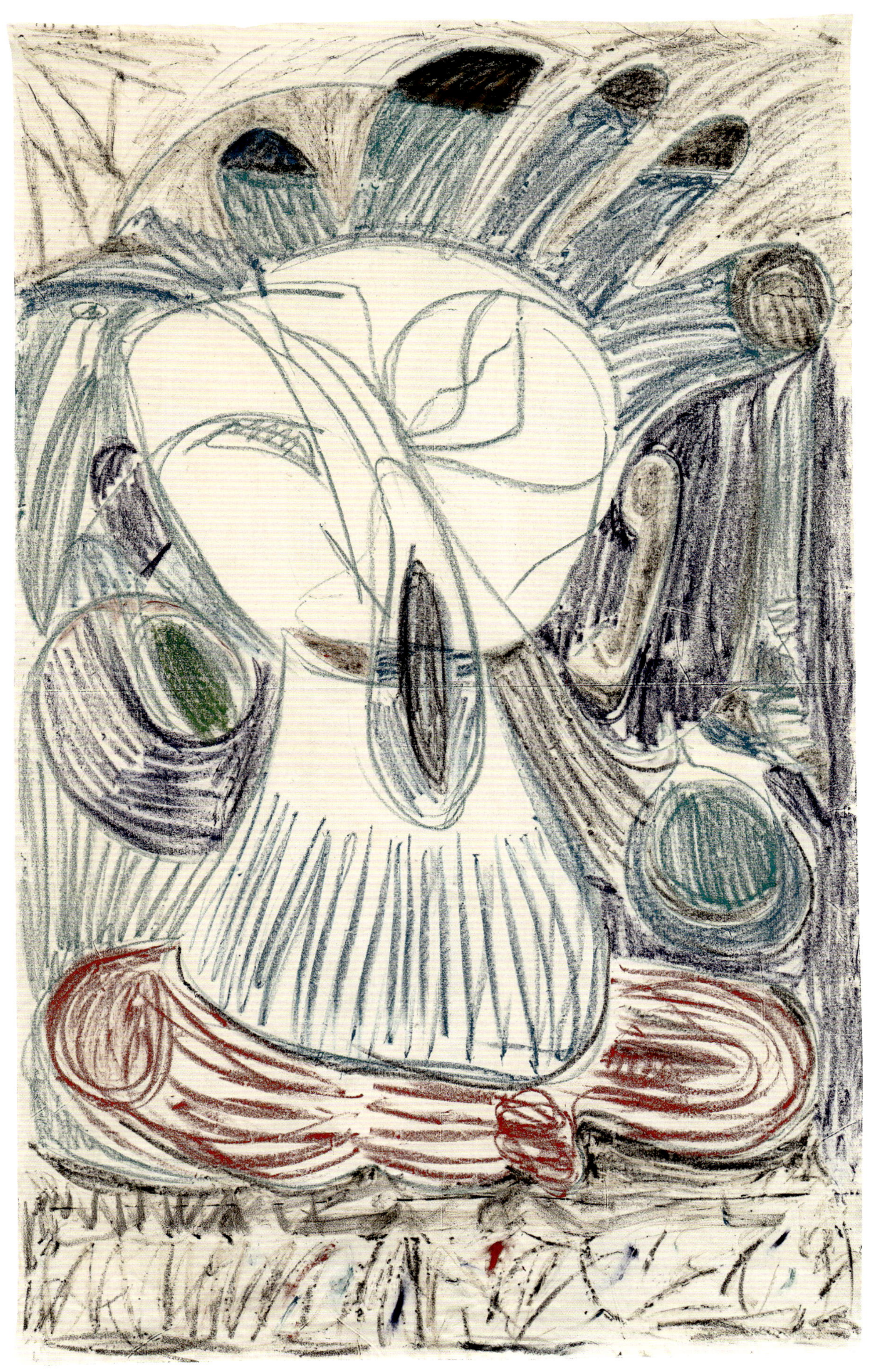

Rebirth Is Always Painful, 2011
oil stick on canvas, 118 ⅛ × 78 ¾ inches | 300 × 200 cm

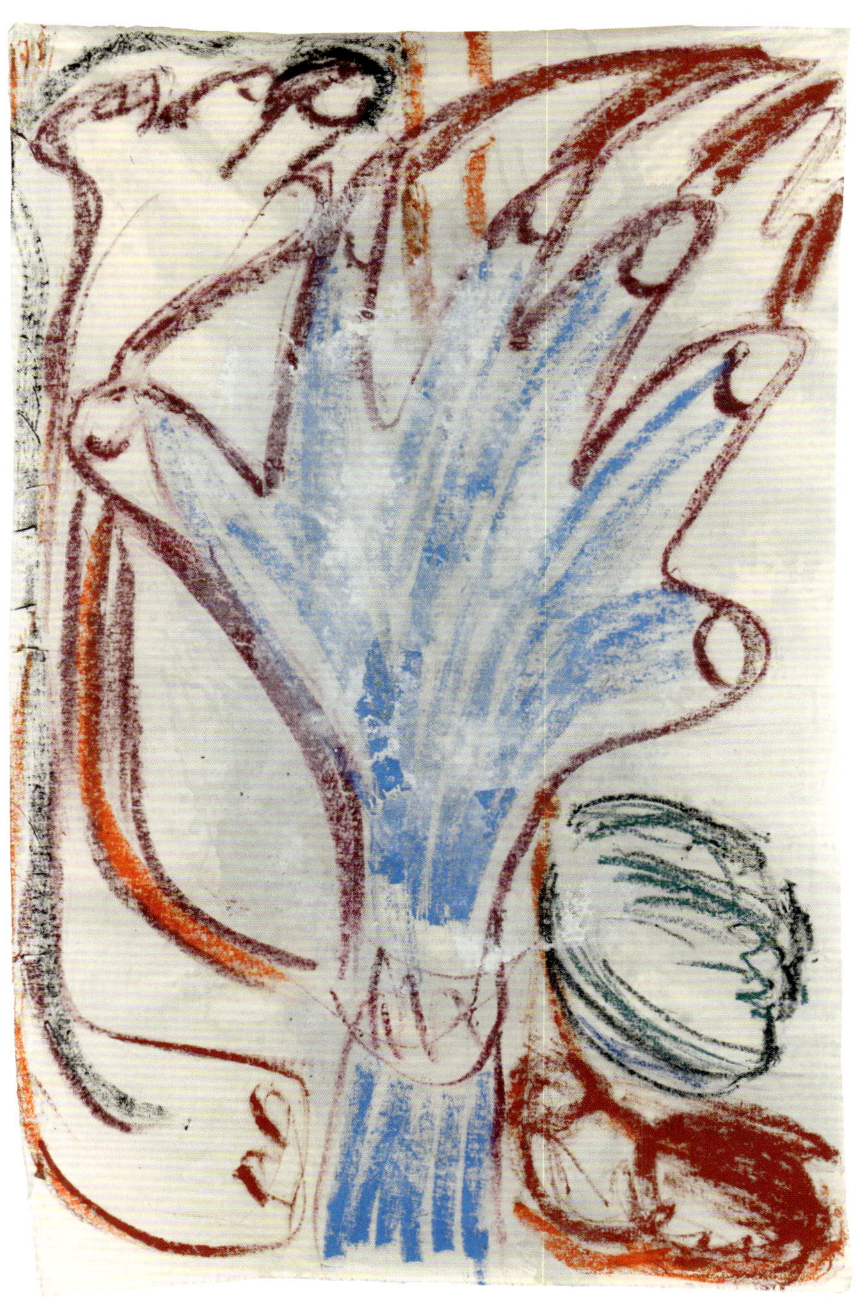

S match, 2012
oil stick and acrylic on canvas, 59 × 39 ¼ inches | 150 × 100 cm

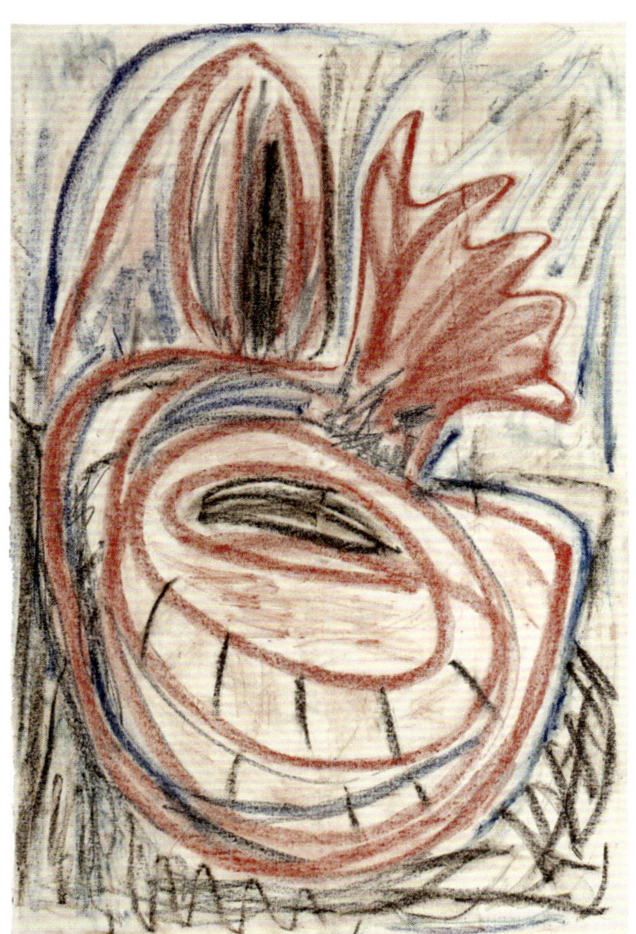

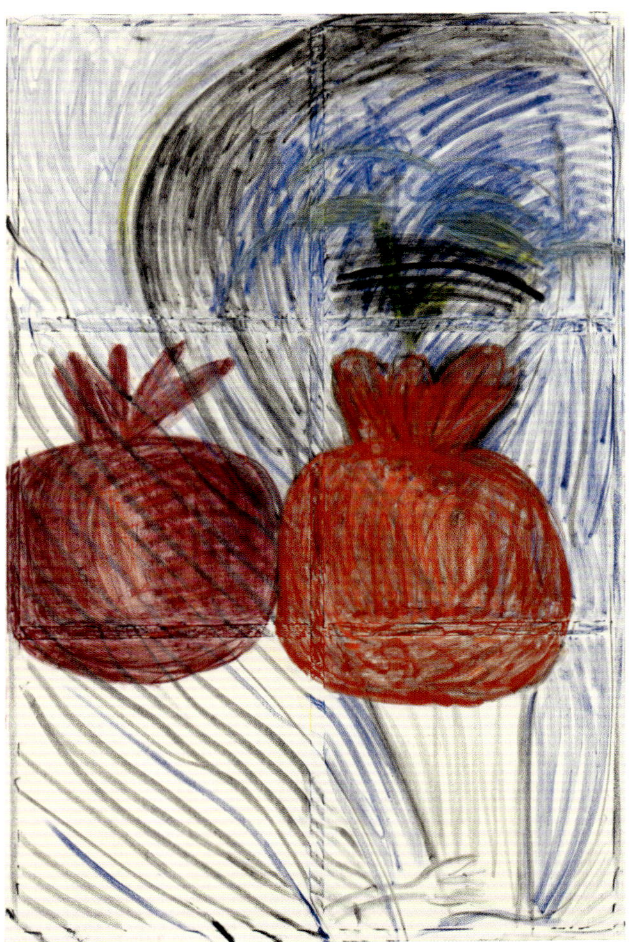

Pomegranate, 2015
oil stick and crayon on canvas
39 ¼ × 19 ¾ inches | 100 × 50 cm

They Made It Because of the Time, 2015
oil stick and pastel on canvas
114 ⅛ × 76 ¾ inches | 290 × 195 cm

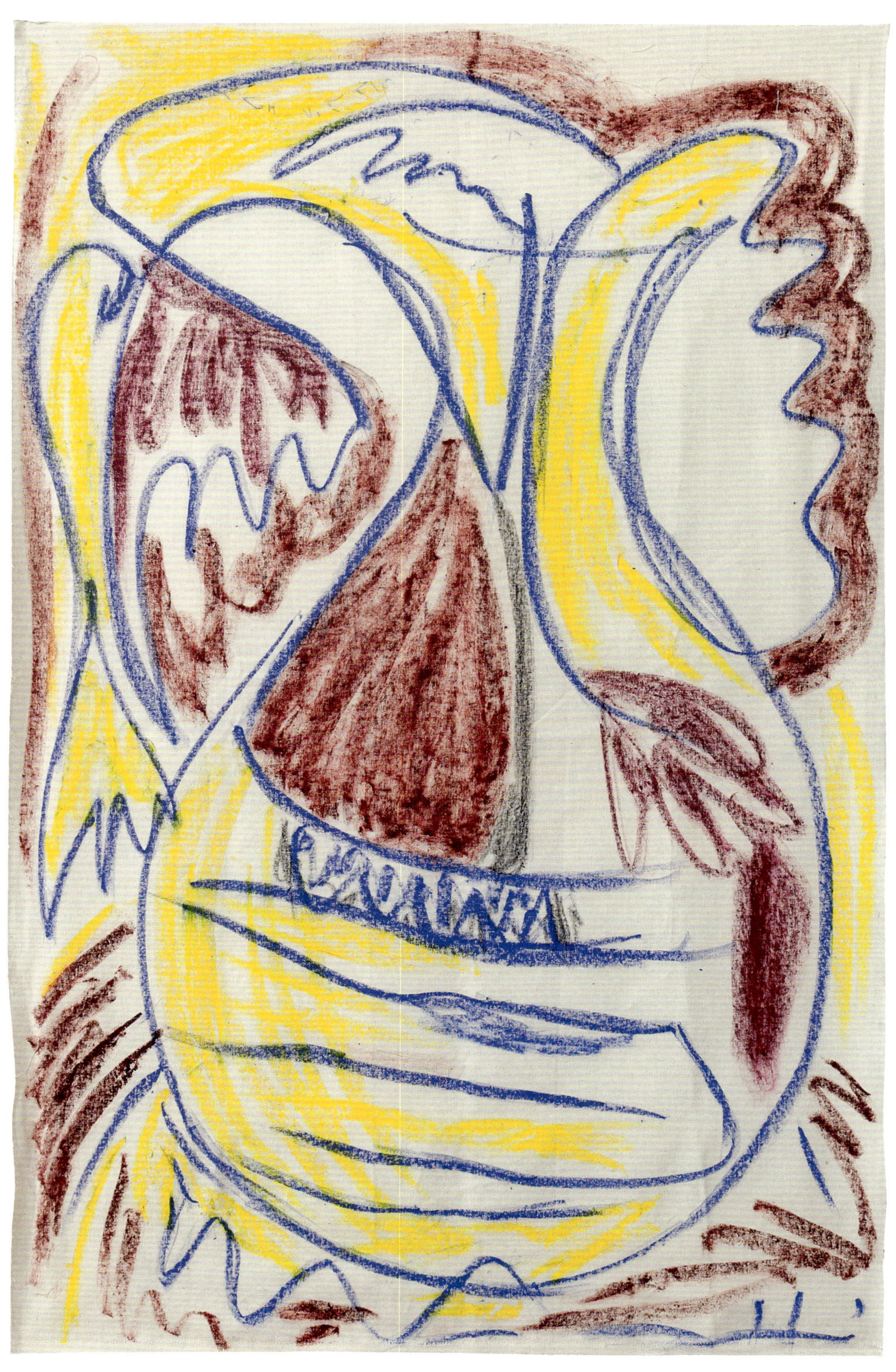

L Vase, 2015
oil stick on canvas, 65 × 35 ⅞ inches | 165 × 91 cm

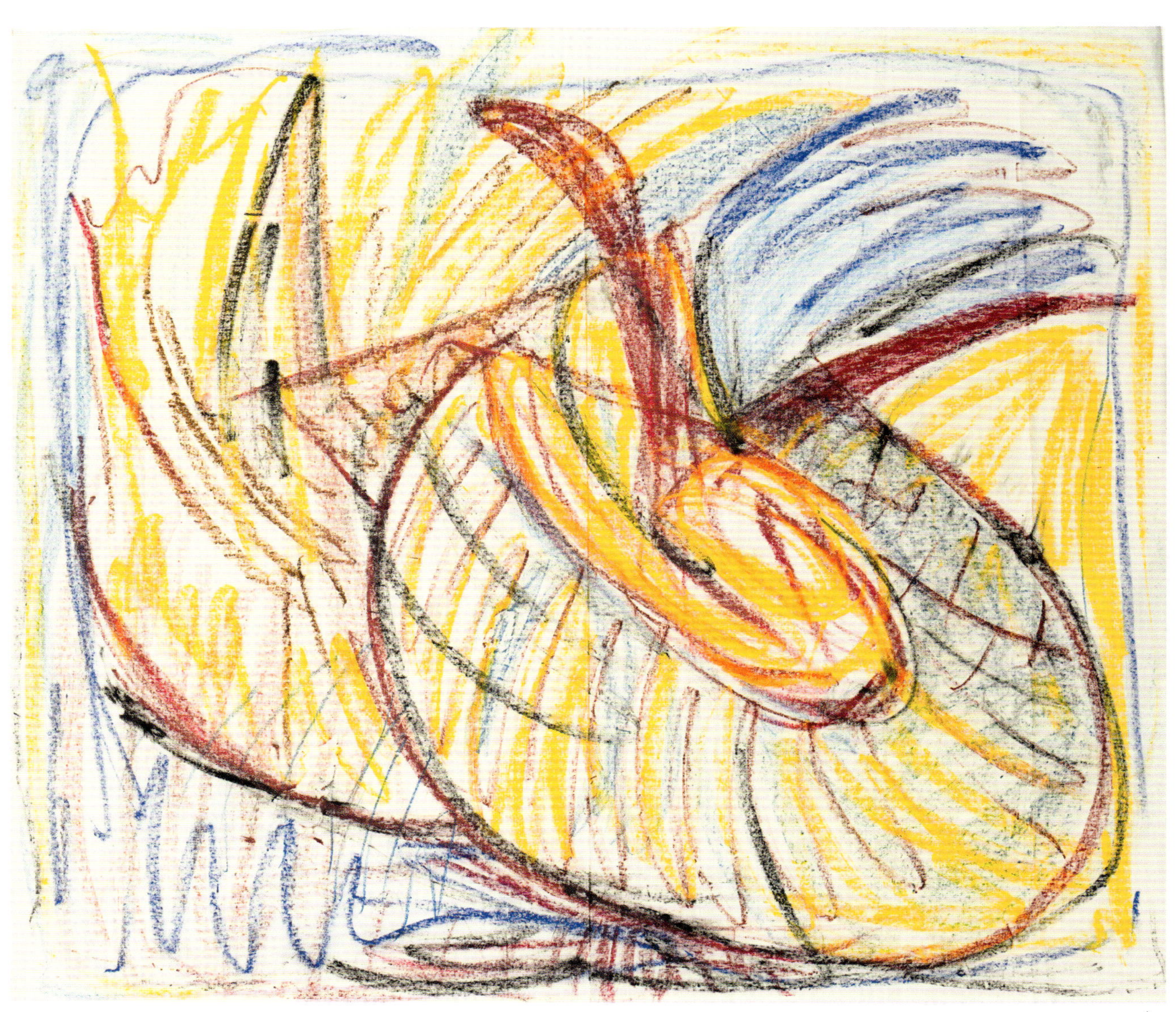

The Seagull, 2015
mixed media on canvas, 65 ⅜ × 77 ⅛ inches | 166 × 196 cm

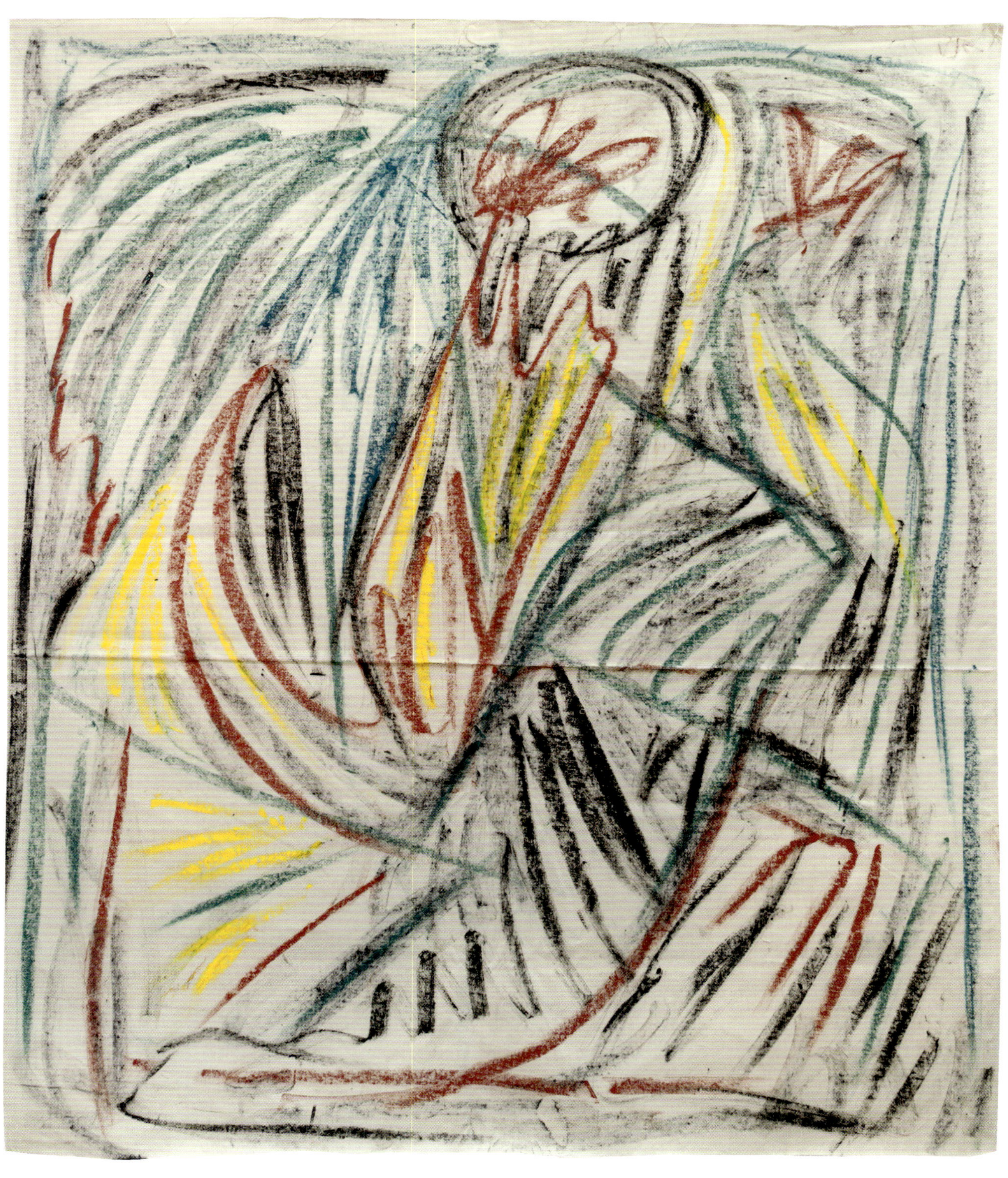

Untitled, 2015
oil stick on canvas, 69 × 59 inches | 175 × 150 cm

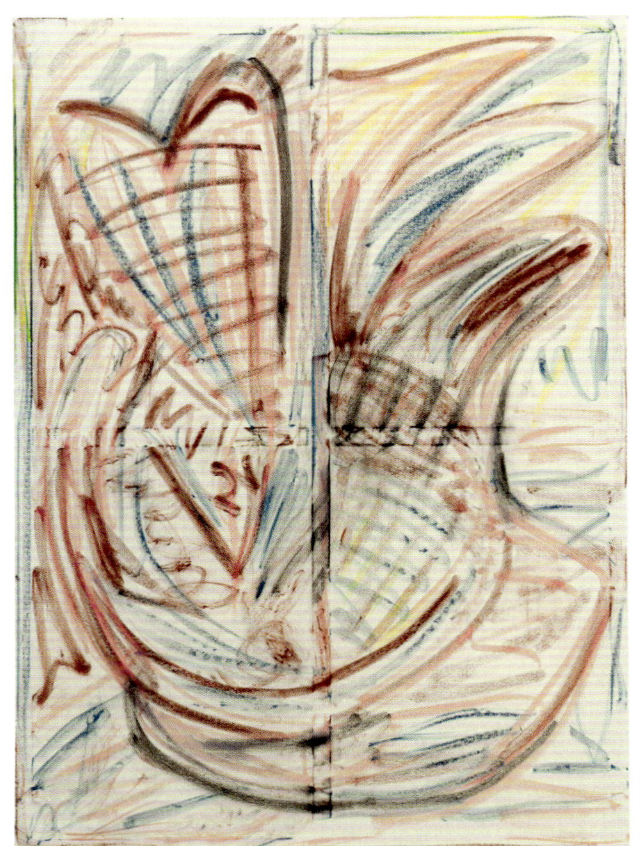

Lotus, 2015
oil stick and pastel on canvas
74 ¾ × 55 ⅛ inches | 190 × 140 cm

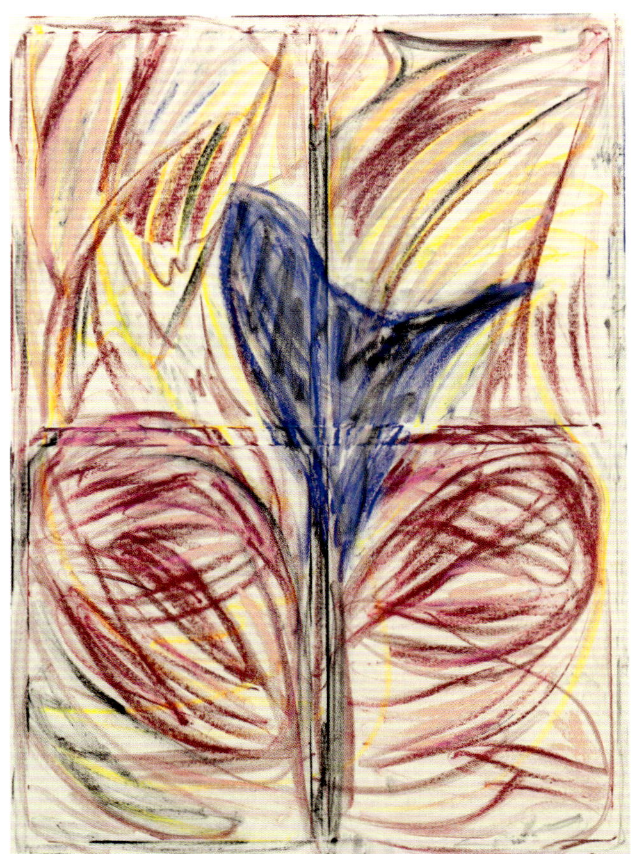

Nymphs, 2015
oil stick and pastel on canvas
74 ¾ × 55 ⅛ inches | 190 × 140 cm

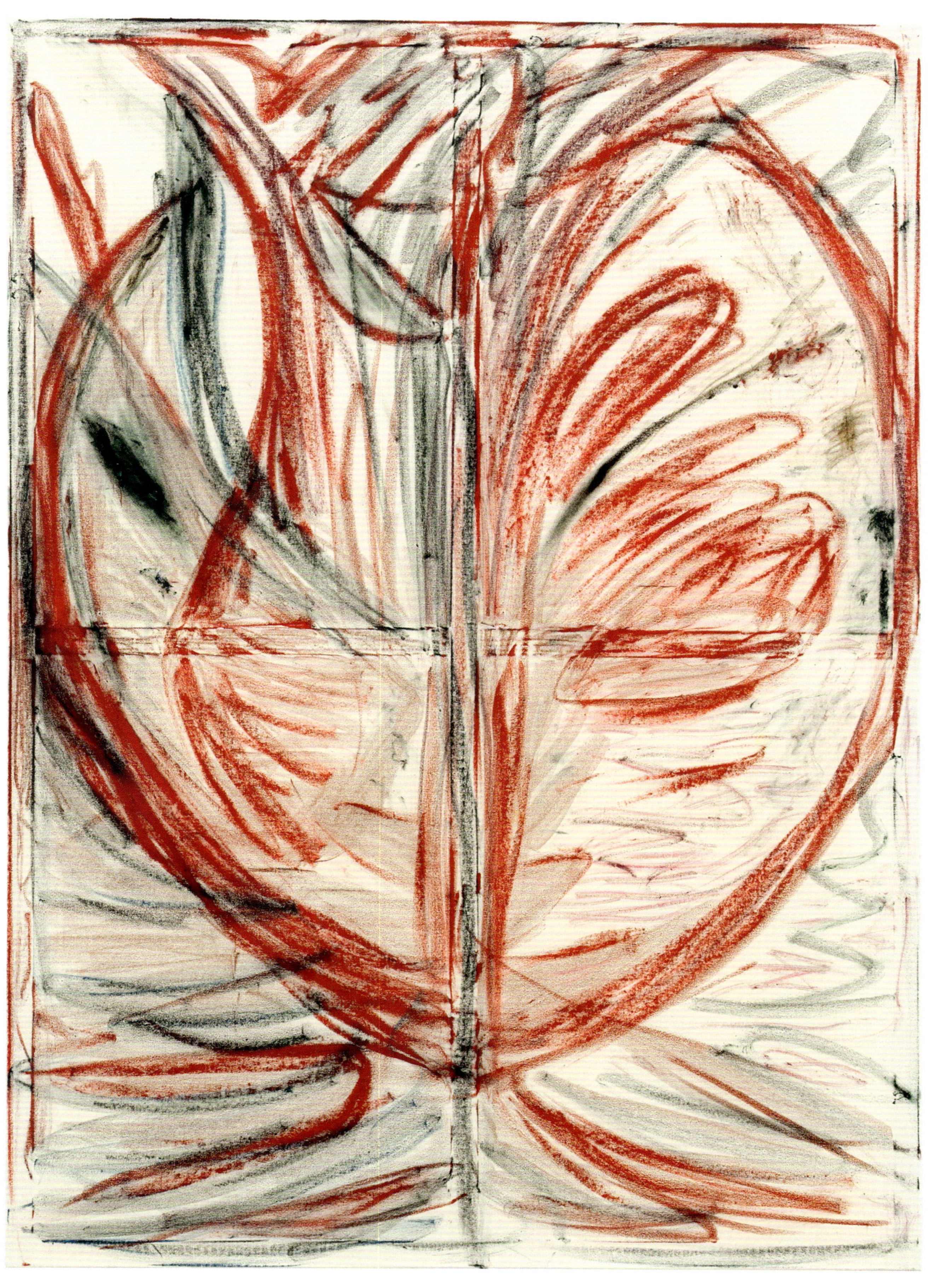

Orchidee, 2015
oil stick and pastel on canvas, 74 ¾ × 55 ⅛ inches | 190 × 140 cm

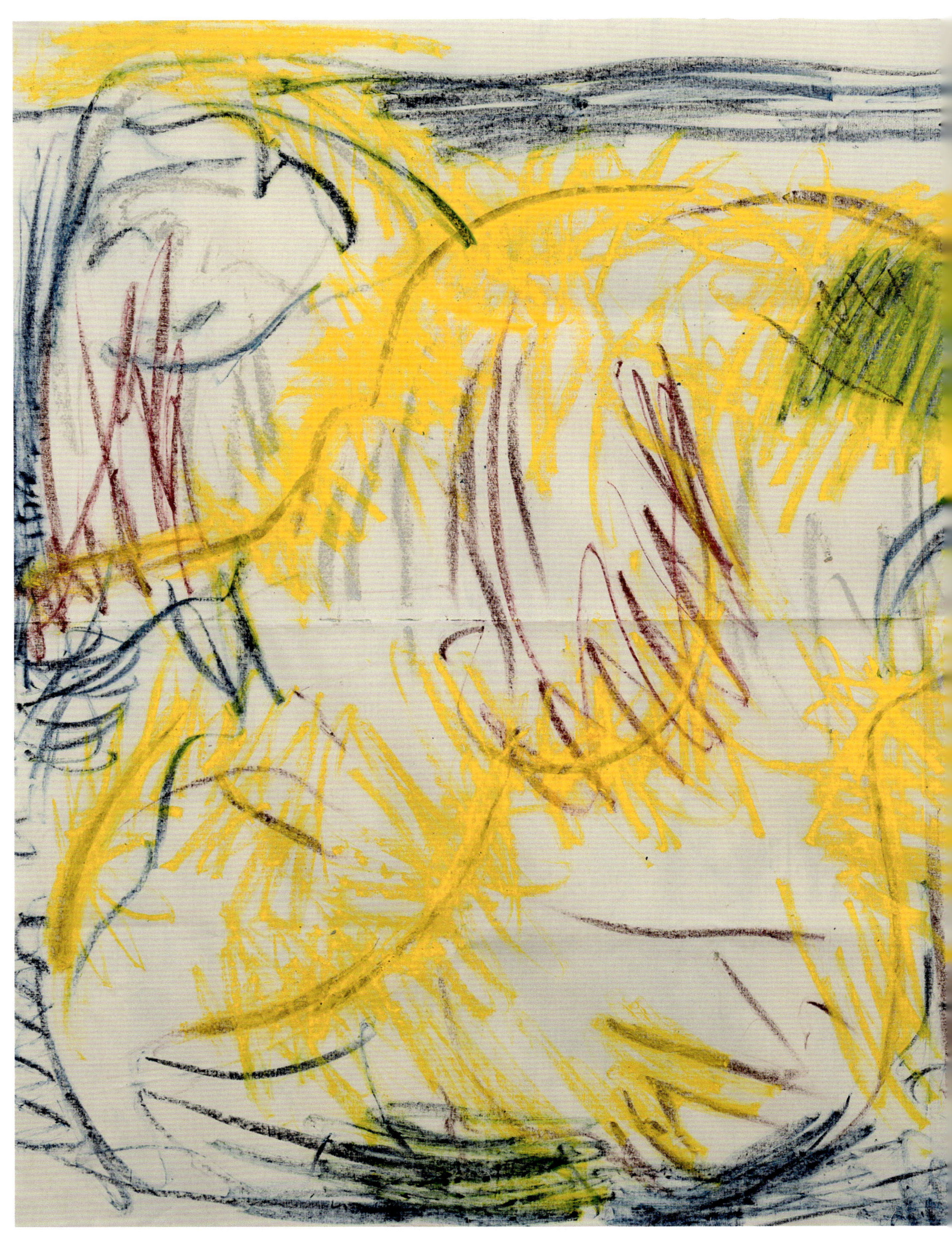

Munchan Dog, 2011
oil stick on raw canvas, 78 ¾ × 118 ⅛ inches | 200 × 300 cm

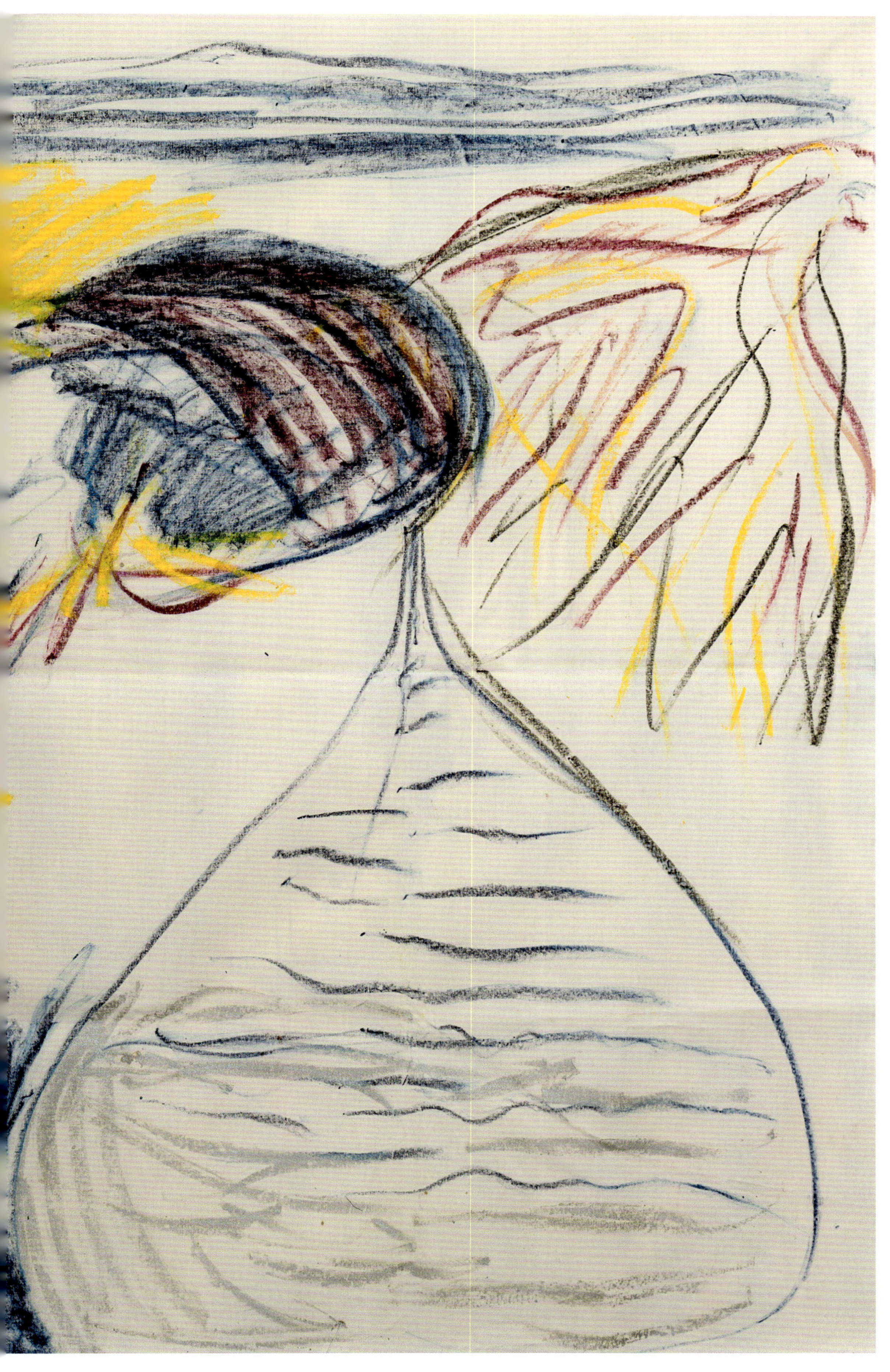

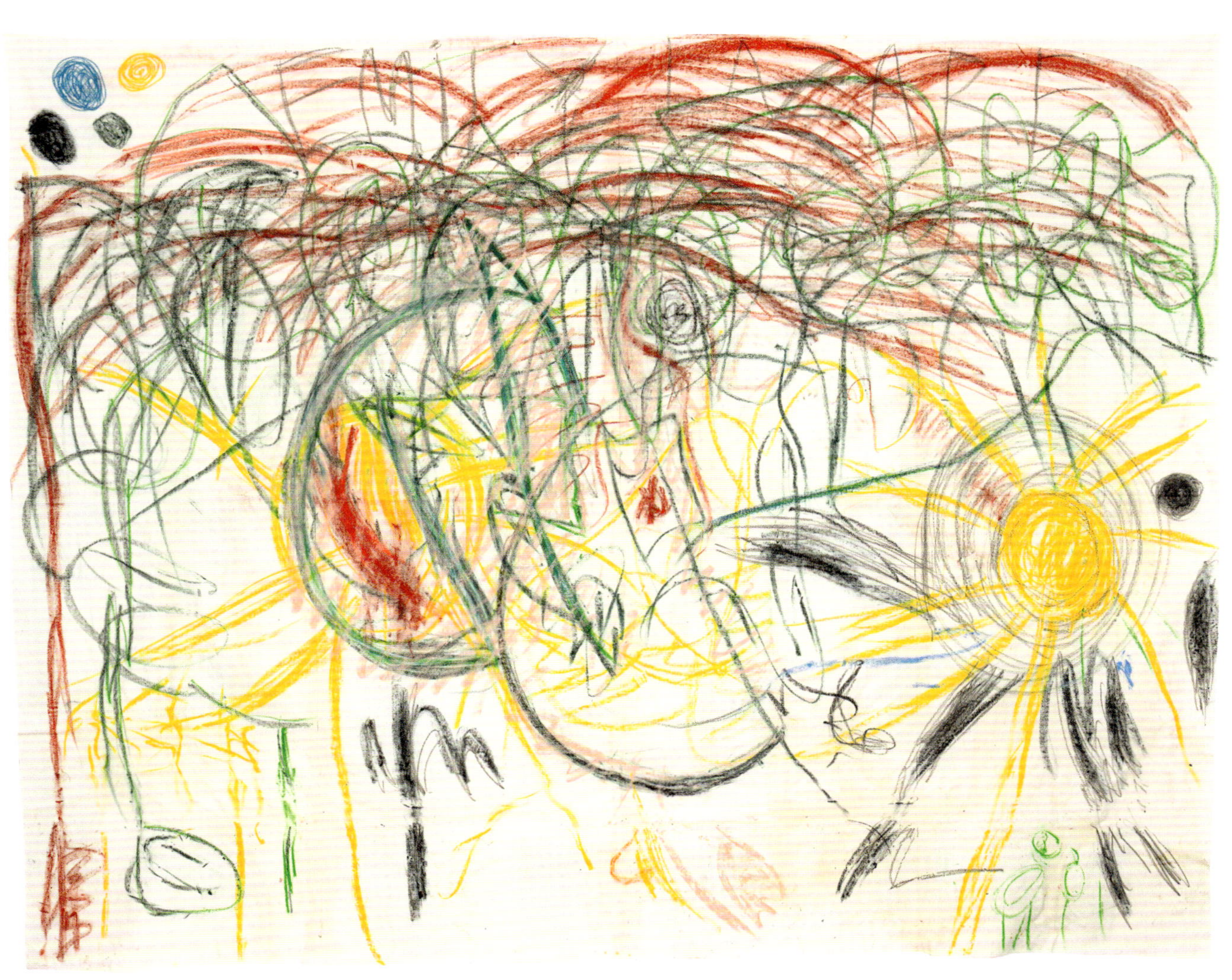

Untitled, 2015
mixed media on raw, unstretched canvas, 117 ¾ × 151 ⅝ inches | 299 × 385 cm

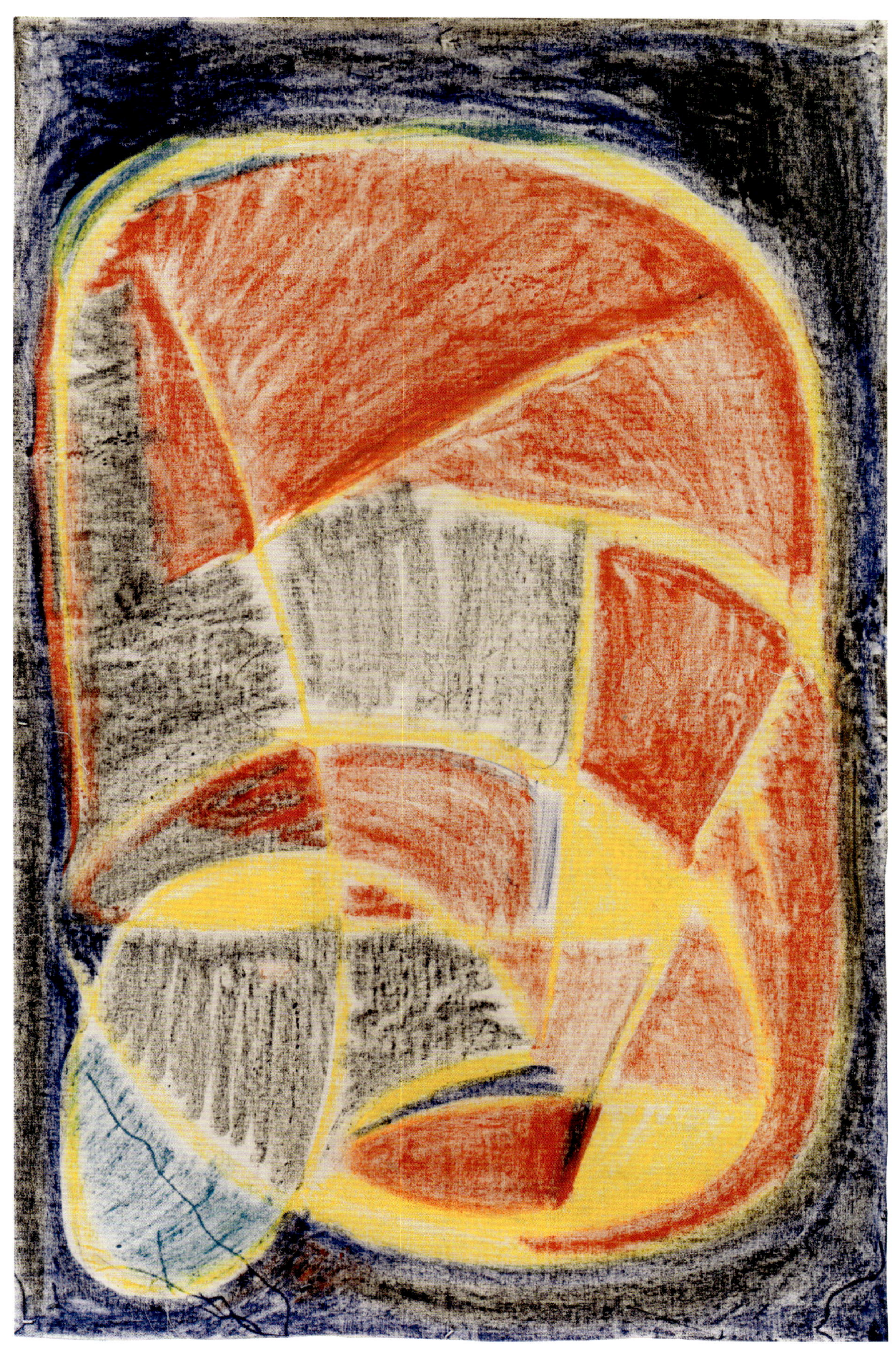

Hello K, 2012
oil stick on canvas, 62 ⅝ × 39 ⅜ inches | 159 × 100 cm

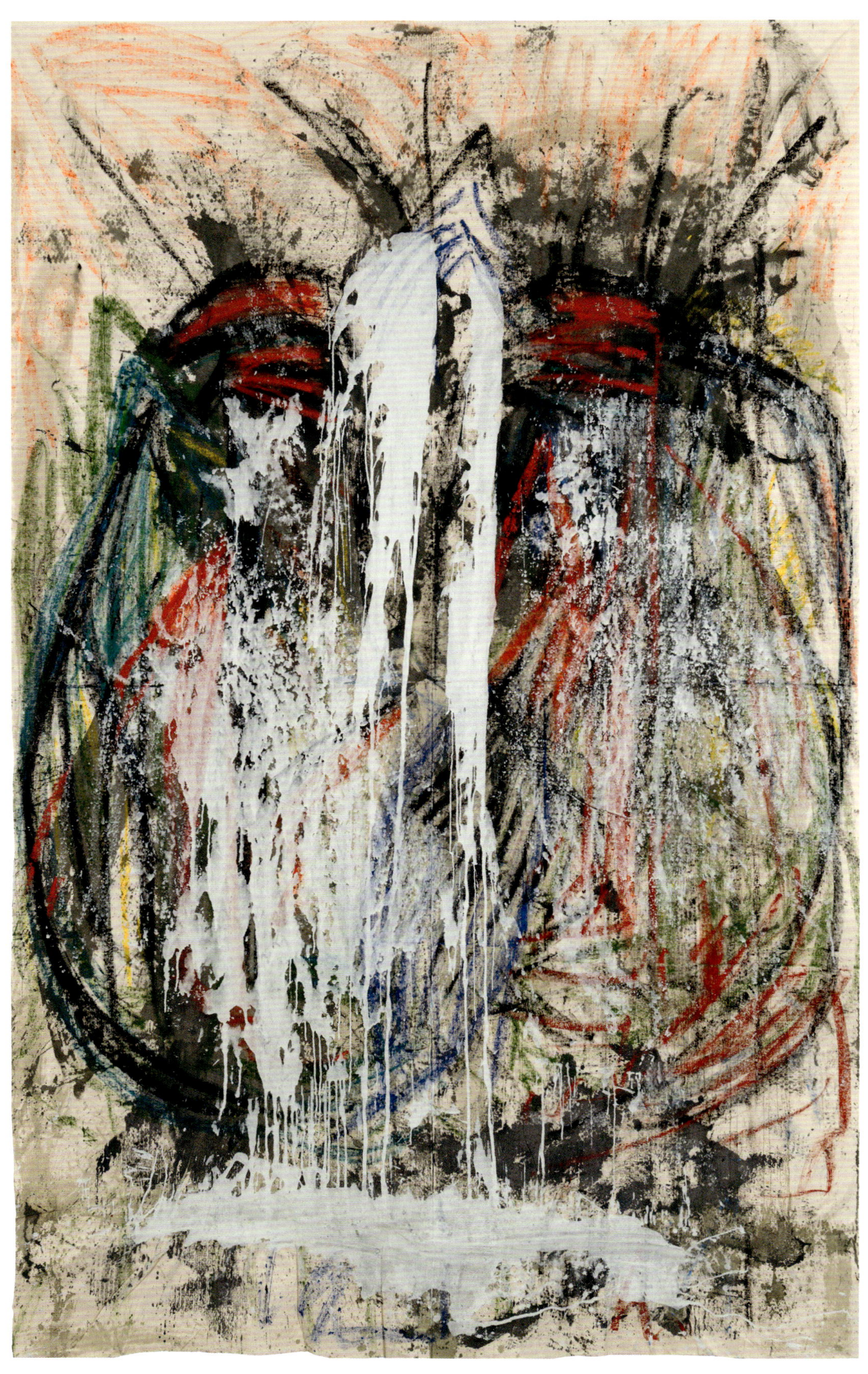

Twins, 2013
oil stick and acrylic on canvas, 118 ⅛ × 78 ¾ inches | 300 × 200 cm

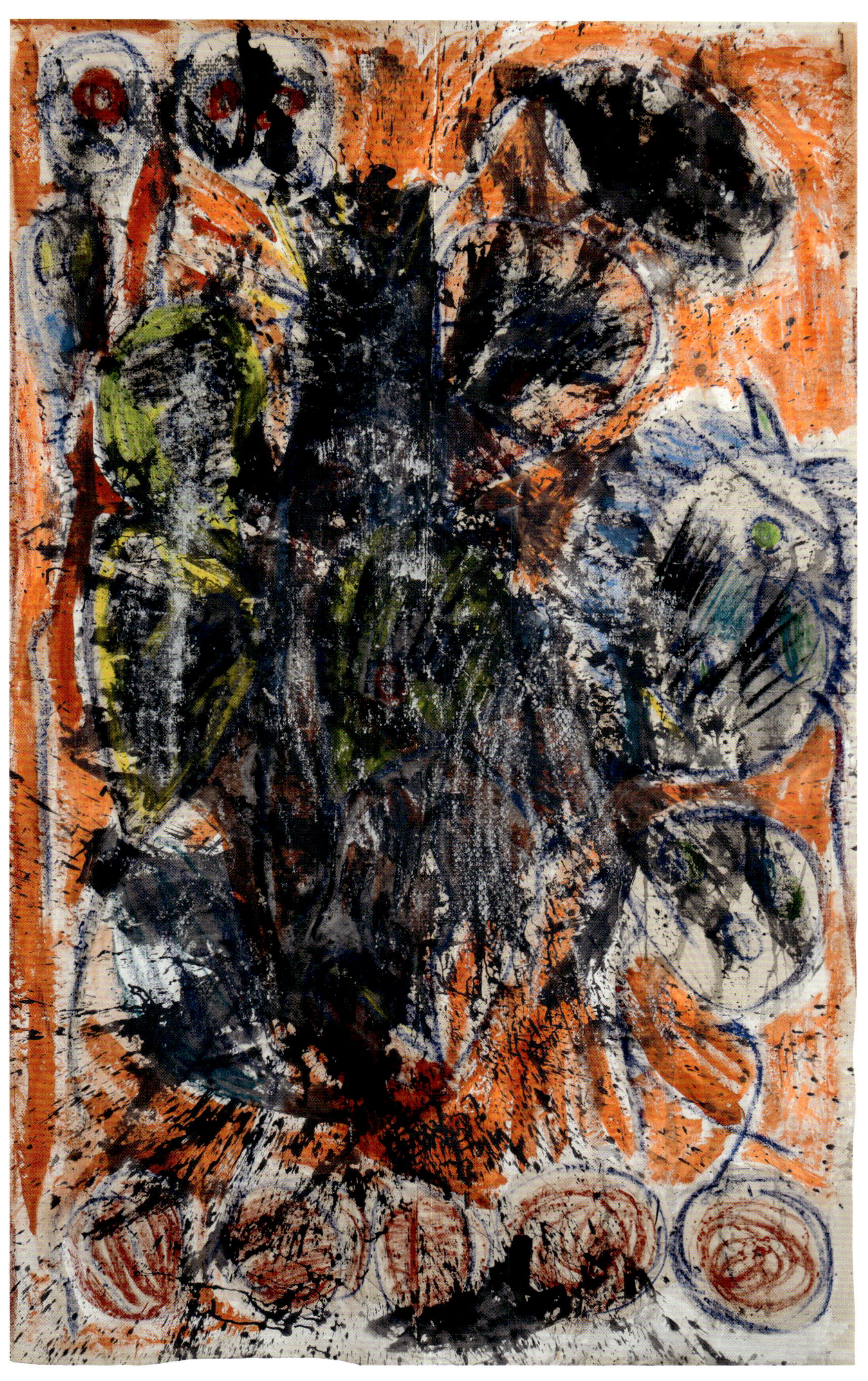

Balloons, 2013
oil stick and acrylic on canvas, 118 ⅛ × 78 ¾ inches | 300 × 200 cm

Still life

Anna Kats

Tamuna Sirbiladze was not a painter of still lifes, not of the traditional sort at any rate, concerned with bourgeois domesticity and fruit arranged just so. She did paint fruit, however, almost habitually. She also painted the male genitalia, portraits of friends and historical figures, the apocalypse, a cheeky abstract reverie titled *pure formalism* (2012), and myriad other subjects, all of them rendered with—in equal measure—an eye for symbolism, serene quietude, and composition borrowed from Dutch Renaissance painting and the arch emotional drama and abstracting formal impulses of the New York School. Her particular creative talent in life was in reconciling the seemingly contradictory tendencies of abstraction and figuration; her canvases remain as testament to her willpower and humor.

Sirbiladze digested the canon of painting, with its overwhelmingly male dramatis personae and their attendant concerns, and adapted its norms to fit a distinctly female-centric (if not explicitly feminist) point of view. If her expressive brushstrokes echo those of Willem de Kooning, to whom she is time and again compared, then her agenda was something else altogether. Indeed, it feels a bit disingenuous to speak of "expressive extremes" in Sirbiladze's oeuvre, that rhetorical trope often applied to de Kooning. Her oeuvre, the oil stick works in particular, are more a study in expressive nuance; her work more often derives its emotive affect not from a wildly arched brushstroke, but from the counterpoint of hand-rendered gesture with text, or from the modicum of formal means with which she animated her subjects. Especially in her late work, Sirbiladze often eschewed thick strata of paint or uninterrupted swathes of pigmented canvas for lengthy, sinuous lines that could communicate volumes in the span of a few expressive strokes.

To be sure, Sirbiladze's debt to modernist sources—Matisse, Chagall, Picasso—was unquestionable. But she replaced these progenitors' sense of heroic drama with a knowing wit everywhere evident in her inaugural New York solo show at Half Gallery, which opened to critical acclaim in August 2015. In swift, expansive strokes that suggested the insouciance of an afterthought, Sirbiladze painted the gallery's standard-issue white walls a shade of bottle green, with only so much care as to leave the decorative fireplace untouched; even the ornamental moldings giving this particular interior an air of respectable domesticity were casually painted over. Her oil stick paintings, produced in a similarly nonchalant manner, were hung on the festooned walls in a demonstration of the title's command: "Take it easy." The room resembled a Parisian salon, a residence in the vein of Gertrude Stein's famed apartment. But because nobody lived there—because the space was not in fact a private home, filled with personal minutia and various inanimate witnesses to everything said or left unsaid, but indeed a gallery space, filled only temporarily with these paintings—this semblance for the Half Gallery gave its environs the aura of a stage set. That is, one might say the same of Sirbiladze's Half Gallery installation as art historian Celeste Brusati observed in her essay "Natural Artifice and Material Values in Dutch Still Life" (1997), concerning painters in the seventeenth century: their strategy was to "perform a double function, on the one hand, simultaneously creating compelling pictorial fictions and inviting the viewer to reflect on the artifice by which those illustrations are produced."

I saw Tamuna for the last time at James Fuentes gallery in October 2015, at the opening of her second, final solo show in New York. I motioned at *They Made It Because of the Time* (2015; p. 34), a canvas of oil stick and pastel that shows two adjacent pomegranates in silhouette. Their blood-red outlines are reduced to basic, flattened forms: a calyx of schematic spikes atop plump circles to denote the fruit's leathery flesh. Rendered in a knowingly messy scrawl reminiscent of childhood, that symbol of fertility and reproduction—everywhere present in the popular imagery of the artist's homeland—became, in Tamuna's hands, a marker of creative vitality. Prompted for an explanation, she simply noted: "They are somehow always with me."

On canvas, along the boundary between abstraction and figuration, Tamuna too remains as palpable and present as ever. Though she is no longer embodied in person, her brushstrokes outlive her physical presence as a gesture realized in perpetuity—a kind of posthumous vitality made possible by the eternal stasis of painting.

Paintings

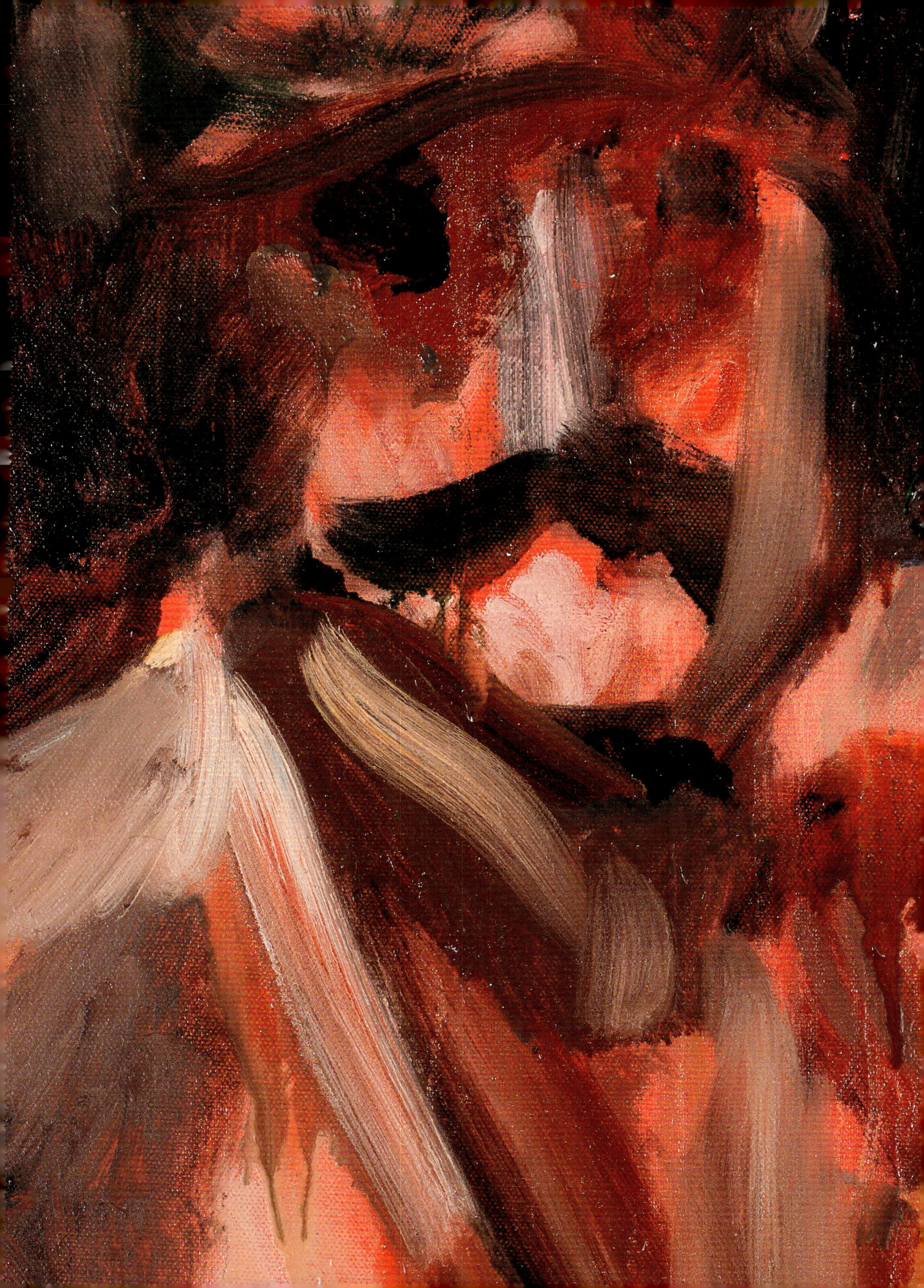

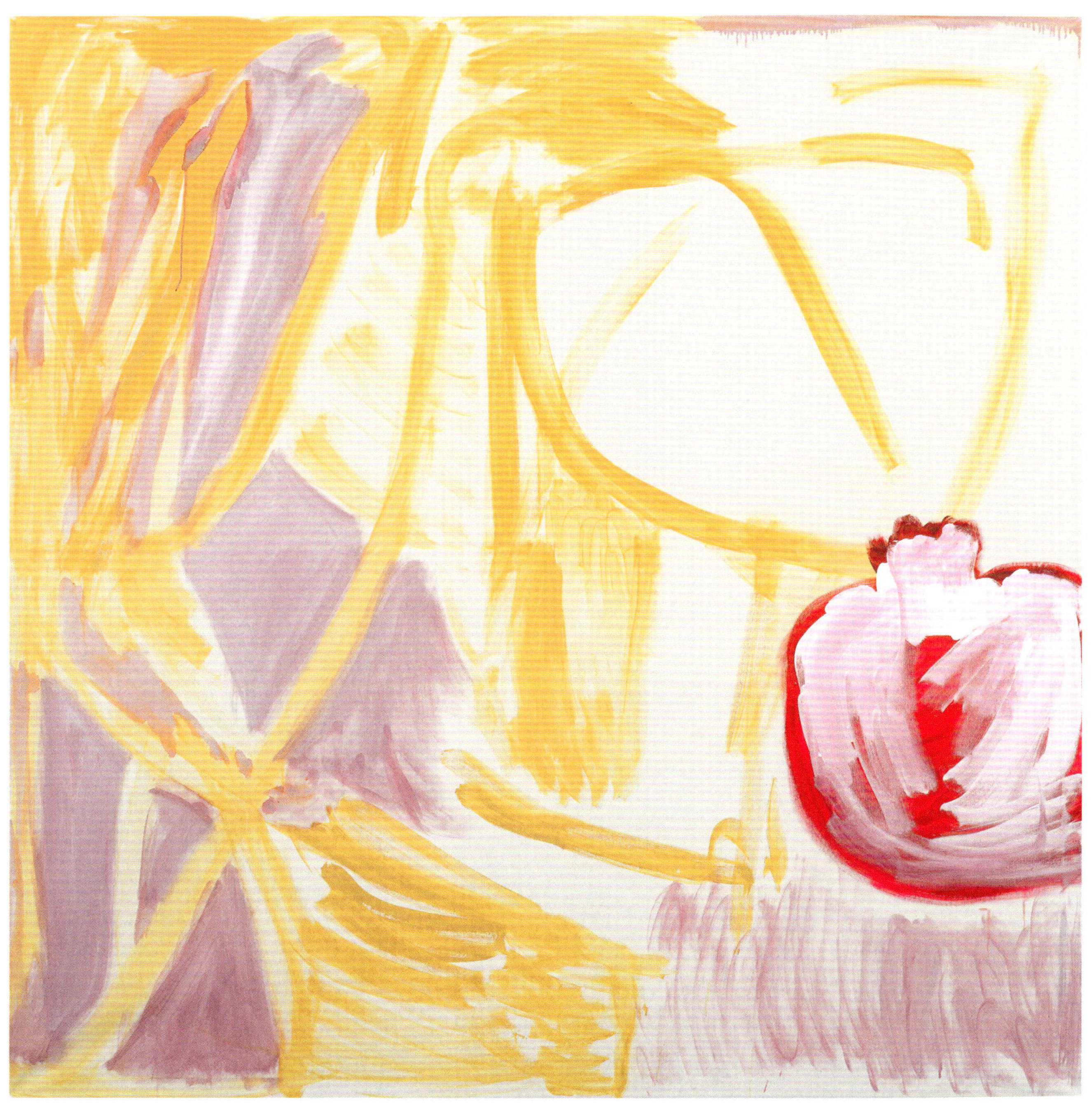

Pomegranate, 2014
acrylic on canvas, 78 ¾ × 78 ¾ inches | 200 × 200 cm

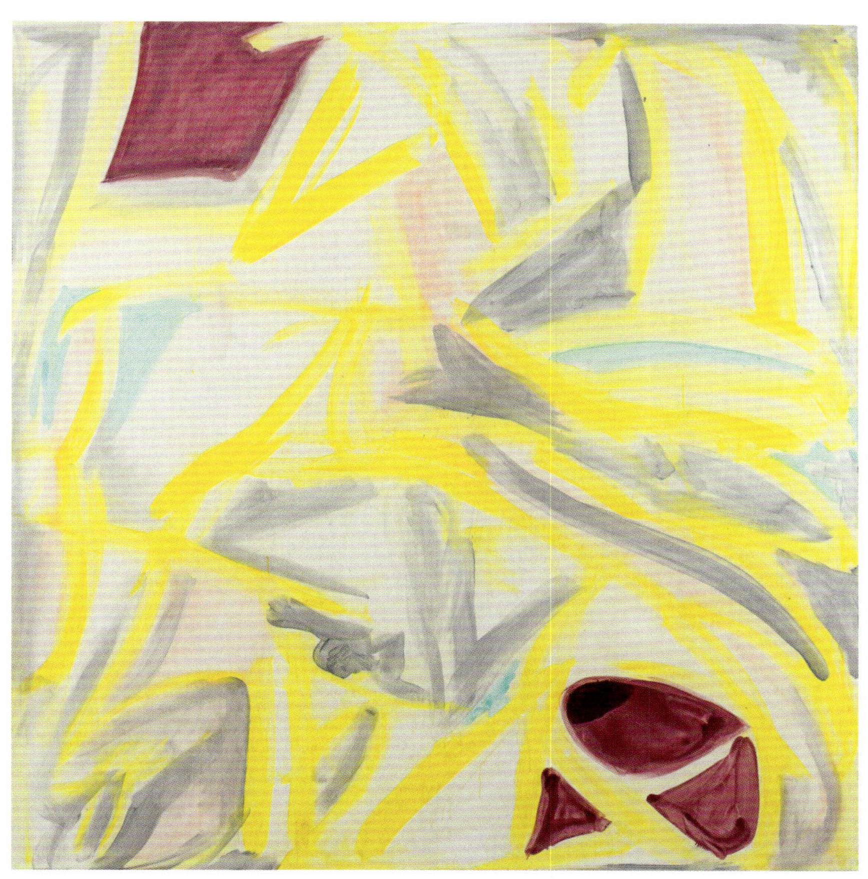

Dedicated, 2014
acrylic on canvas, 78 ¾ × 78 ¾ inches | 200 × 200 cm

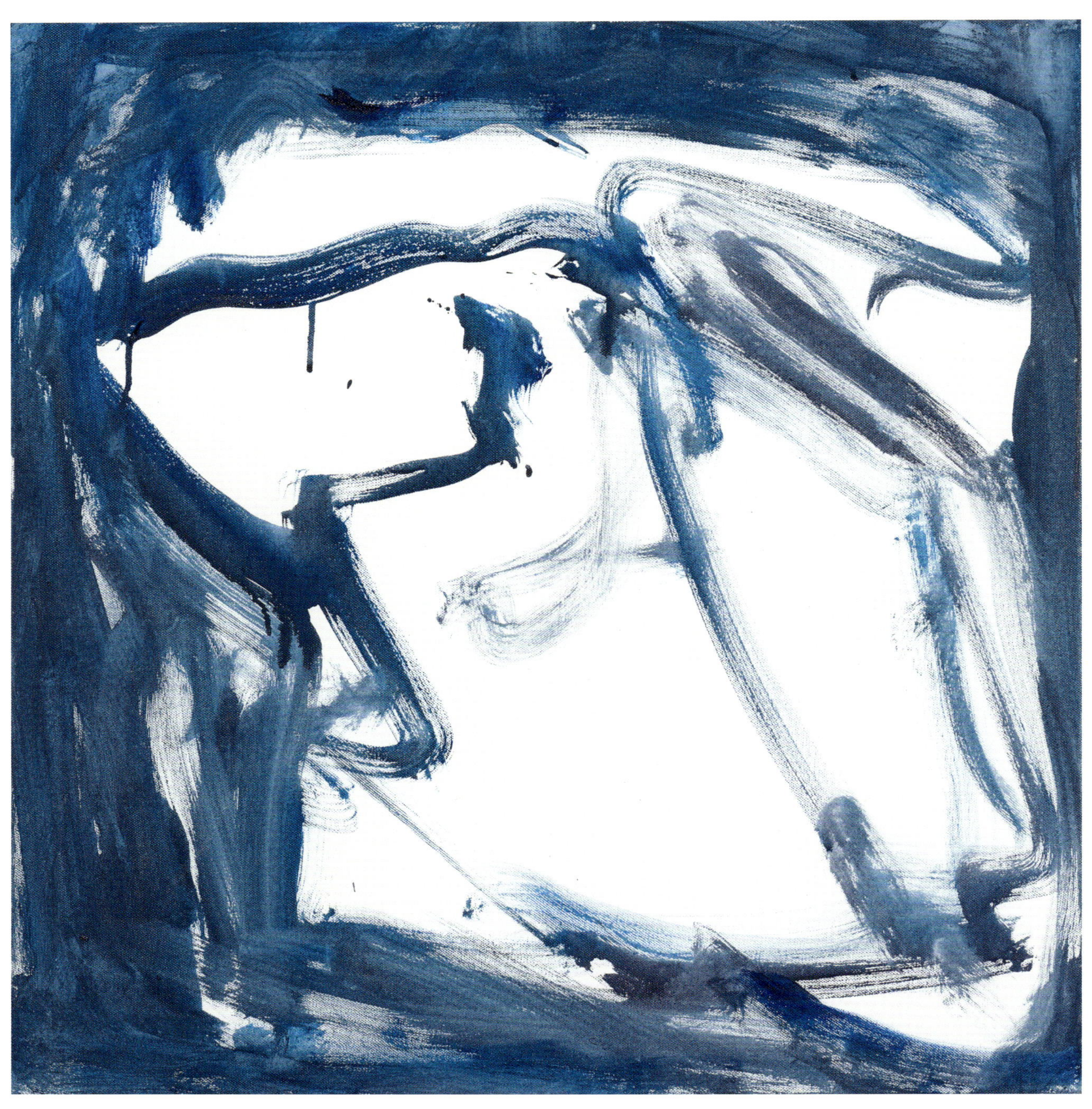

B & W, 2010
acrylic on canvas, 27 ½ × 27 ½ inches | 70 × 70 cm

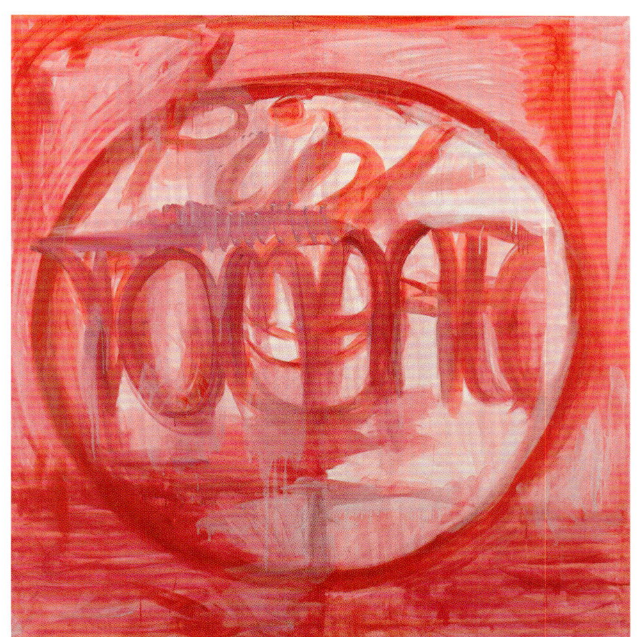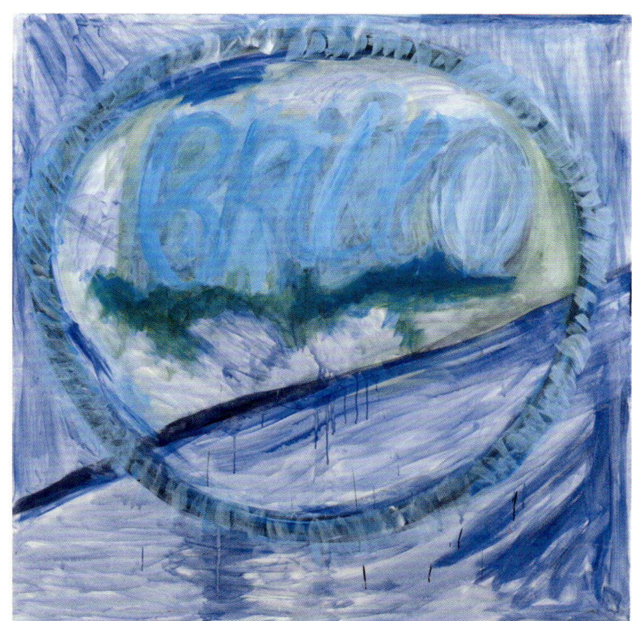

Pink Tomato, 2013
acrylic on canvas, 78 ¾ × 78 ¾ inches | 200 × 200 cm

Brillo, 2014
acrylic on canvas, 78 ¾ × 78 ¾ inches | 200 × 200 cm

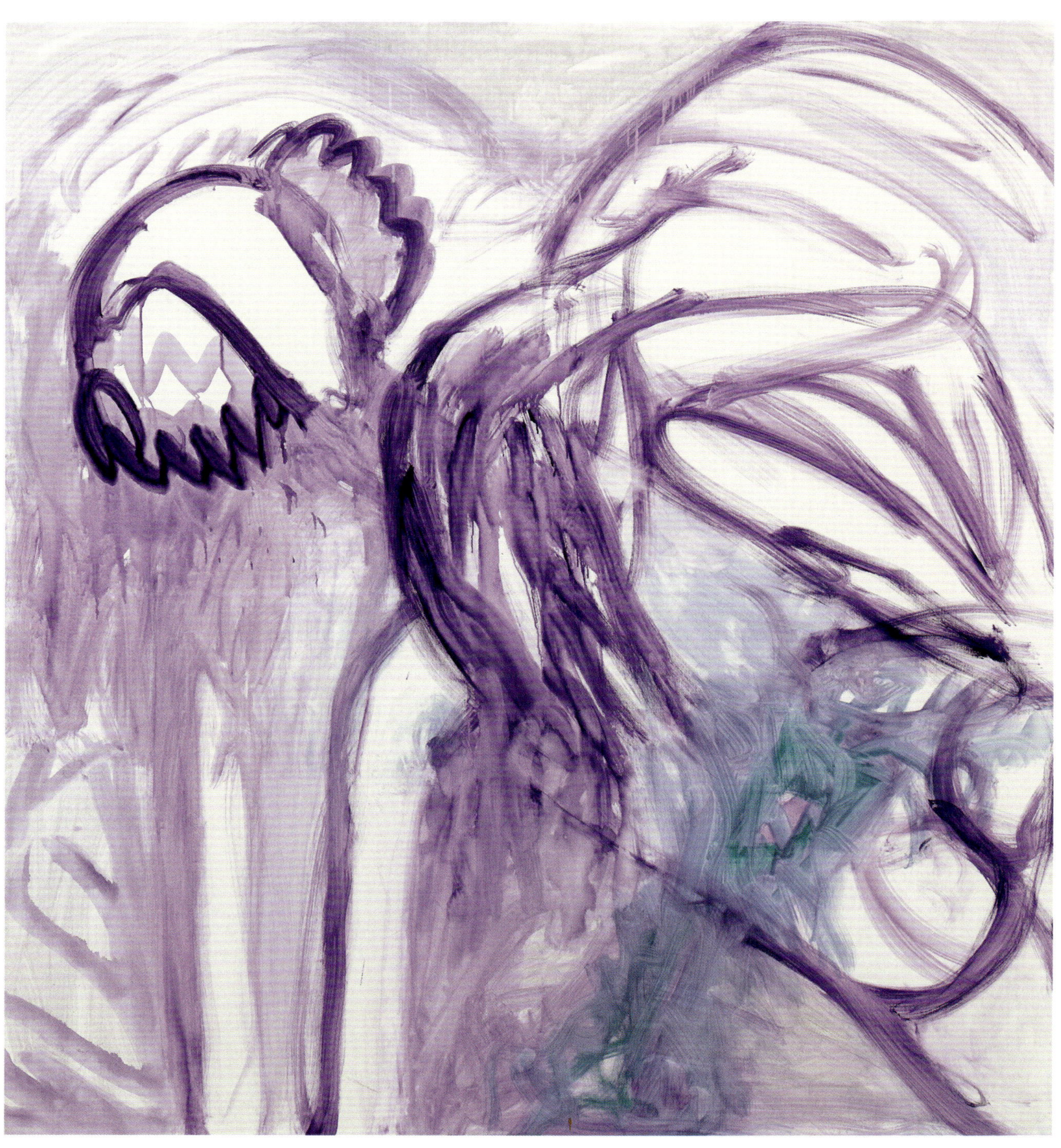

Not Regularly / Violet Violence, 2006
acrylic on canvas, 78 ¾ × 74 ¾ inches | 200 × 190 cm

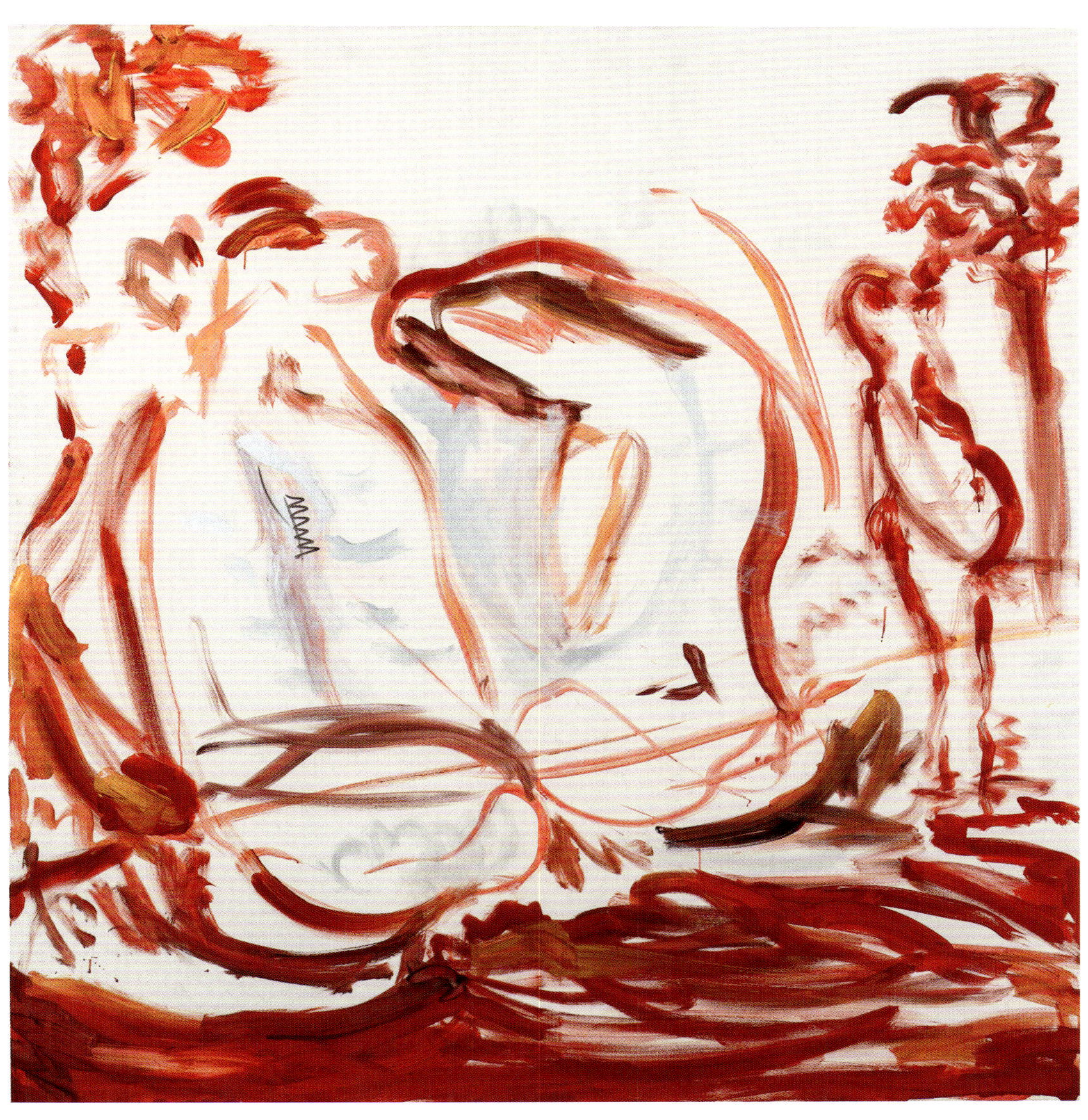

When a Baby Was Pissing In Her Belly, 2006
acrylic on canvas, 78 ¾ × 78 ¾ inches | 200 × 200 cm

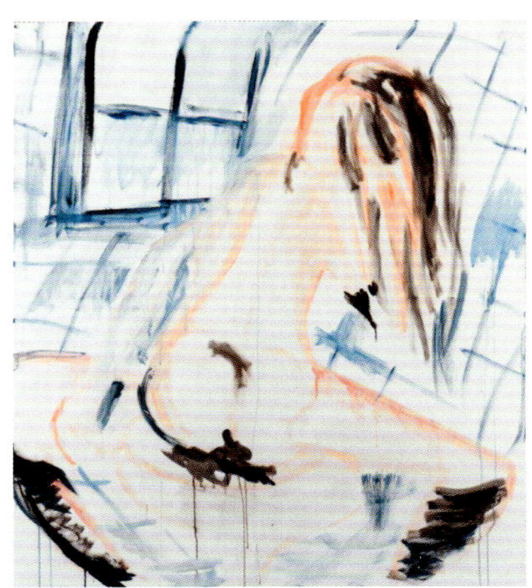

Untitled, n.d.
acrylic on canvas, 78 ¾ × 70 ½ inches | 200 × 179 cm

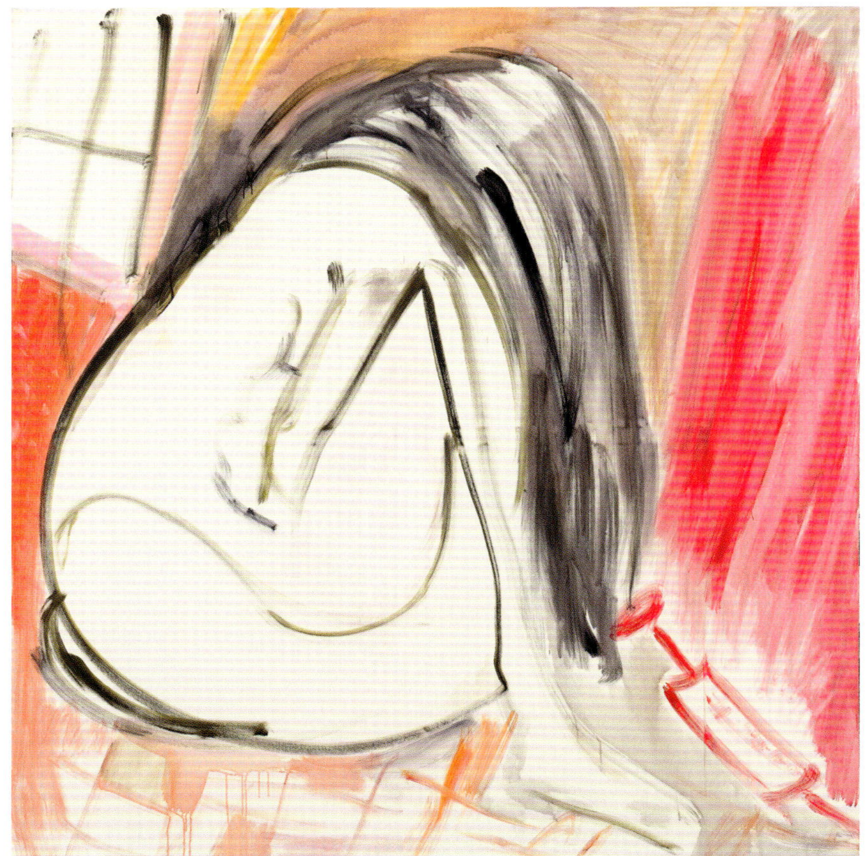

Tryangel, 2007
acrylic on canvas, 78 ¾ × 78 ¾ inches | 200 × 200 cm

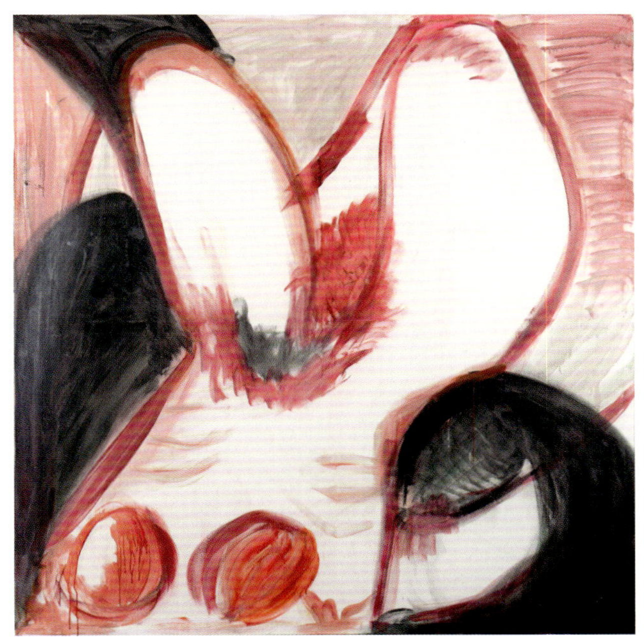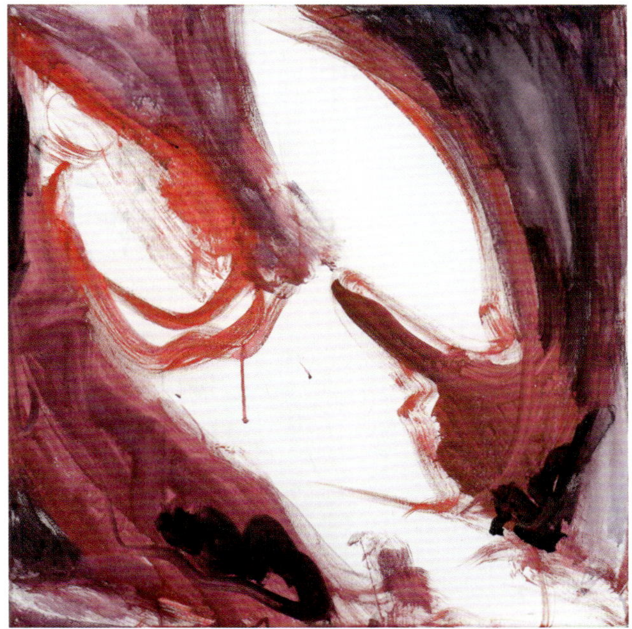

Tits, 2014
acrylic on canvas, 78 ¾ × 78 ¾ inches | 200 × 200 cm

Torso, 2015
acrylic on canvas, 27 ½ × 27 ½ inches | 70 × 70 cm

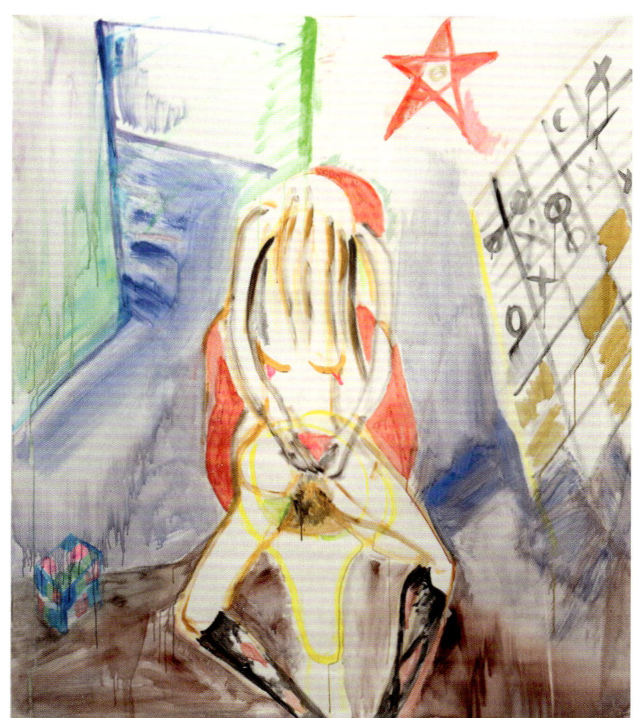

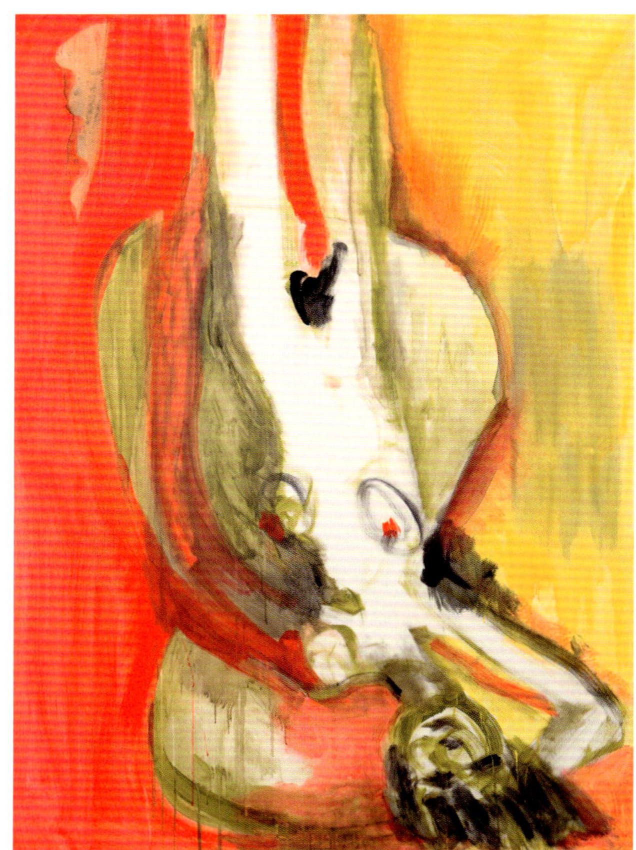

Unter den roten Sternen / Cubic Rubic (Communist), 2005
acrylic on canvas, 82 ¾ × 63 inches | 210 × 160 cm

Expectation in Venice, 2005
acrylic on canvas, 63 × 47 ¼ inches | 160 × 120 cm

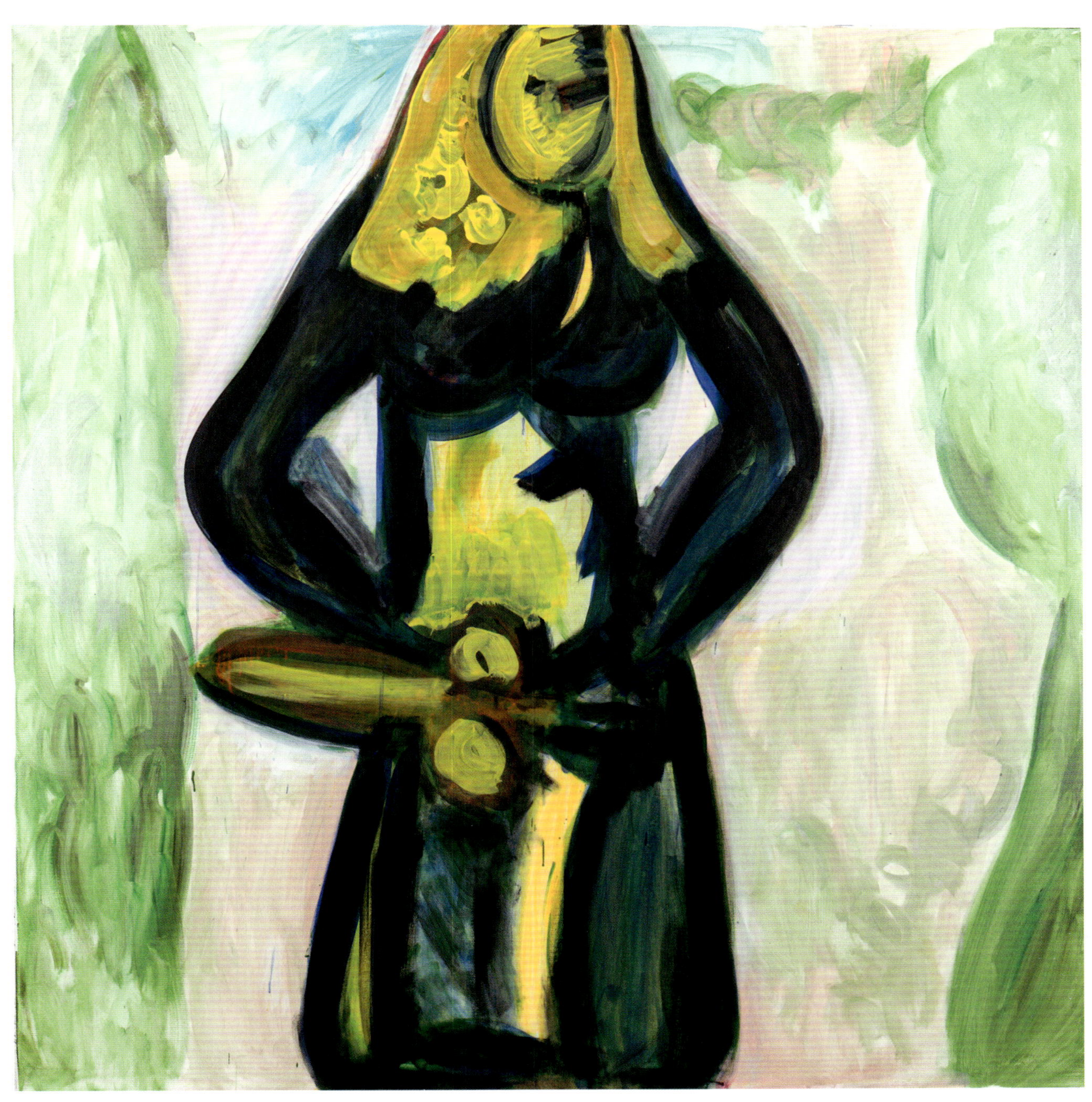

Almost Mona Lisa, 2014
acrylic on canvas, 78 ¾ × 78 ¾ inches | 200 × 200 cm

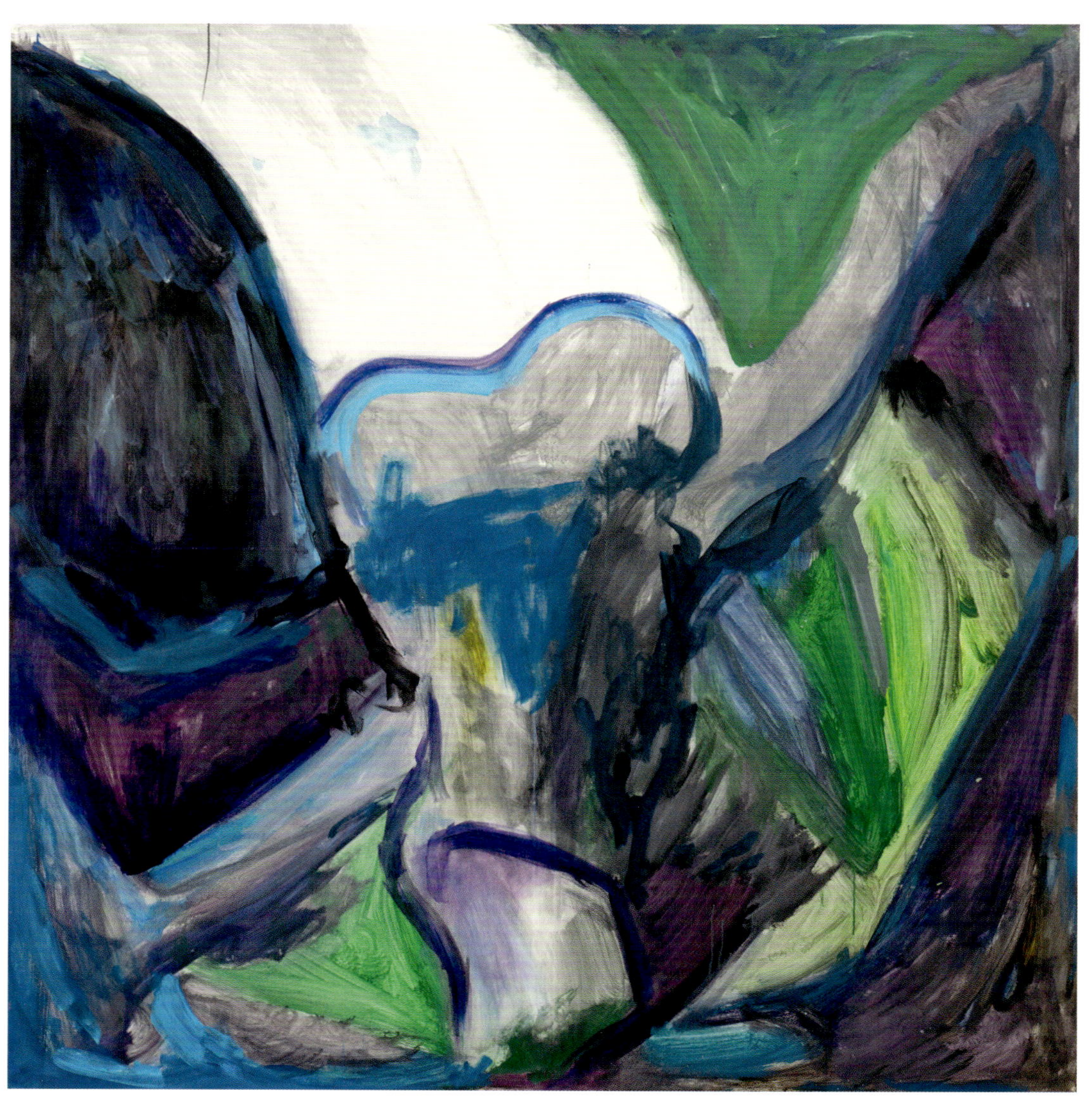

Earth, 2011
acrylic on canvas, 78 ¾ × 78 ¾ inches | 200 × 200 cm

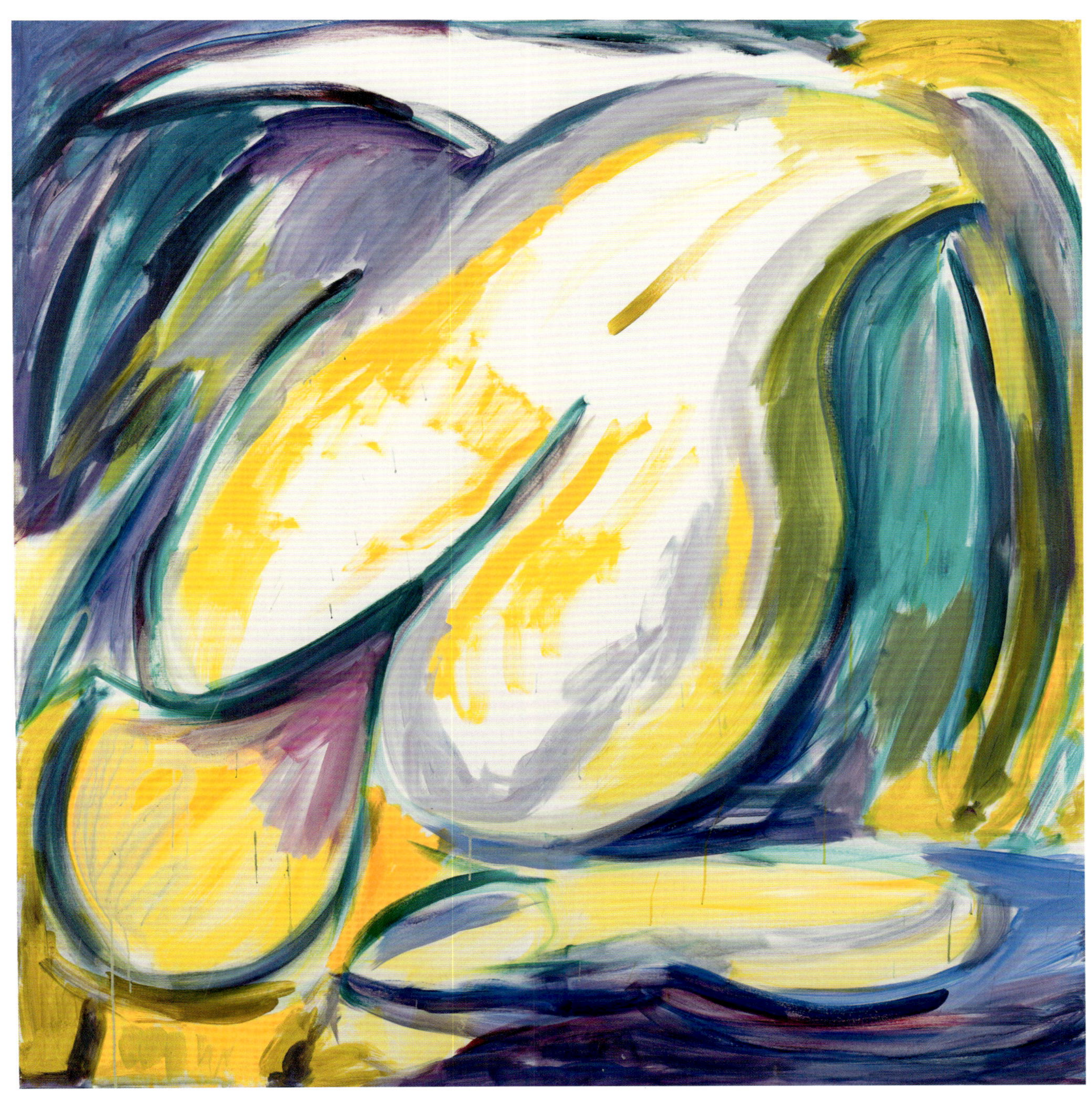

Matisse, 2012
acrylic on canvas, 78 ¾ × 78 ¾ inches | 200 × 200 cm

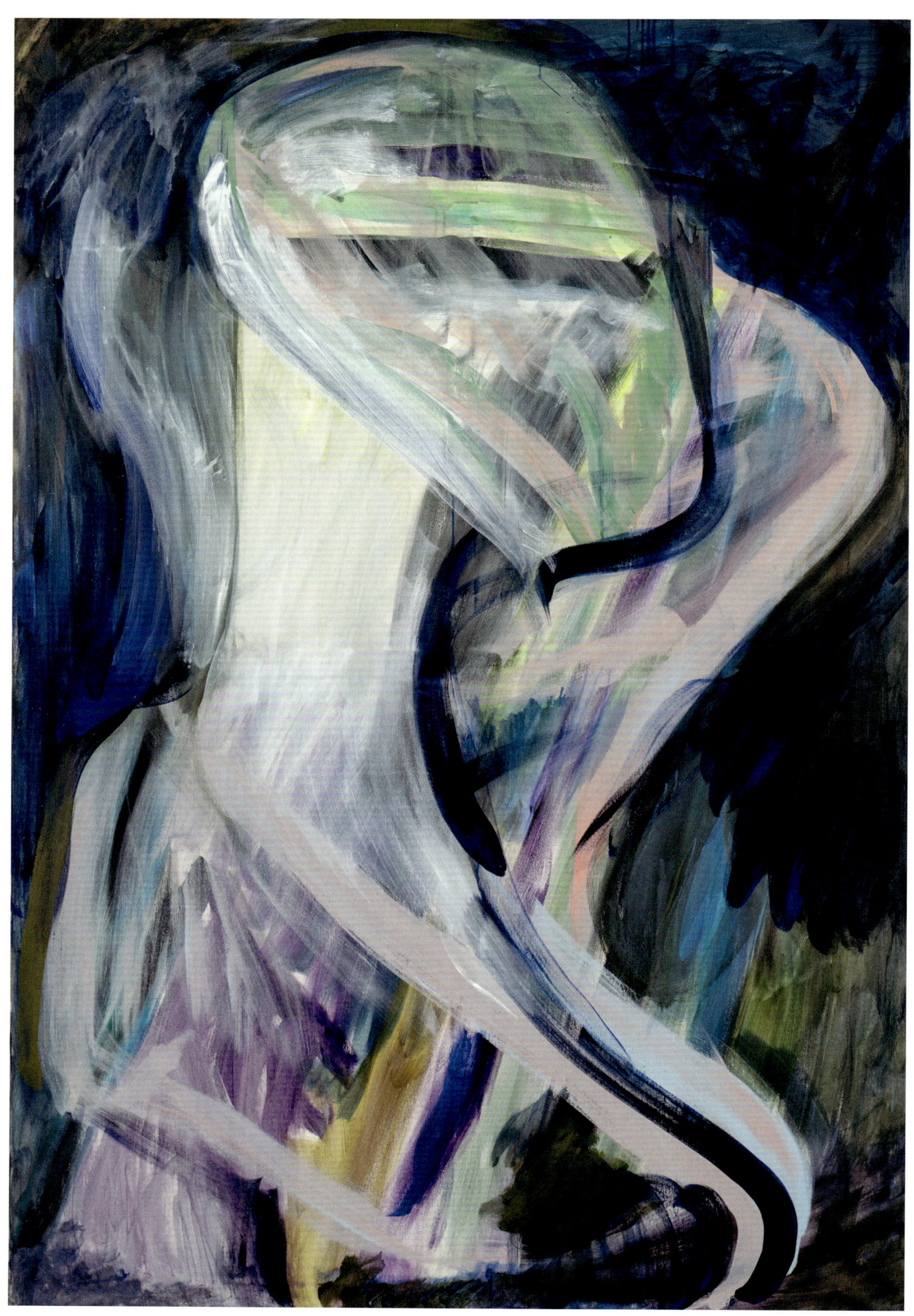

Untitled, 2005
acrylic on canvas, 76 ¾ × 53 ¼ inches | 195 × 135 cm

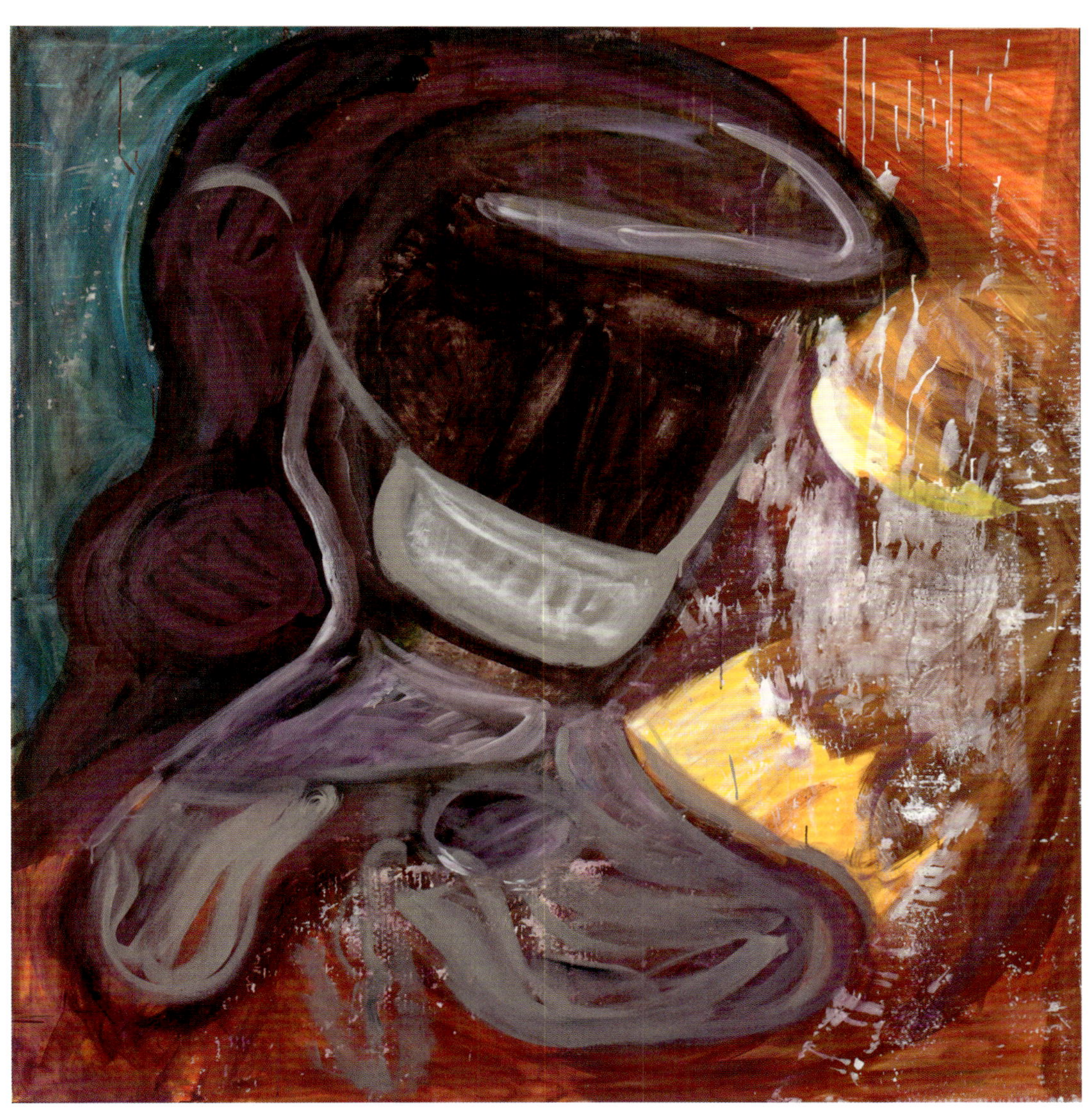

Birdshit Pigeon, 2014
acrylic on canvas, 78 ¾ × 78 ¾ inches | 200 × 200 cm

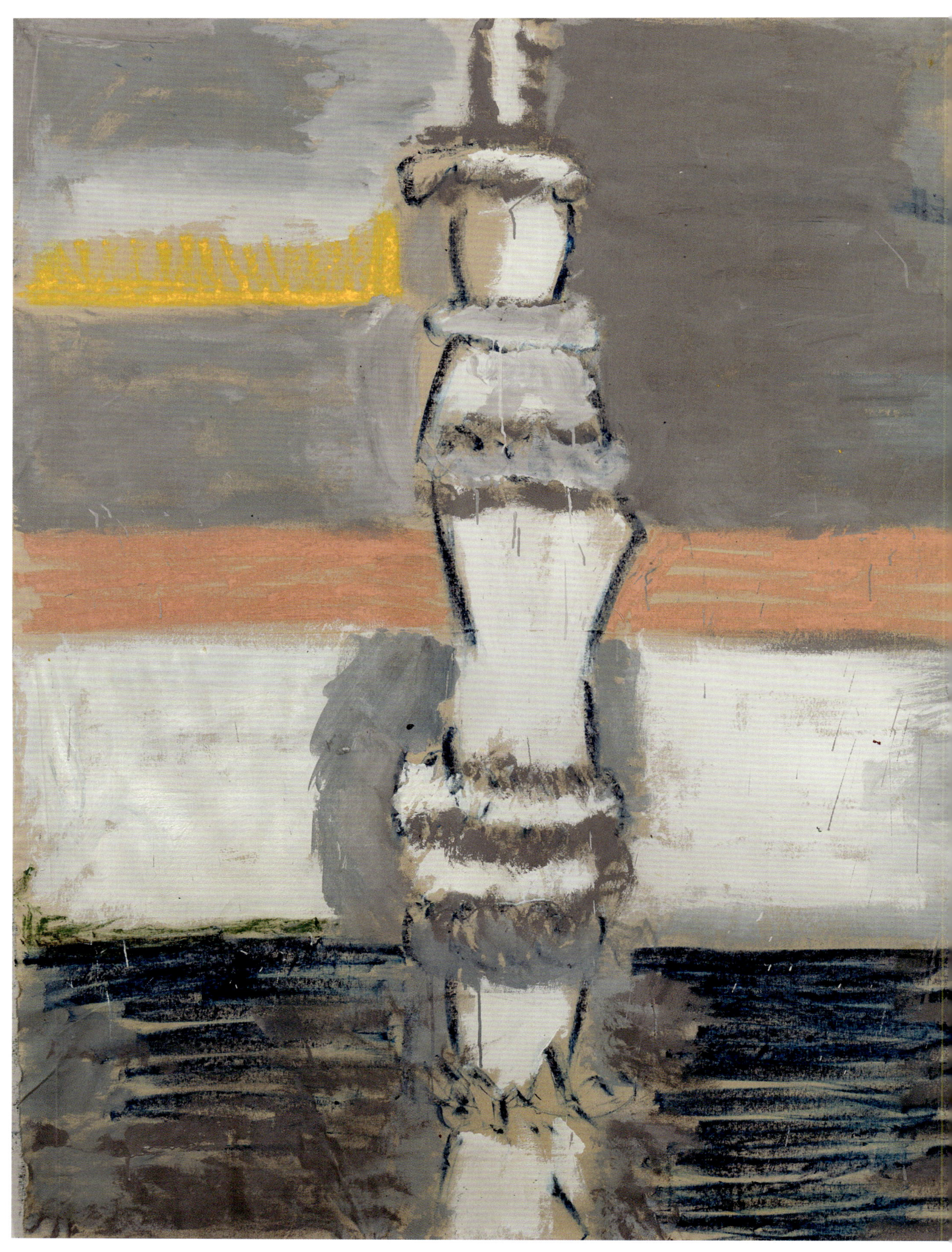

White Columns, 2011
oil stick and acrylic on canvas, 78 ¾ × 118 ⅛ inches | 200 × 300 cm

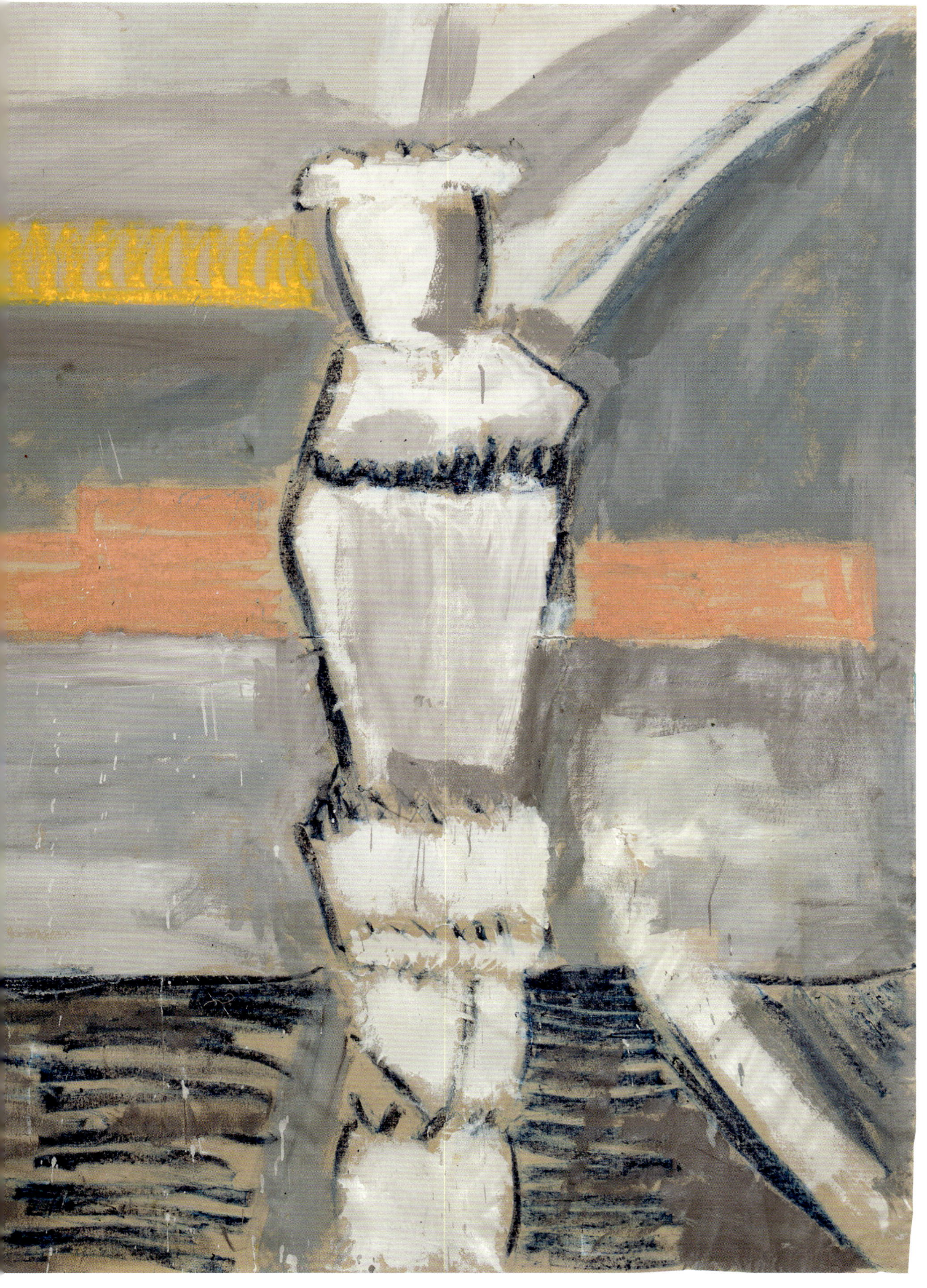

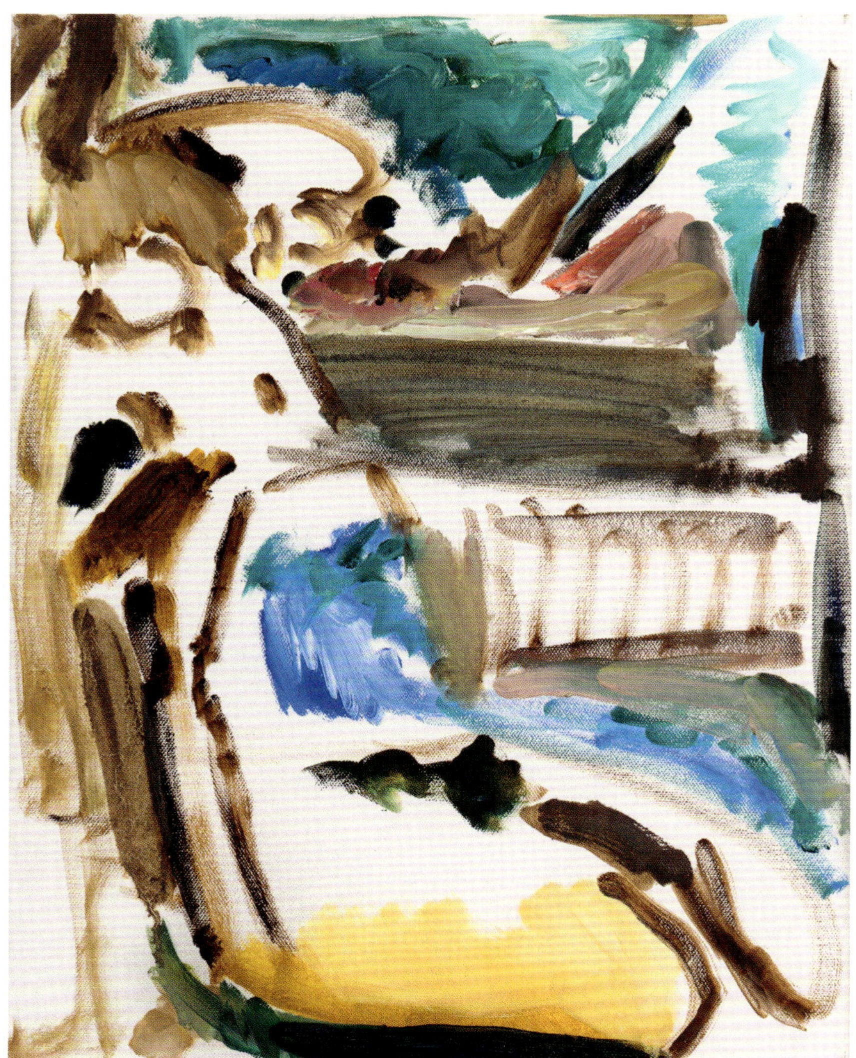

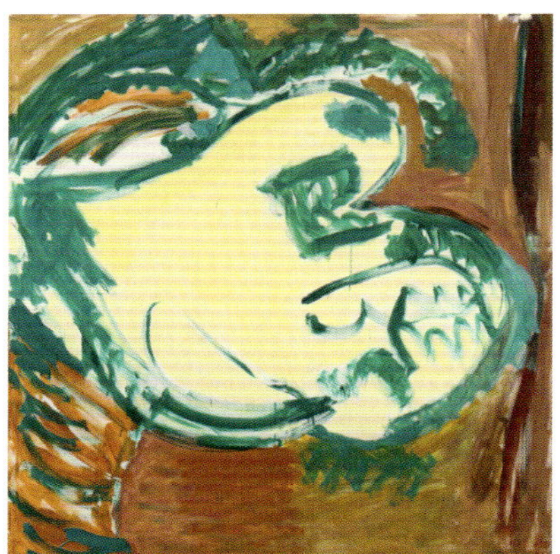

At the Beach, 2002
acrylic on canvas, 19 ¾ × 15 ¾ inches | 50 × 40 cm

UNDEAD, 2008
acrylic on canvas, 78 ¾ × 78 ¾ inches | 200 × 200 cm

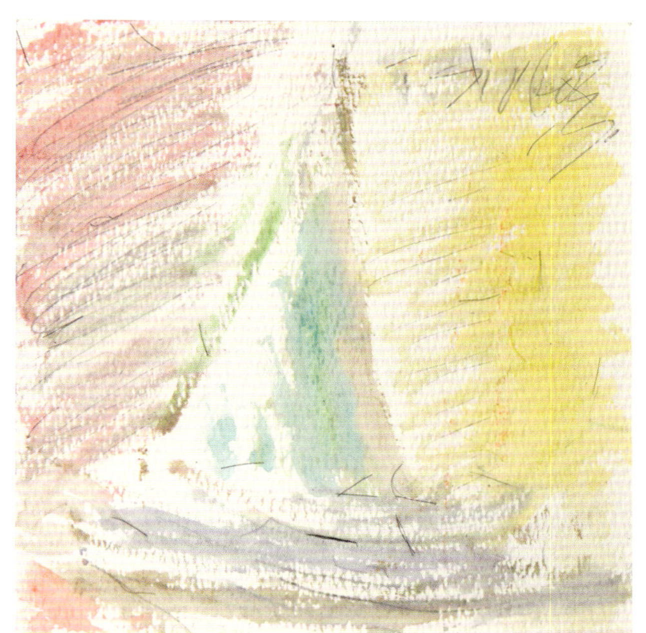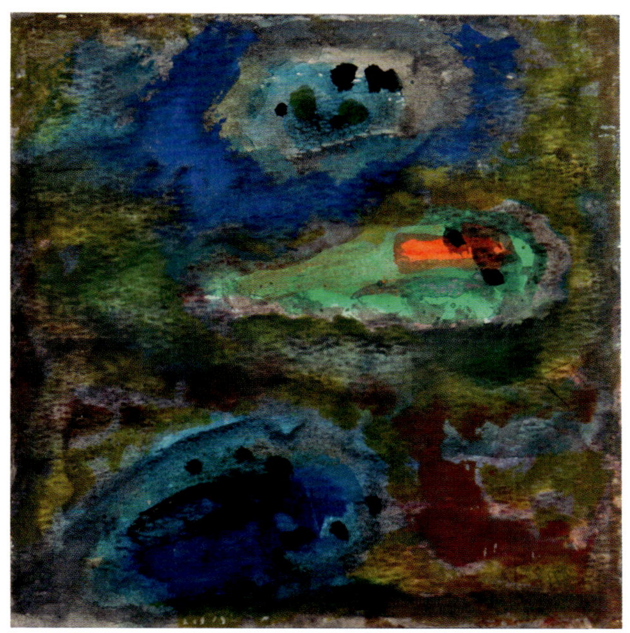

2 Aquarells, 2004
watercolor on paper; two parts, each: 7 ⅞ × 7 ⅞ | 20 × 20 cm

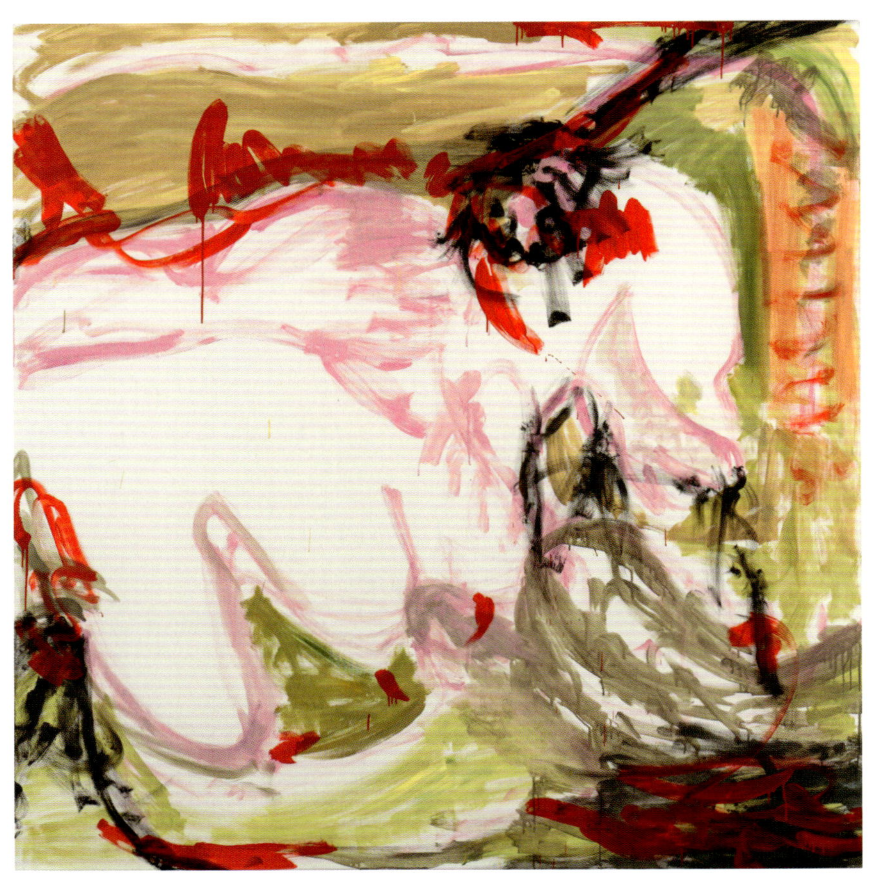

St. Dragon, 2008
acrylic on canvas, 78 ¾ × 78 ¾ inches | 200 × 200 cm

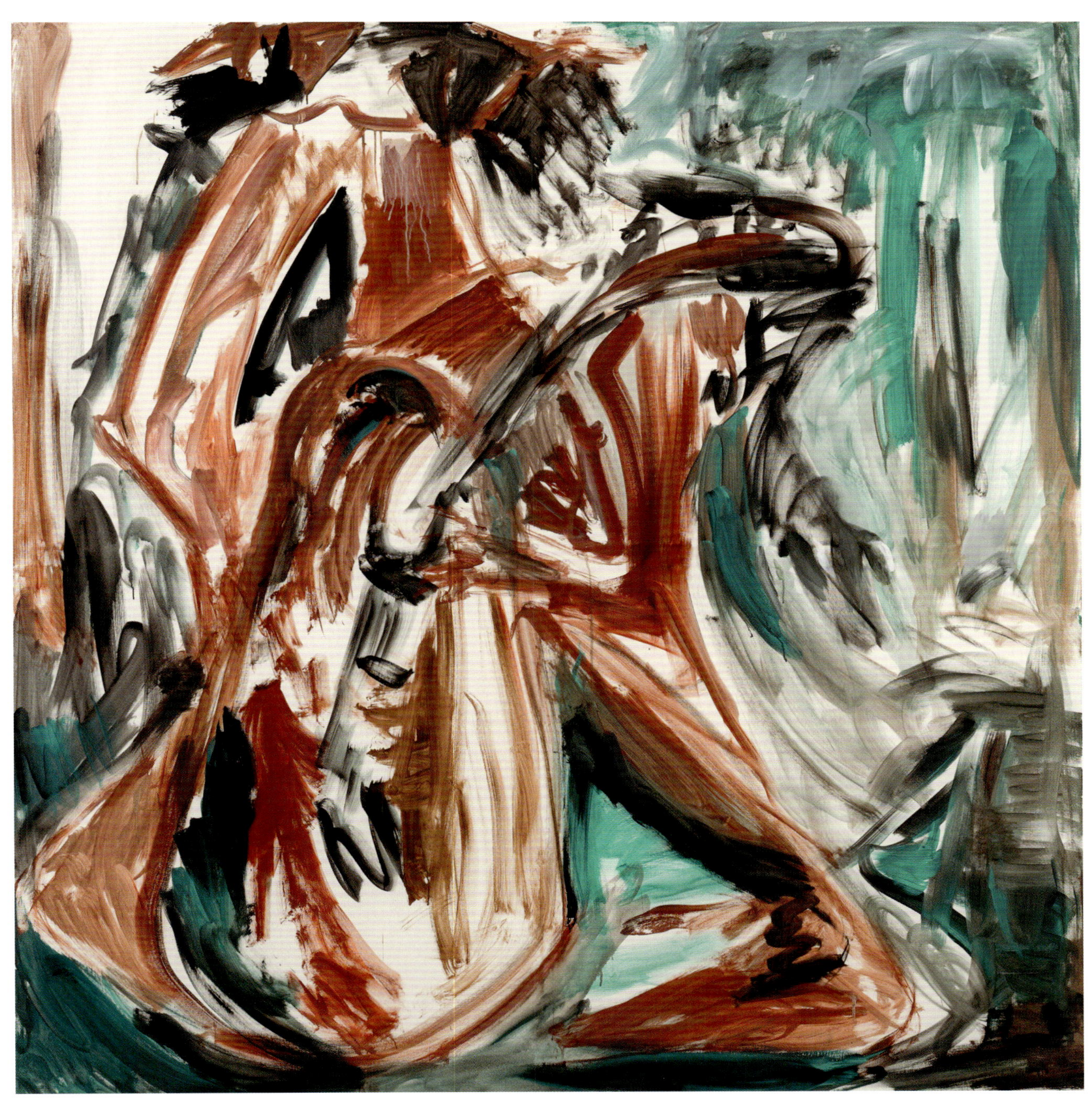

Guitar, 2010—2015
acrylic on canvas, 78 ¾ × 78 ¾ inches | 200 × 200 cm

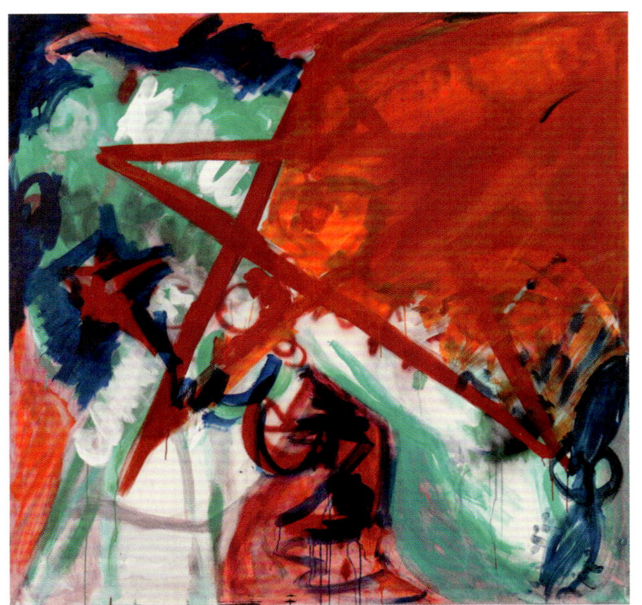

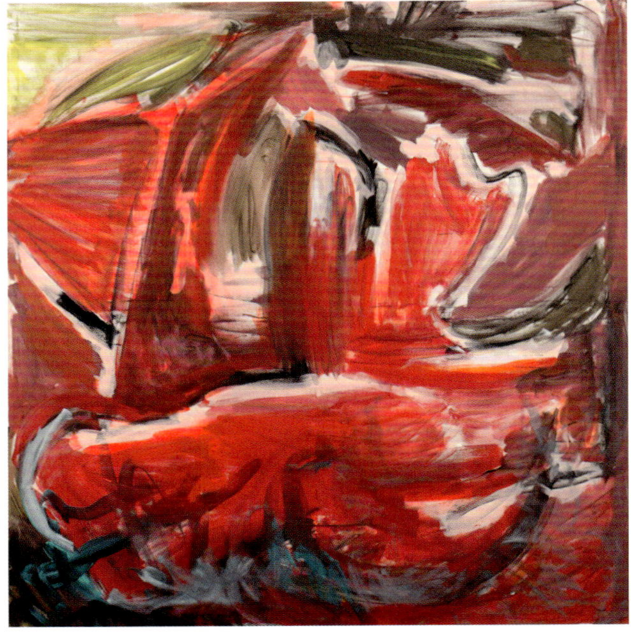

Eraserhead, 2008
acrylic on canvas, 74 ¾ × 78 ¾ inches | 190 × 200 cm

Concentrate on Metaphor, 2011
acrylic on canvas, 78 ¾ × 78 ¾ inches | 200 × 200 cm

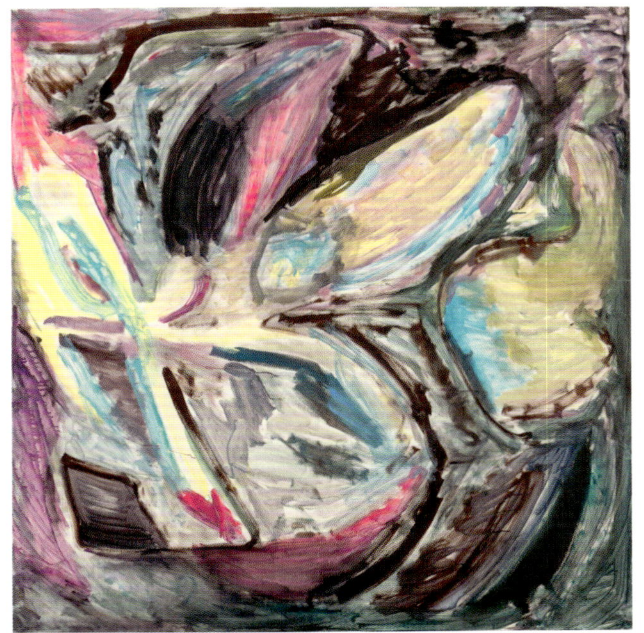

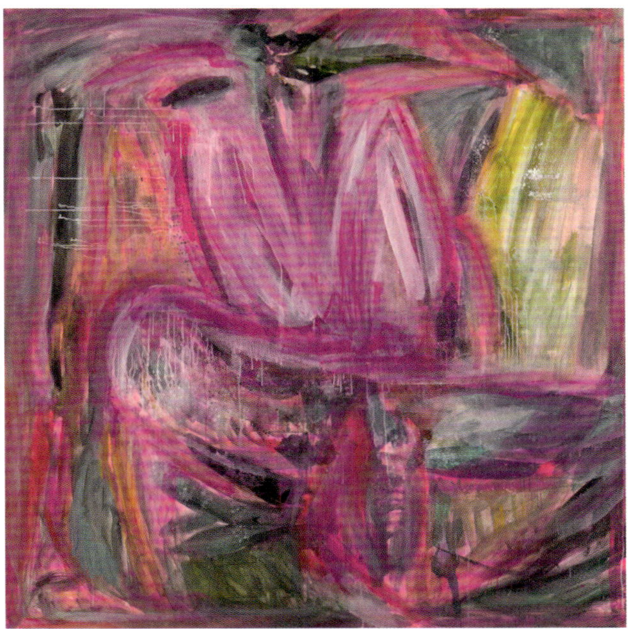

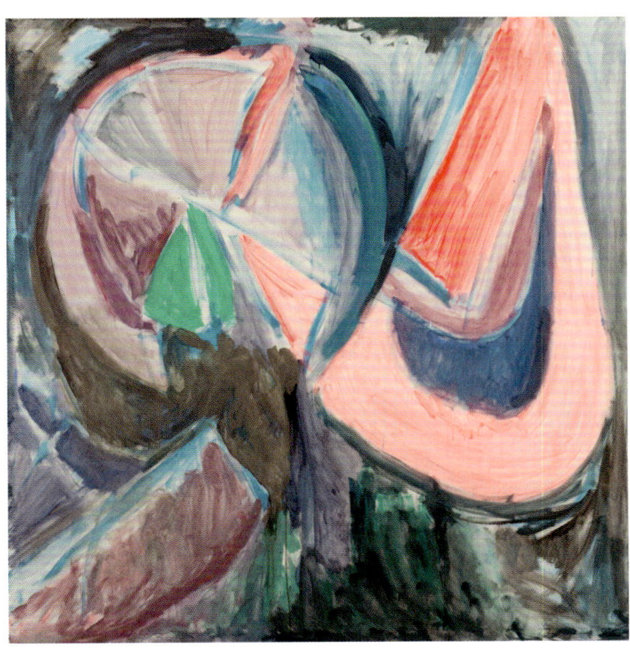

FLORA, 2012
acrylic on canvas, 78 ¾ × 78 ¾ inches | 200 × 200 cm

Literary Cachet, 2014
acrylic on canvas, 78 ¾ × 78 ¾ inches | 200 × 200 cm

Fukushima Mon Amour, 2011—2015
acrylic on canvas, 78 ¾ × 78 ¾ inches | 200 × 200 cm

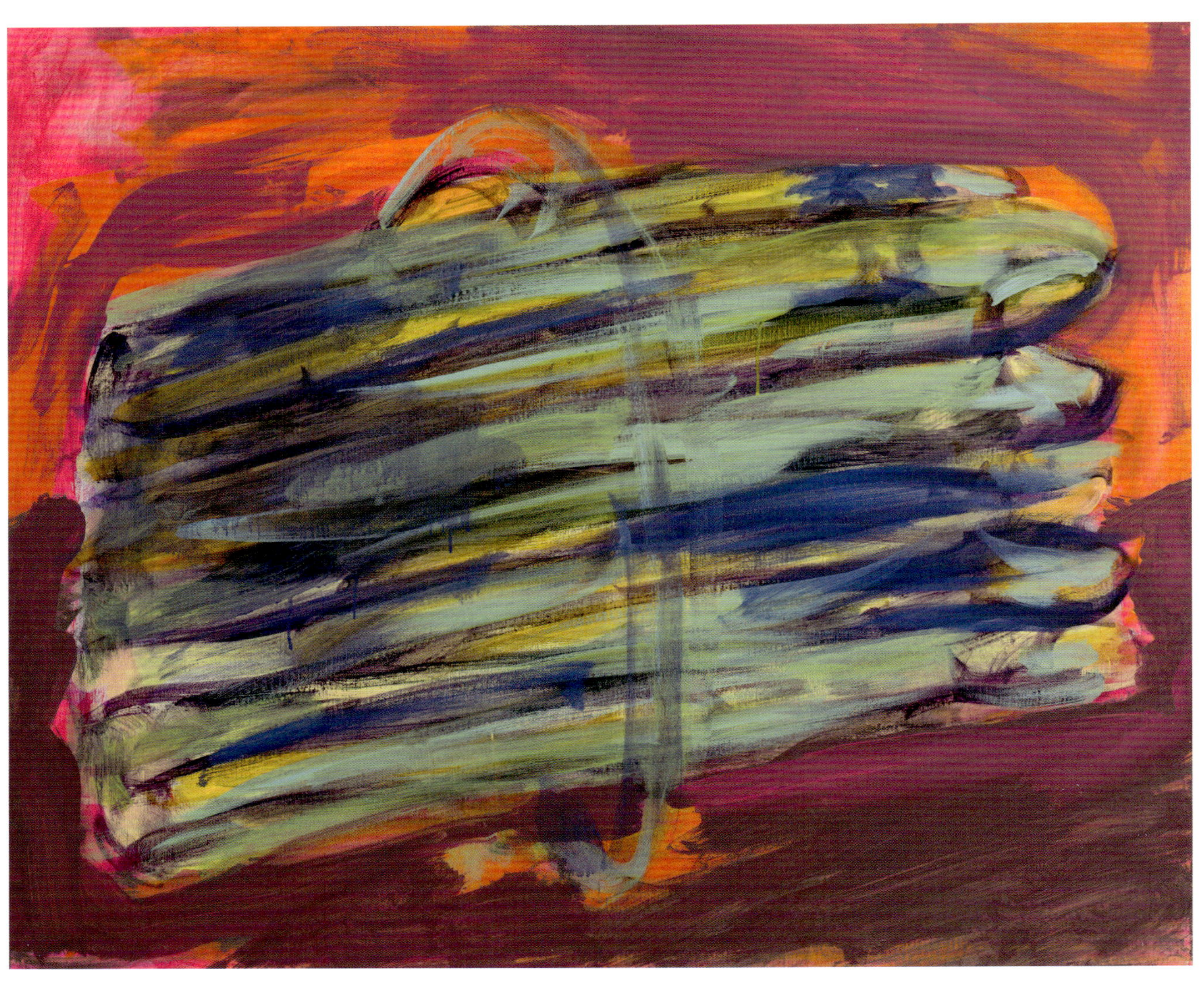

Asparagus, 2010
acrylic on canvas, 31 ½ × 39 ⅜ inches | 80 × 100 cm

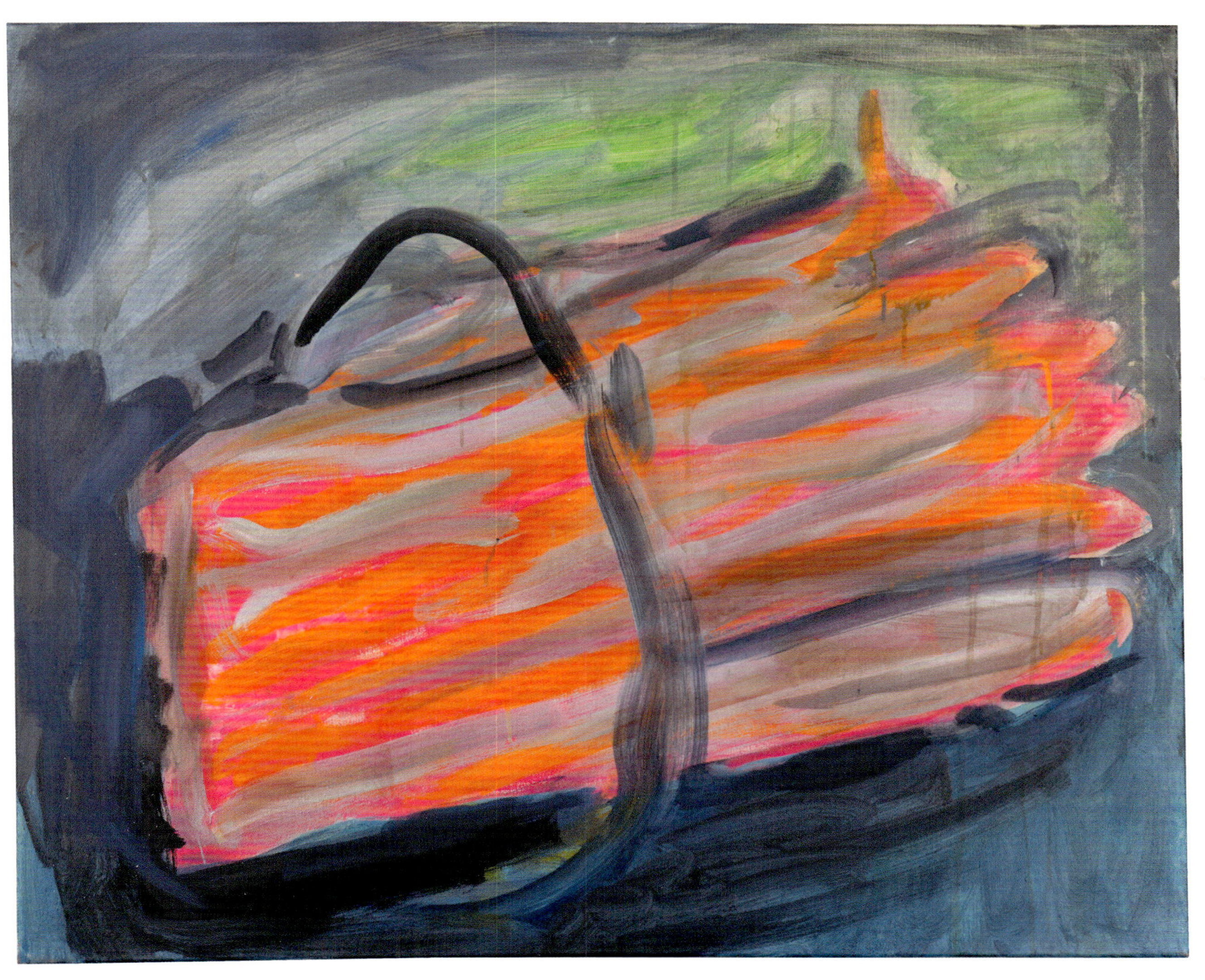

Asparagus 2, 2010
acrylic on canvas, 31½ × 39⅜ inches | 80 × 100 cm

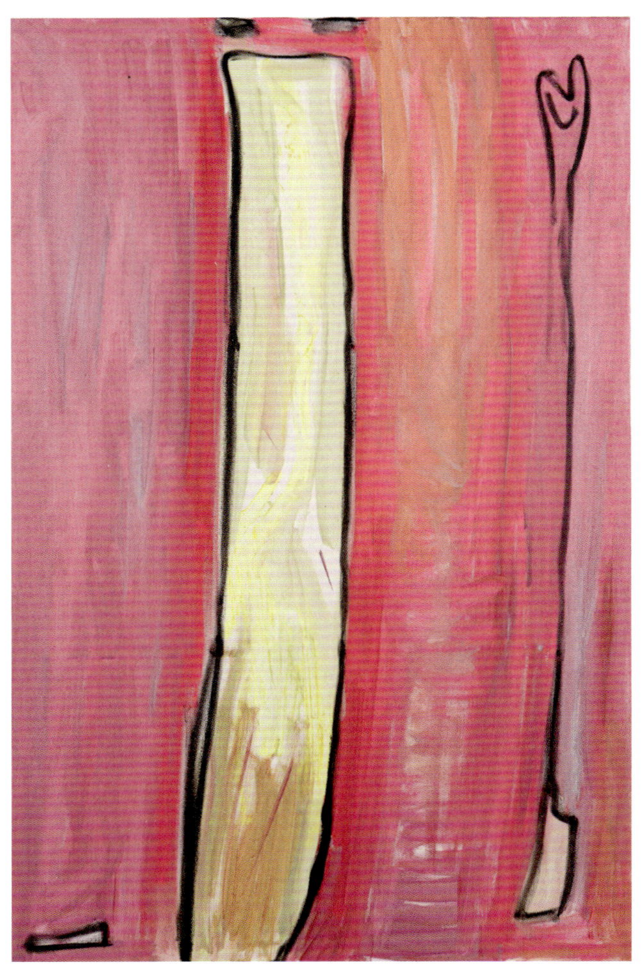

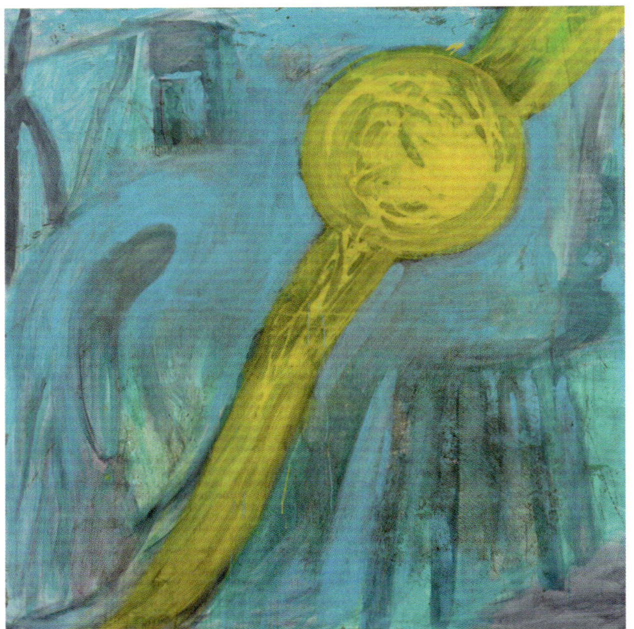

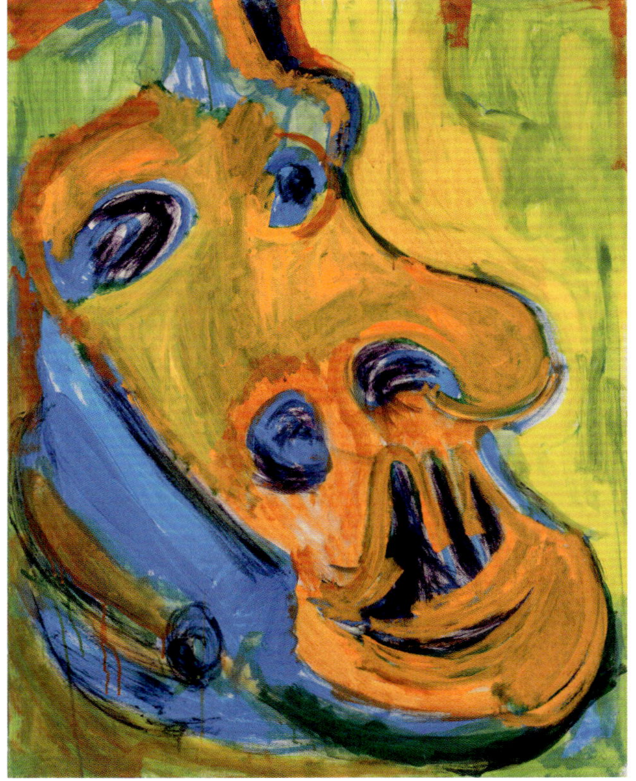

Asparagus–1 Proust, 2011–2015
oil on canvas, 59 × 39 ⅜ inches | 150 × 100 cm

Suwiny, 2013
acrylic on canvas, 78 ¾ × 78 ¾ inches | 200 × 200 cm

Portrait of Van Gogh, 2009
acrylic on canvas, 39 ⅜ × 31 ½ inches | 100 × 80 cm

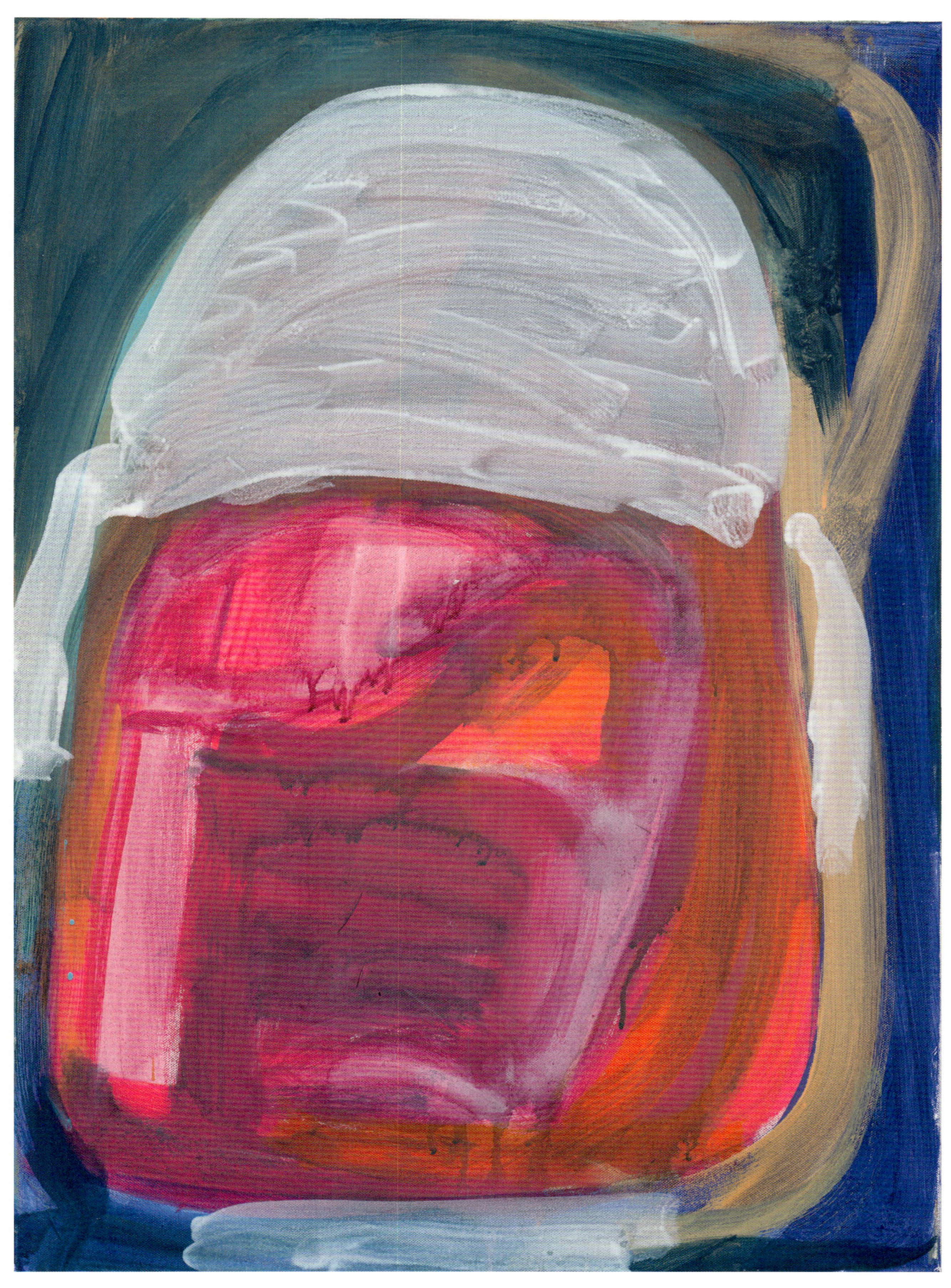

Kippi, 2010
acrylic on canvas, 31½ × 23⅝ inches | 80×60 cm

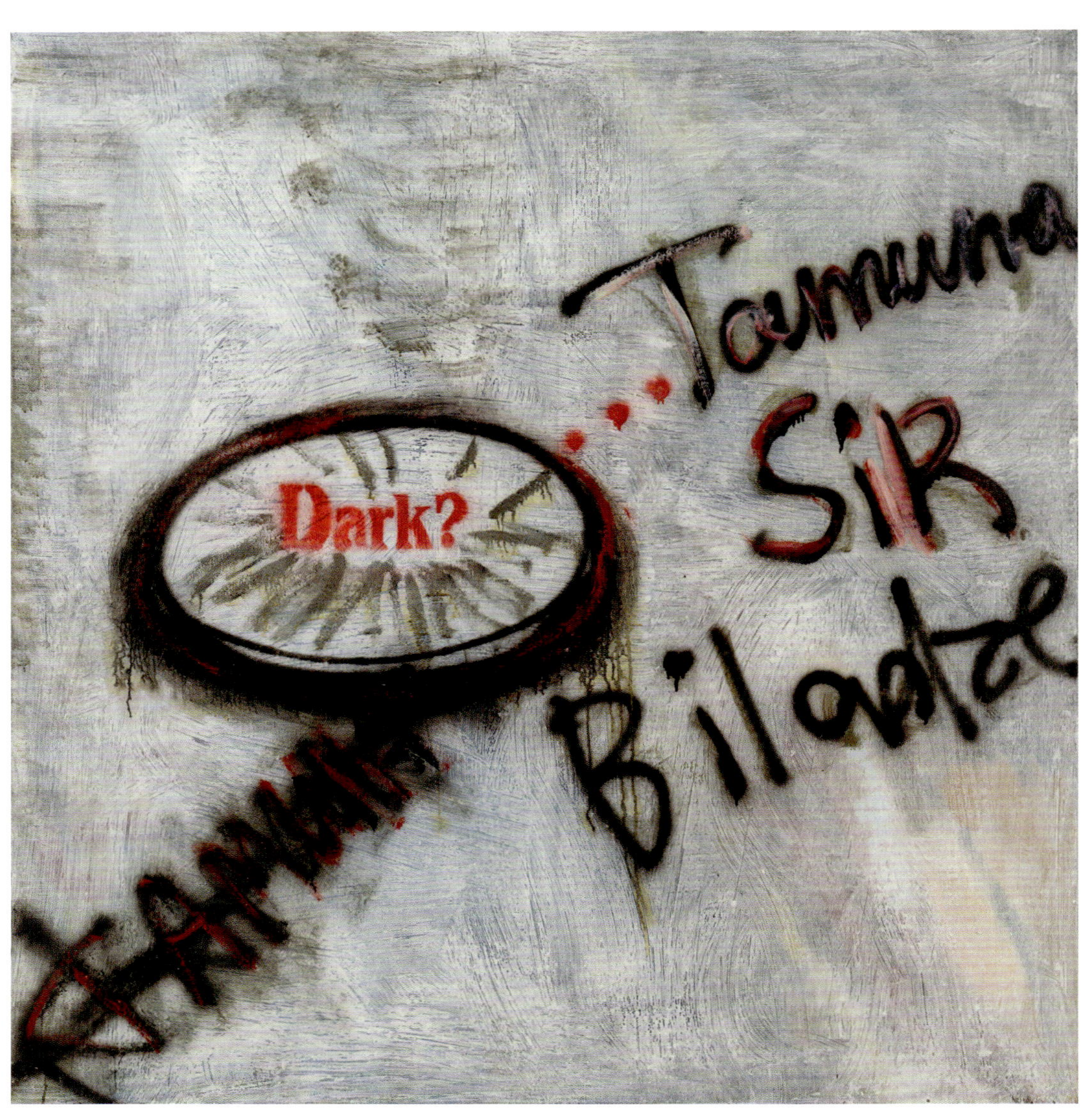

Tamuna Sir Biladze, n.d.
acrylic on canvas, 63 × 63 inches | 160 × 160 cm

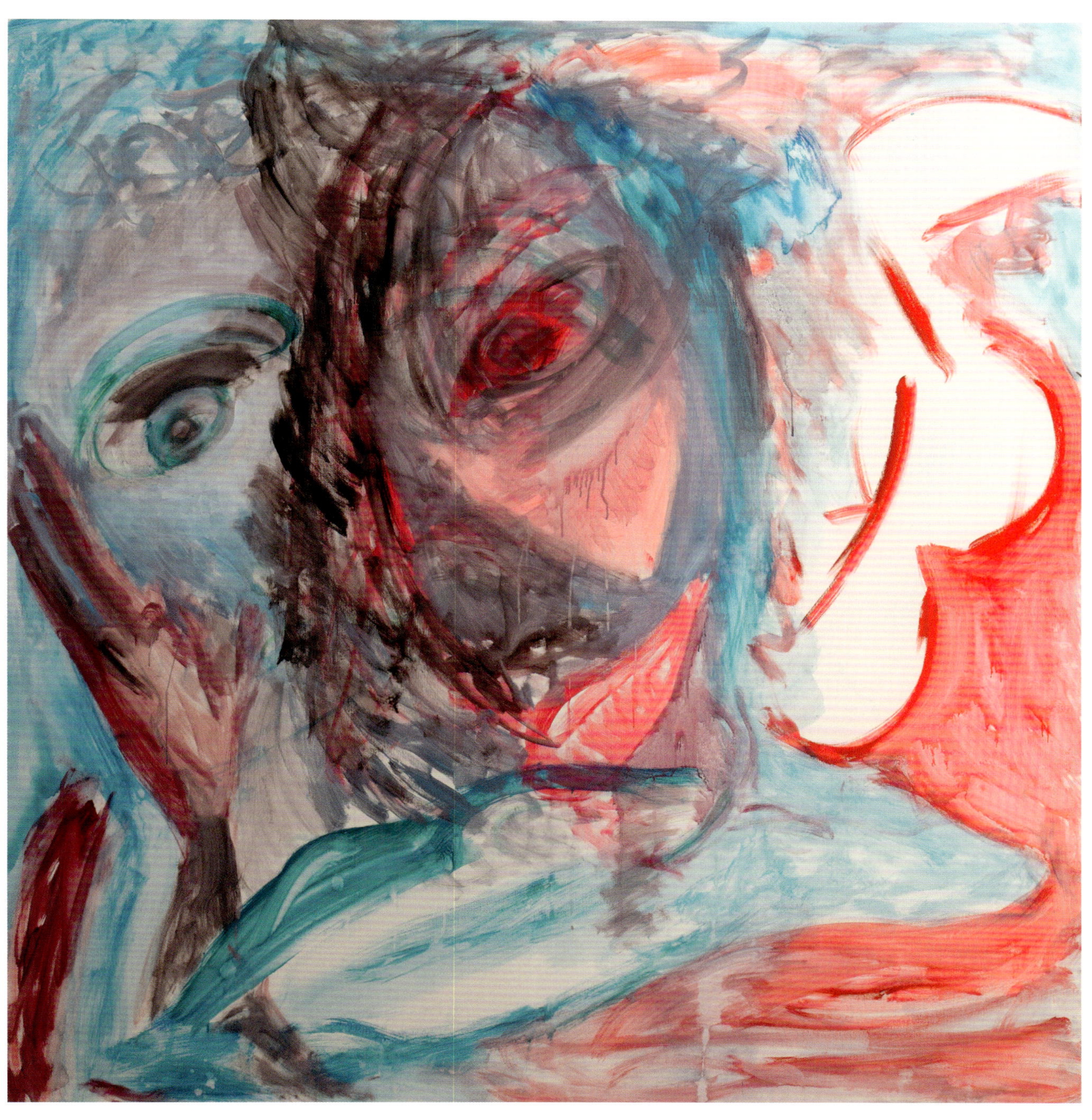

T. Predicted B. Fear "With Love", 2006–2010
acrylic on canvas, 78 ¾ × 78 ¾ inches | 200 × 200 cm

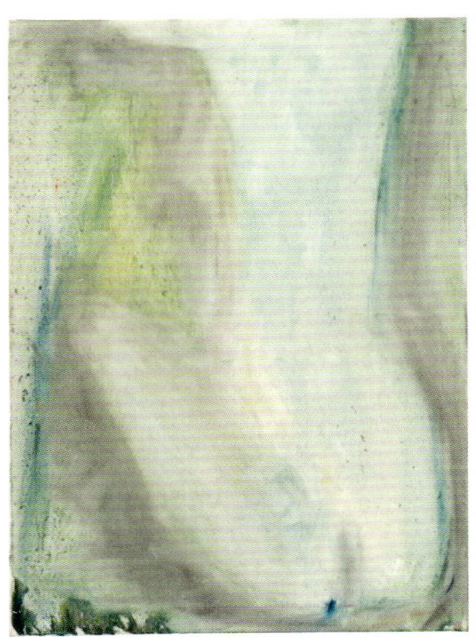

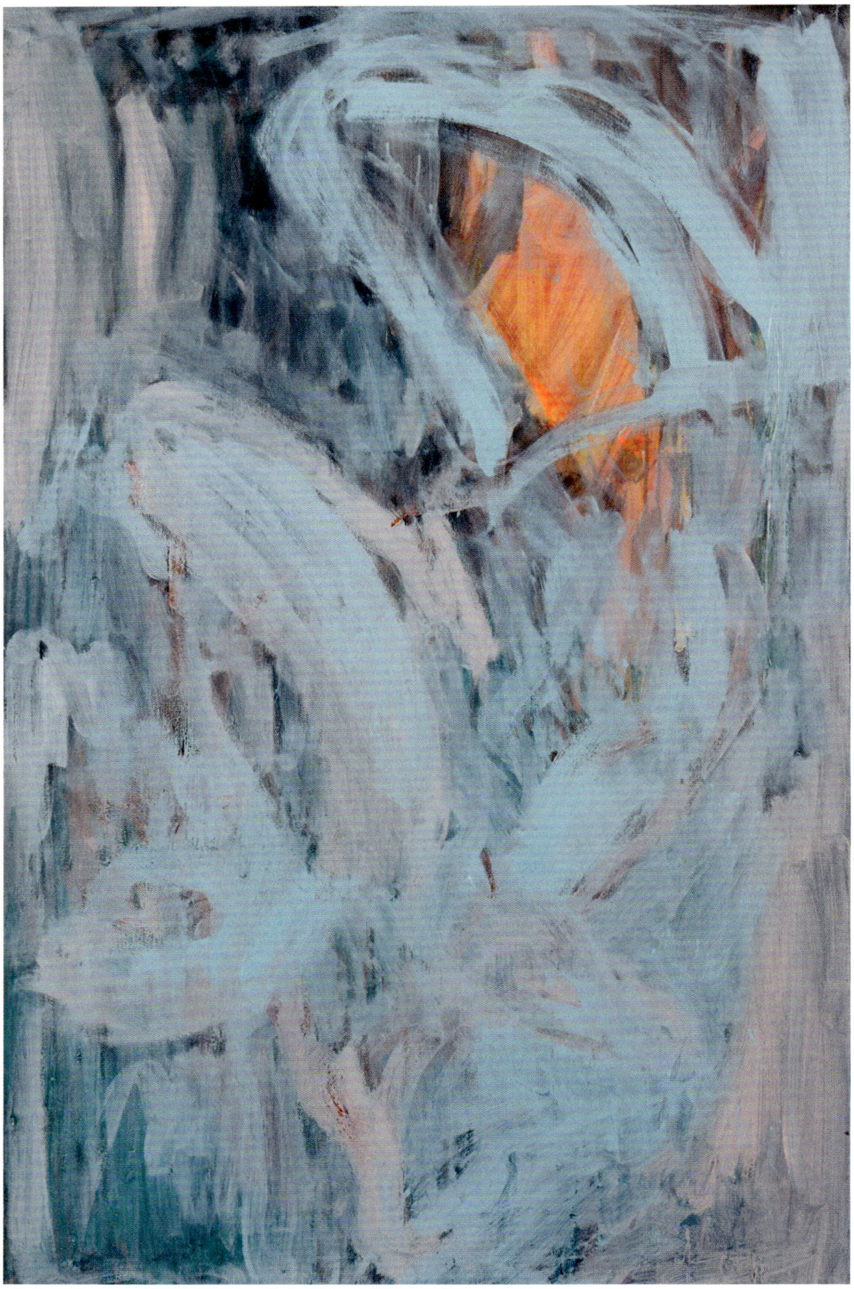

Torso in Sfumato, 2010
oil on canvas, 31 ½ × 23 ⅝ inches | 80 × 60 cm

Light Blue, Orange, 2011
acrylic on canvas, 59 × 39 ⅜ inches | 150 × 100 cm

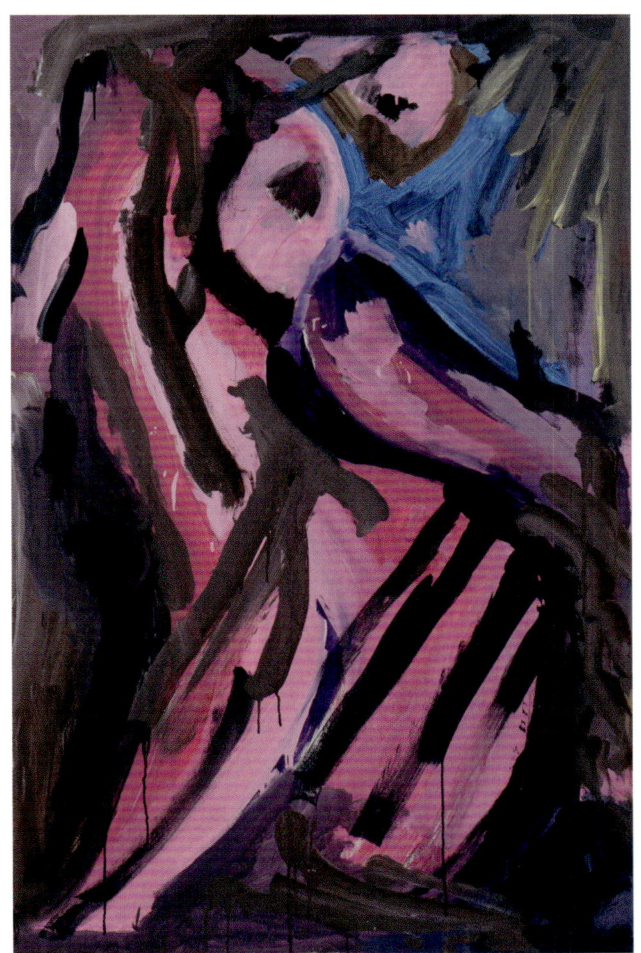 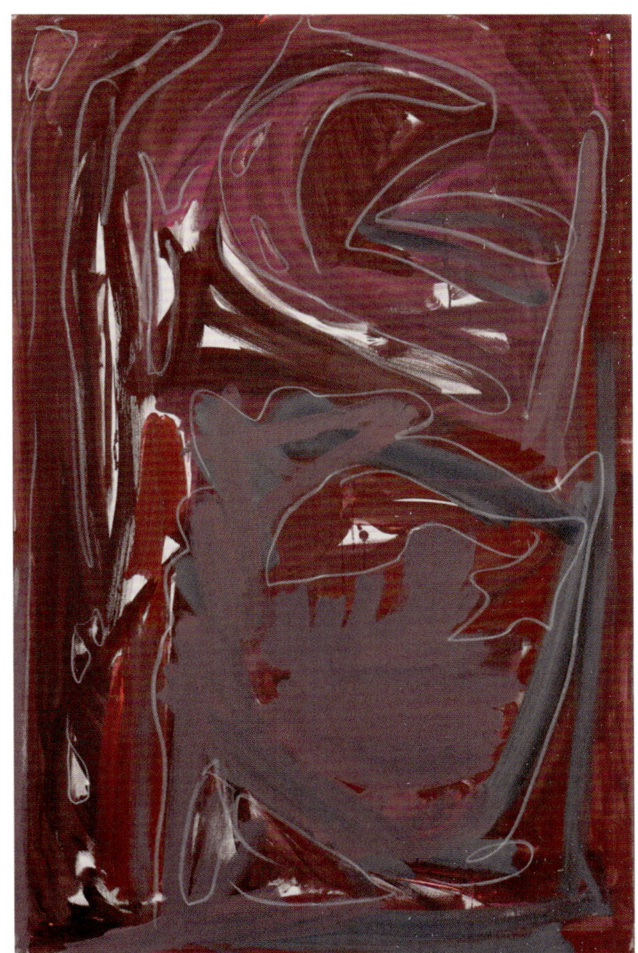

Nipple, 2008
acrylic on canvas, 59 × 39 ⅜ inches | 150 × 100 cm

Violett, 2011—2015
acrylic on canvas, 59 × 39 ⅜ inches | 150 × 100 cm

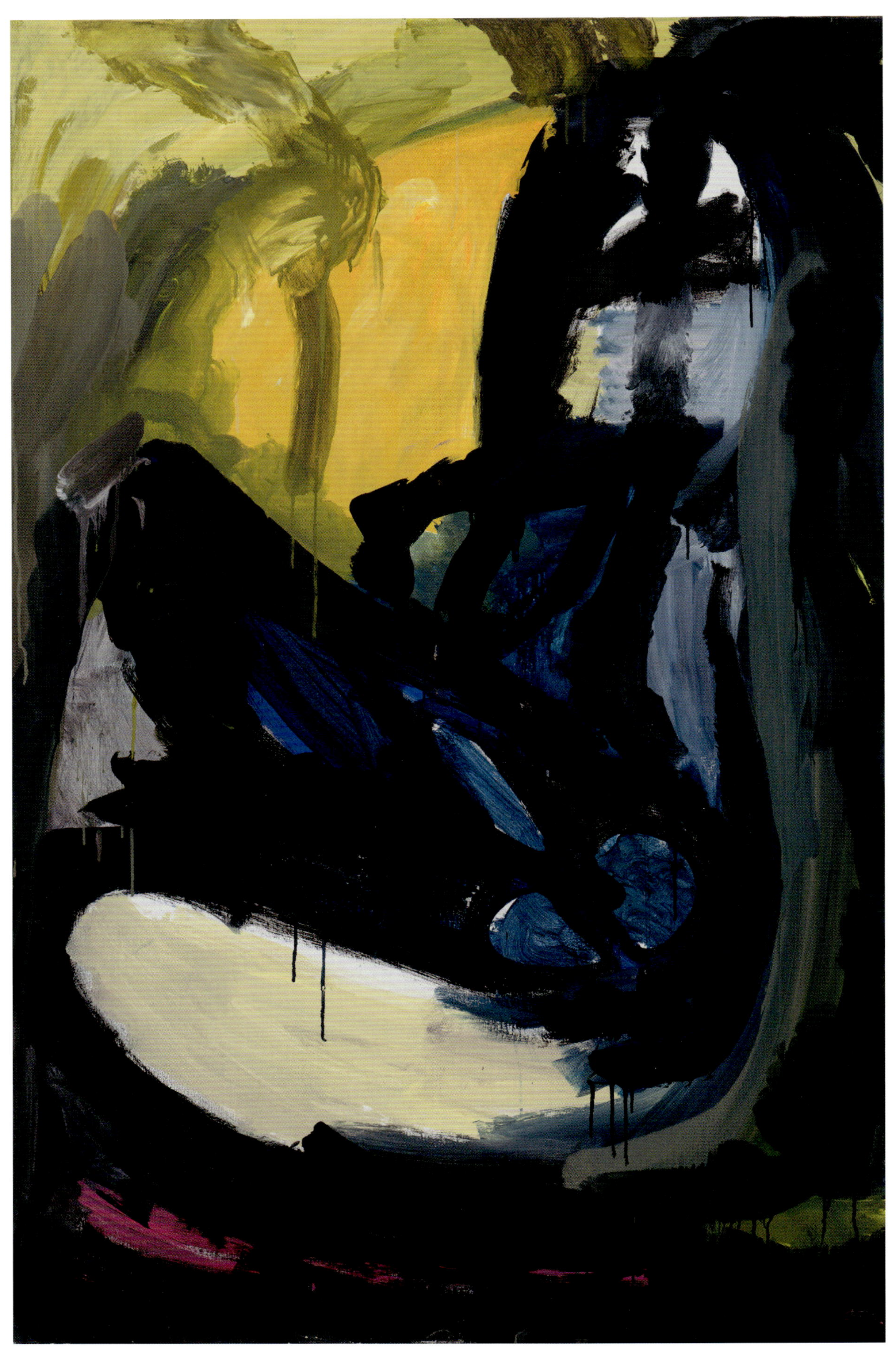

NAPOLITANA, 2008
acrylic on canvas, 59 × 39 ⅜ inches | 150 × 100 cm

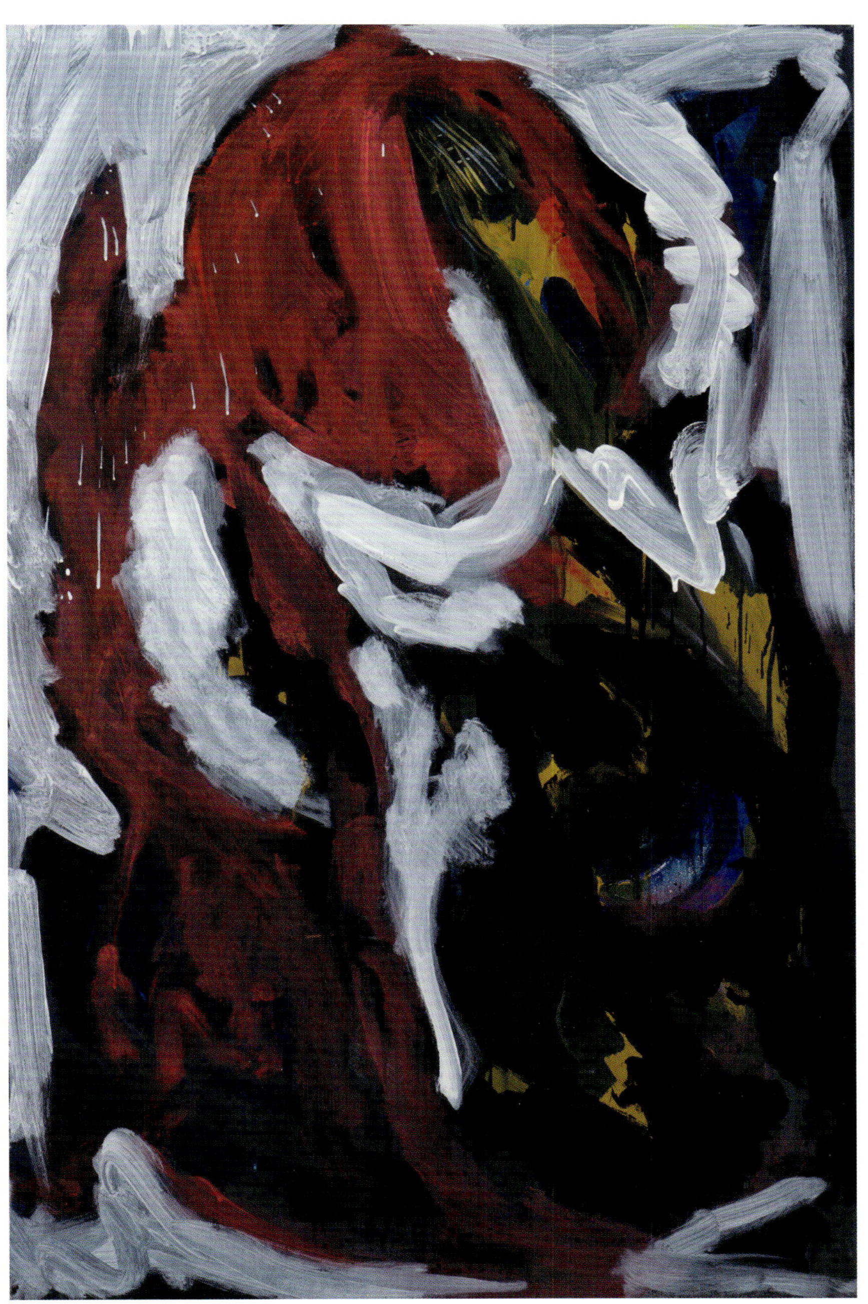

DOGHEAD, 2008
acrylic on canvas, 59 × 39 ⅜ inches | 150 × 100 cm

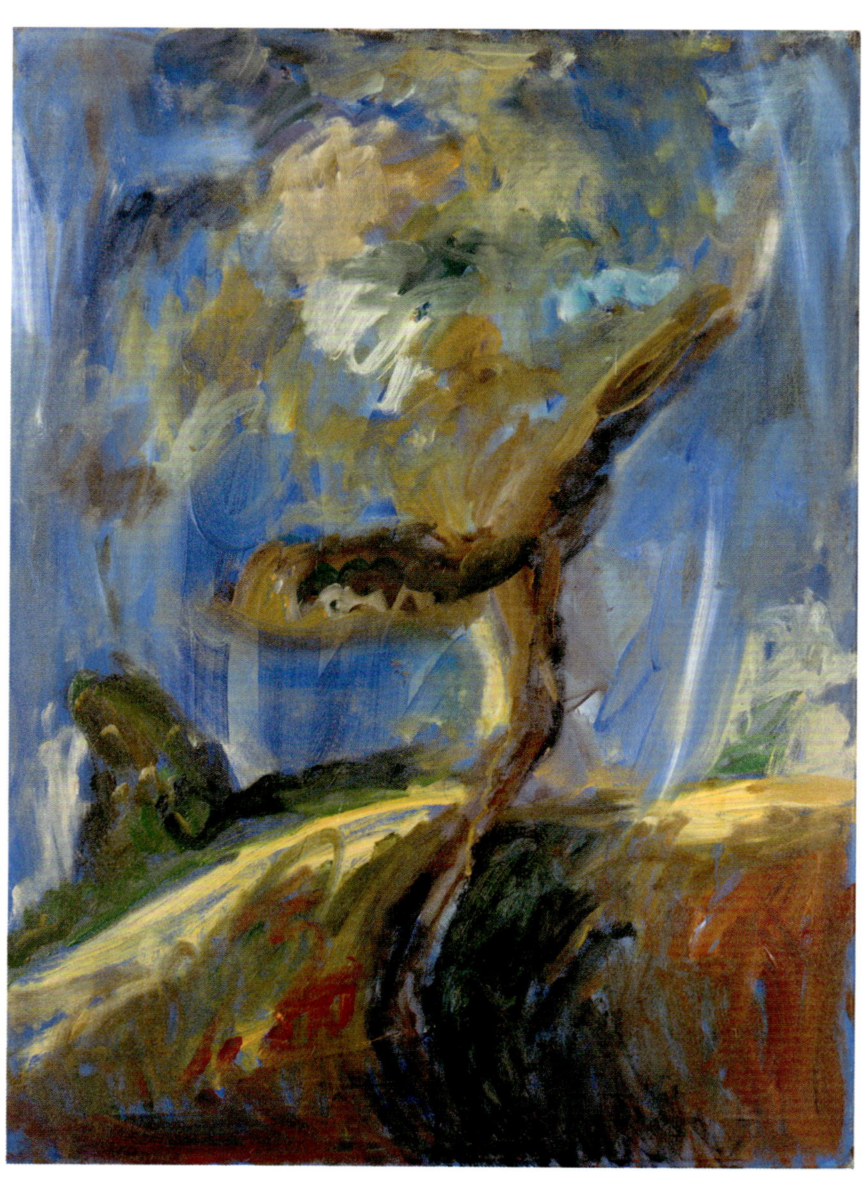

treesome, 2012
oil on canvas, 31½ × 23½ inches | 80 × 60 cm

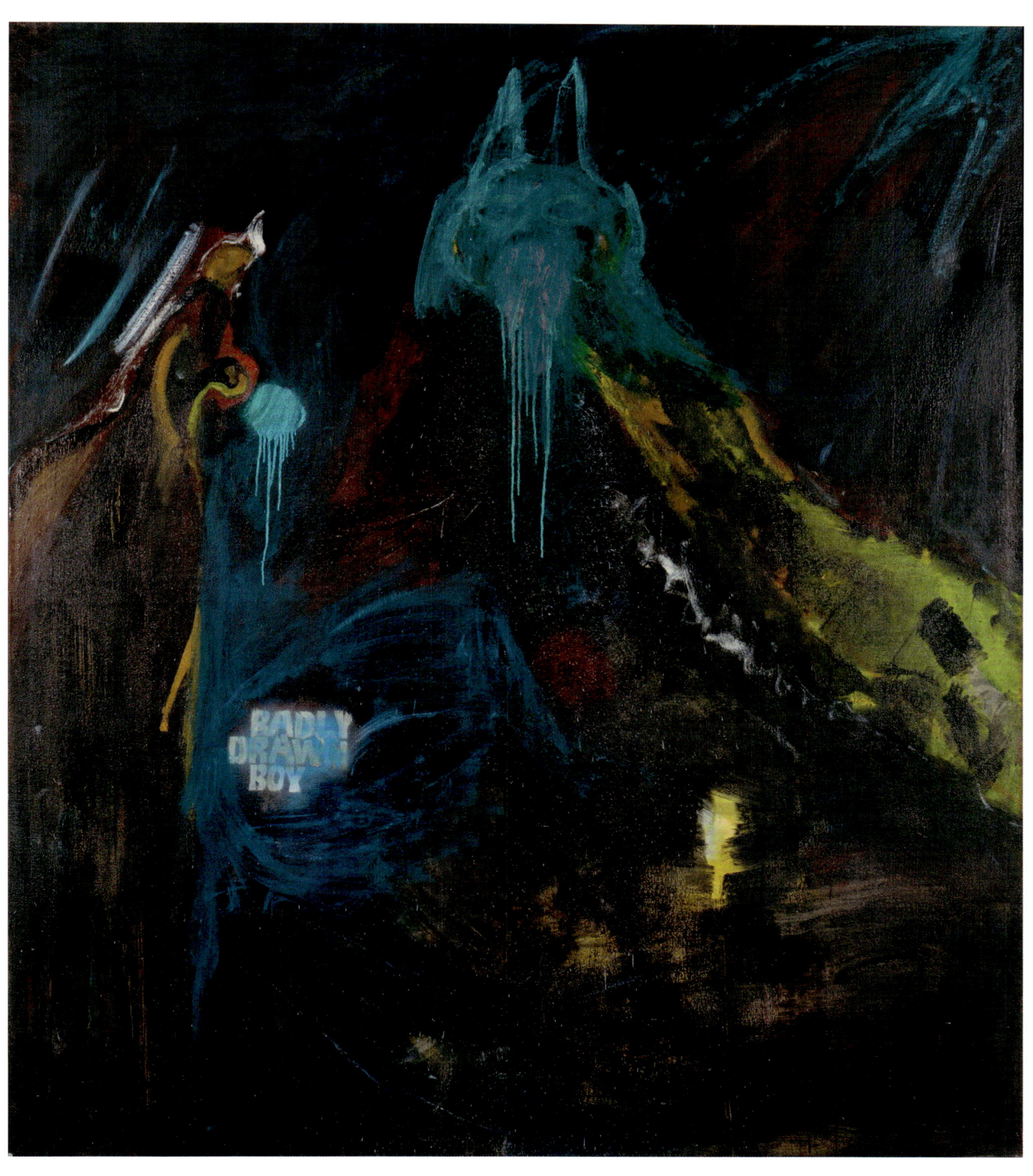

BadlyDrawnBoy, c. 2002
acrylic and oil on canvas, 78 ¾ × 70 ½ inches | 200 × 179 cm

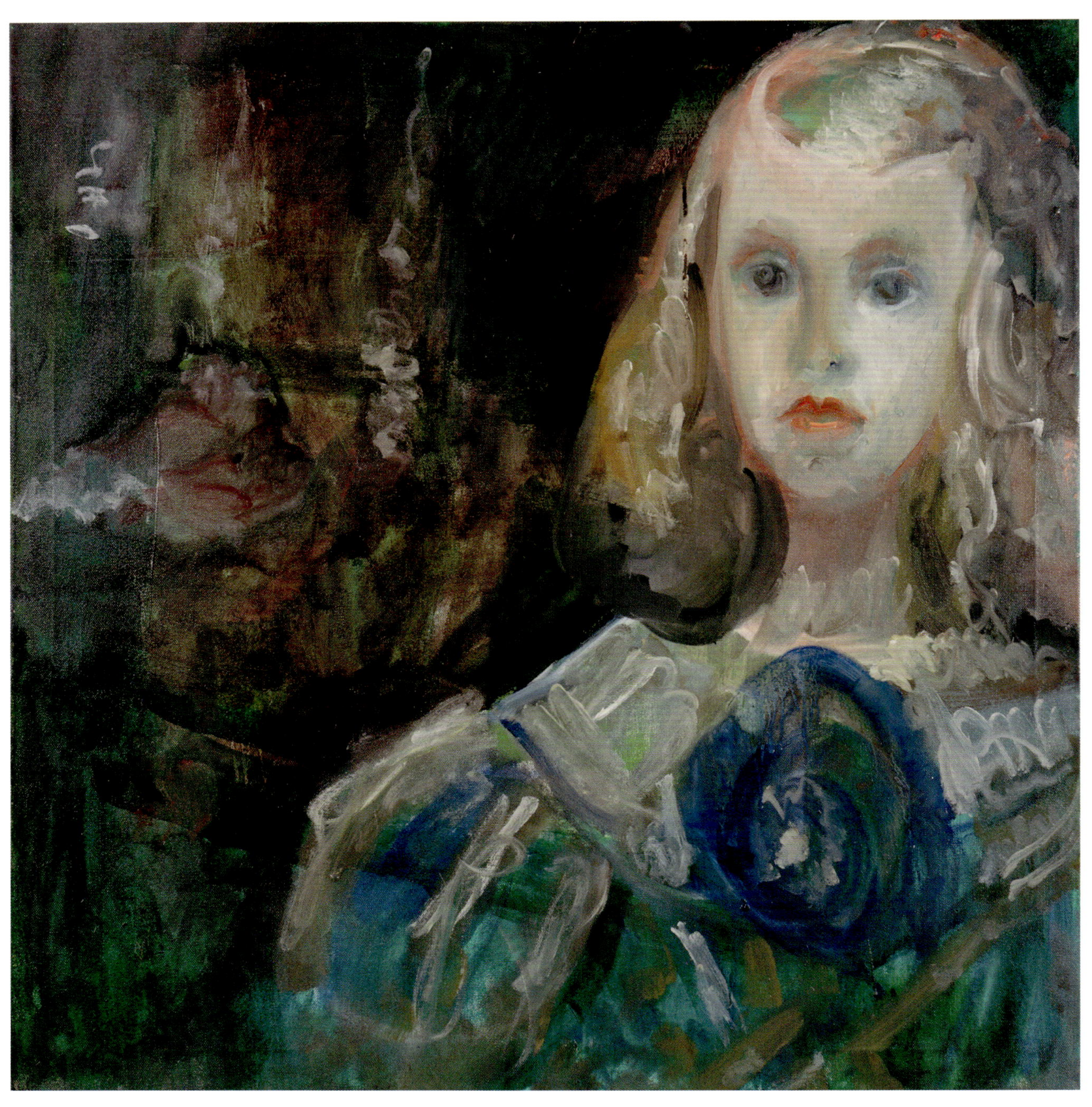

Girl, 2012
oil on canvas, 31½ × 31½ inches | 80 × 80 cm

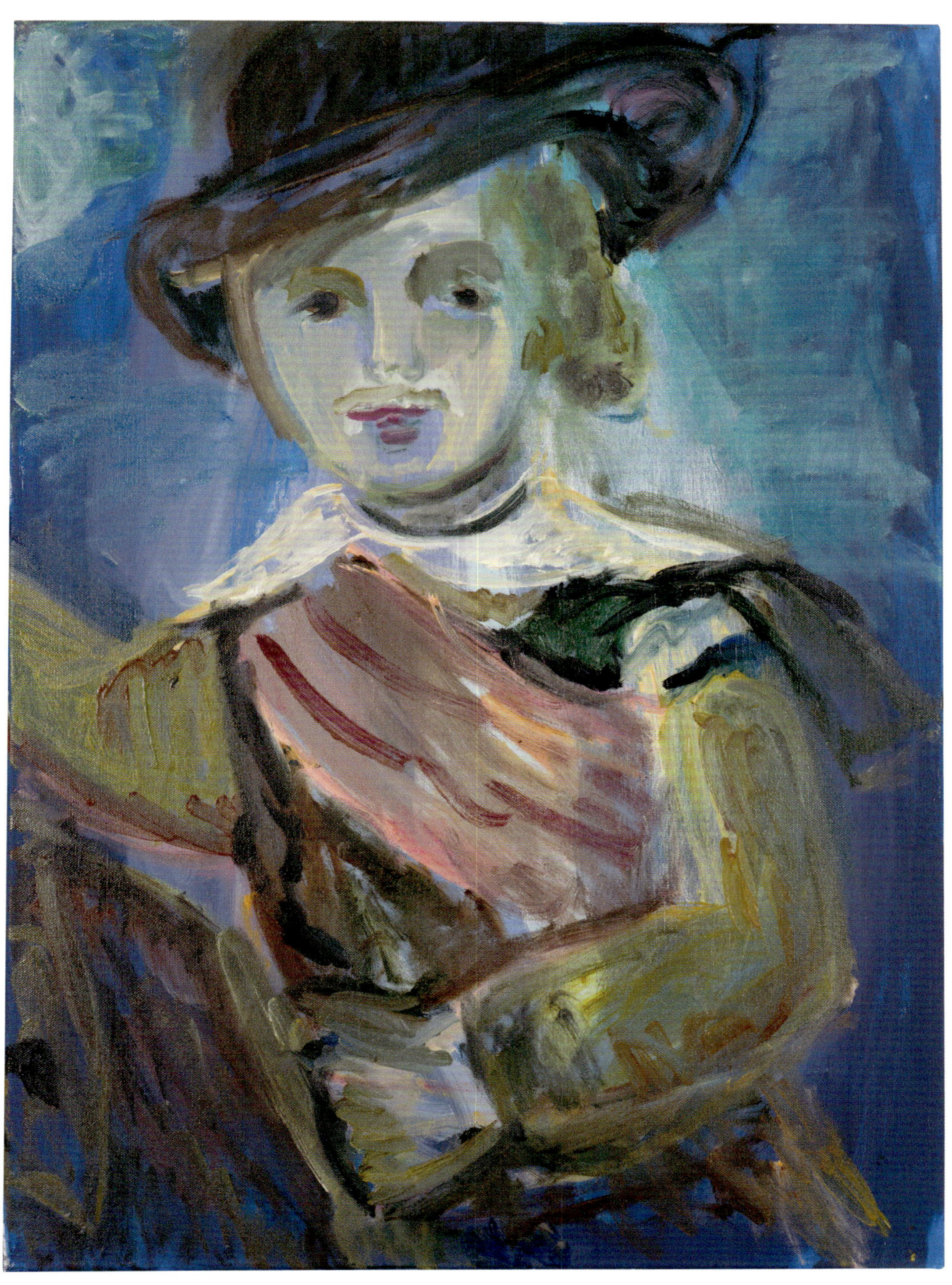

Boy, 2012
oil on canvas, 35 × 23 ½ inches | 89 × 60 cm

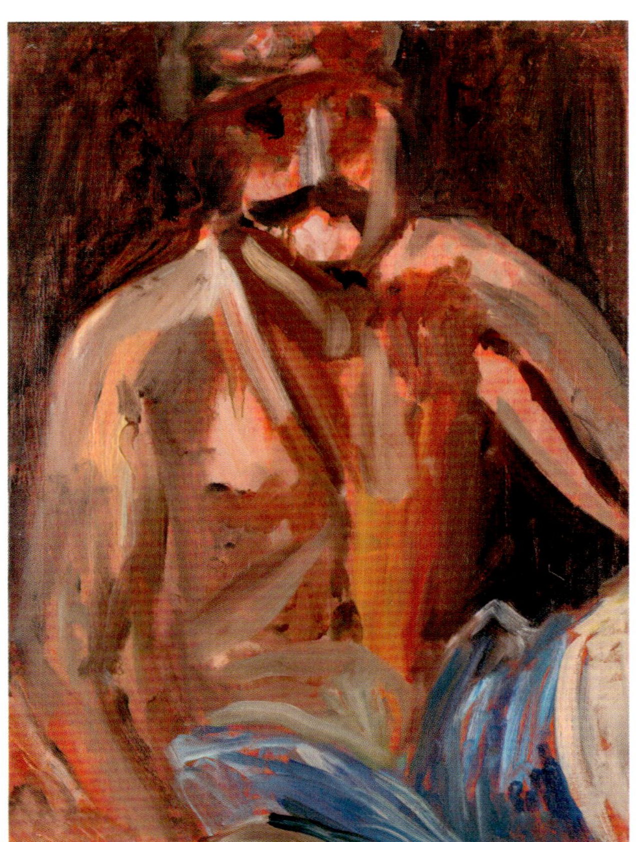

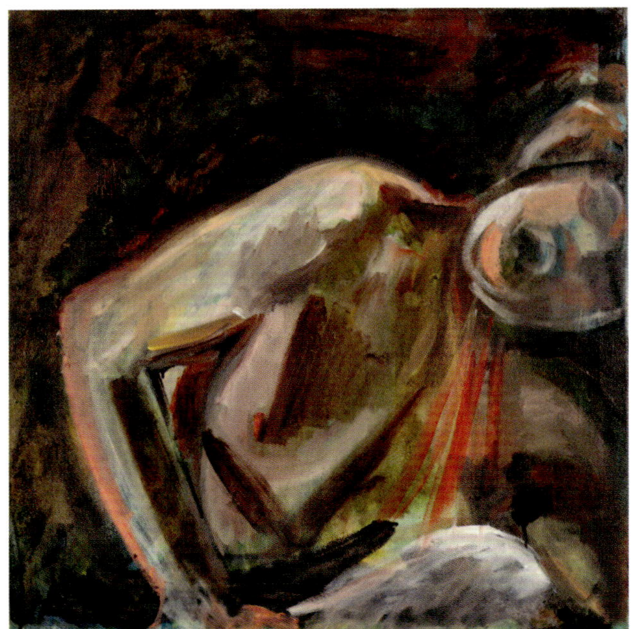

Moustage, 2012
oil on canvas, 31 ½ × 23 ½ inches | 80 × 60 cm

Scream, 2012
oil on canvas, 27 ½ × 27 ½ inches | 70 × 70 cm

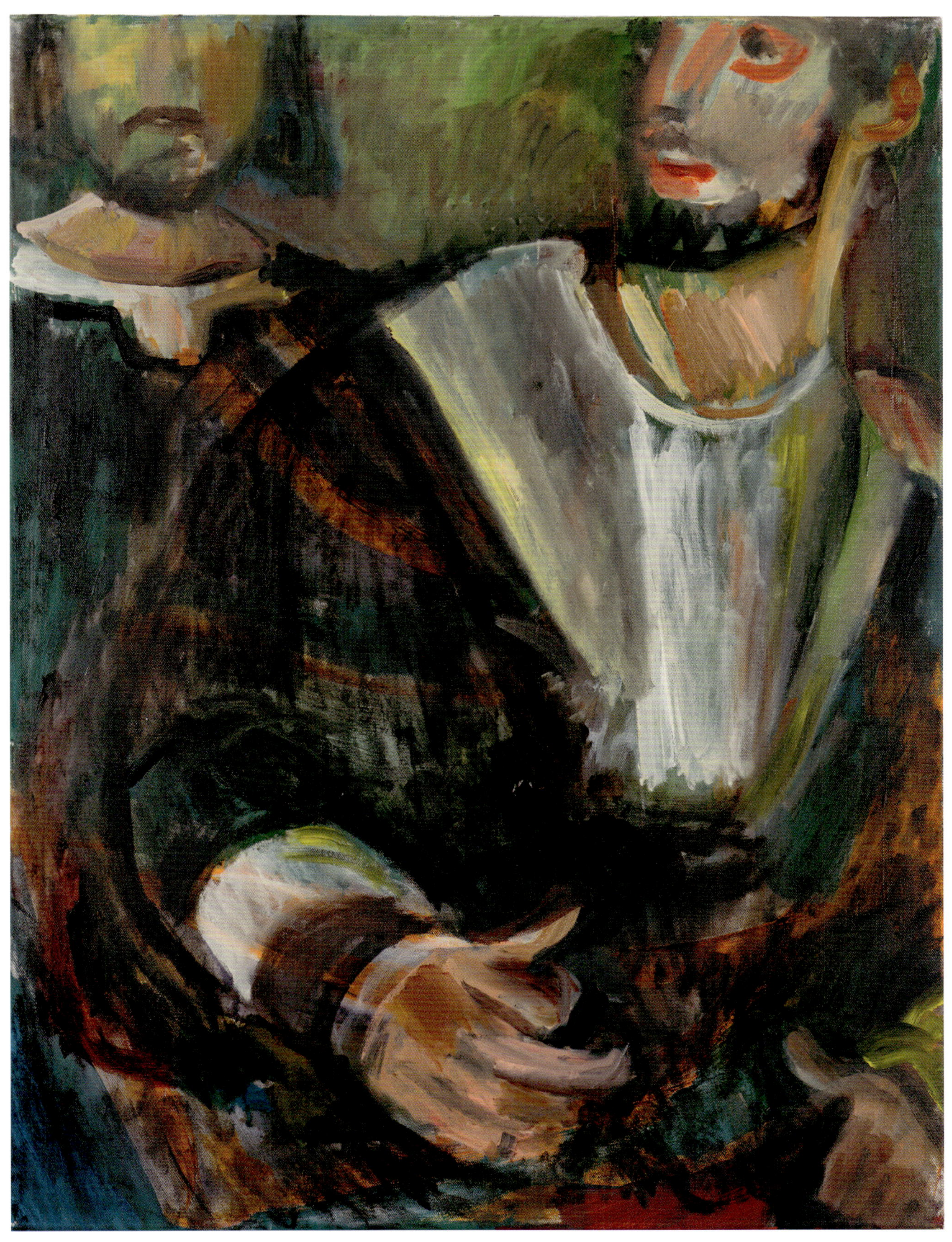

Bodyguard, 2012
oil on canvas, 35 ½ × 27 ½ inches | 90 × 70 cm

Image breaker
Julie Ryan

Combining a flair for visual nonchalance and highly specific modes of display, the artist Tamuna Sirbiladze concentrated swift, straightforward parlance into epic images. The resulting body of work is as intelligent as it is wry, rich with allusions to fecundity, sexuality, family, and mortality.

The work is iconoclastic, as was the artist herself; in an emboldened contemporary sense that also recalls the literal origins of the word *iconoclast*, from the medieval Greek *eikon*, meaning "image," and *klastes*, meaning "breaker." But first the iconoclast must destroy preconceived notions of image and expectation. Implicit in this process is the eventuality of a larger and unexpected vision. For Sirbiladze, that meant a continual confrontation with hypermasculinity, hierarchy, and minimalist and formalist traditions. The work bends in on itself and doubles back, assembling and disassembling simultaneously (often on the same canvas); each resulting image—an *image breaker*.

Motif

The earliest paintings by Sirbiladze date back to a time when she was a student in her native Georgia, at the state academy in Tbilisi. These works show a highly proficient and mannered style with subject matter appropriate to the time and place. However rote and regimented the mechanizations of the Soviet bloc academic experience were, they instilled in Sirbiladze a baseline subject matter, while also affording the artist opportunity to break with the rules, to resist.

Sunny Days (1990), made when Sirbiladze was just nineteen years old, is a bold divergence from her carefully rendered still lifes and portraiture of the time. The yellow "sun" sinks into waves of blue brushstrokes (moon), closely resembling in both format and temperament the paintings *Canada* and *Andy's Hair* (both 2014). More than twenty years later, she would exhibit these "flower" paintings in 2016 at Almine Rech Gallery, Brussels.

Sirbiladze returned in one way or another throughout her life to a personal portfolio of "iconic" motifs. The lotus, pomegranate, flora, and daily still life detritus found their way overtly or suggestively onto the canvas. Having this arsenal of "ready-made" subjects allowed the work to be realized quickly, utilizing repeated motifs as armatures for mark-making.

The self-described banners, in oil stick, have an unrehearsed lineality, existing almost in spite of themselves. Sirbiladze seems to have simultaneously rendered subjects through gesture and taken a stab at them. The lotus plant, a heavily symbolic bloom, grows through muddy waters; its arrival can symbolize purity, beauty, love, and victory. Or luck! In *Lotus* (2015; p. 30), one sees all of this—the massive achievement of the image's victorious arrival under a hail of rapidly restrained gestures. This contradictory emergence of subject matter and motif through repeated linear gestures is recurring and foundational.

Traditions

The video camera, Google, and appropriated images from Sirbiladze's photographs taken at the Kunsthistoriches Museum Wien were all source material for series of paintings, works in and of themselves—pieces such as *BadlyDrawnBoy* (c. 2002; p. 83), with its crushing space and impulsive layering reminiscent of Albert Oehlen's methodology; a ruthless obliteration of images (in order to make an image), a partnering of painterly technique as subject with computer interface and new technologies. Omnivorous engagement with multiple platforms of image-gathering and making, with little to no regard for traditional art historical hierarchies, is the "spirit" of the paintings. There is a resourcefulness that drives each image.

Ab Ex

In these emotive, body-centered works by Sirbiladze, larger and smaller visual stories yield to gestural aggravated surfaces. The sparse lines and dashes of the *Fold* series come to mind, like tablecloths or bedsheets marked by an evening, then folded and set aside. *Rebirth is Always Painful* (2011; p. 32) and *Pomegranate* (2015; p. 34) epitomize the decisive gesture. What is "pleasurable" in experiencing these paintings is that we feel them as much as we see them. Their physicality, scale, and unrefined materiality trigger a visceral response.

In the 1940s, New York City became the center of abstract expressionism, a movement that represented a shift in art-making to prioritize the physical act of painting itself. Sirbiladze loved New York City, and like the ab ex giant Lee Krasner, explored the liminal space between the objective and nonobjective; both artists frequently returned to subjects of gender roles and identity. *In Which It Is Whether They Went With It* (2015; p. 29) is an expansive work by Sirbiladze that can be interpreted (in title and form) as an "inevitability," or fate. *The Seasons* (1957), an epic work by Krasner, also reflects on inevitability, life cycles, and rebirth, using powerful generic forms. Sirbiladze differed from her predecessor, though, in excising the sentimental in favor of the symbolic, and in wrestling with ugly truths, as in *Hey, you big ass (Spiegel)* (2008).

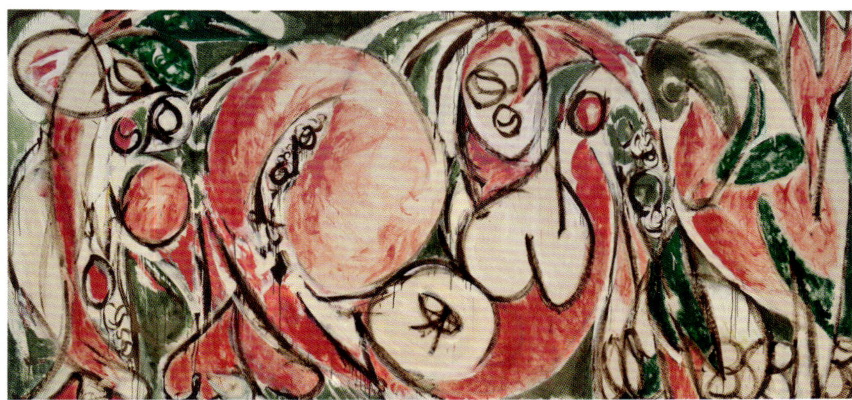

Lee Krasner
The Seasons, 1957
oil and house paint on canvas
92 ¾ × 203 ⅞ inches | 235.6 × 517.8 cm

Identity—difference

Sirbiladze delved into female "messiness" extensively throughout her career,
but most graphically from 2005–2008, for example in the works *Unter den roten
Sternen / Cubic Rubic (Communist)* (2005; p. 58) and *Diana in the bathroom* (2005).
With scantily applied paint, the colors are more symbolic than "colorful," and the
subjects vie for position between bathrooms and bedrooms. The whole series
reads as a mammoth "Sagas of Womanhood." These are Sirbiladze's iconoclastic
genre paintings: irreverent, scatological, and unabashed, this highly narrative series
illustrates the underpinnings of many (more abstract) later paintings such as *Eve's
apple* (2015; p. 23) or *Birdshit Pigeon* (2014; p. 63). Sirbiladze's readiness to dish
out unflattering observations about her subject matter (herself included) echoes
Susan Sontag's statement "The only interesting answers are those that destroy the
questions." This *breaking* of subject matter, pictorial plane, and rules Sirbiladze
embraced, as a visual agitator.

Status—speed

Throughout the centuries, the grand castles of the United Kingdom and Europe
have housed enormous framed paintings, hung on salon walls. Of course, fire was
always feared; saving the valuables was paramount to preserving wealth and status.
But how to evacuate these large canvases quickly when every minute counts?
A knife: a dagger in its sheath was set below the paintings so that, in case of fire,
they could be quickly cut out of their frames and tossed out the window. This
pragmatic expediency, built into the very presentation of the paintings, comes to
mind most obviously in the unstretched banners, but also in other loose canvas
works. Cognizant that a painting's presence serves both as signifier and platform,
Sirbiladze stepped up production in her last years. The artist was also aware of
the short-lived supports/surfaces movement of the late 1960s in southern France,
which included the artists Claude Viallat and Louis Cane, who did away with
conventional substrates, opting instead for free-form hanging and presentation
methods, to thereby act in opposition.

Take Cane's piece *Toile découpée (Cut Canvas)* (1971), where the material
extends beyond the surface of the wall and is also part of the wall's surface. This
duplicitous relationship of the art object, extending itself into the space and away
from the wall, is a tool that Sirbiladze employed seemingly casually in her studio
practice and then intentionally in the public domain, in Vienna at Galerie Lisa Ruyter
in 2012 and Secession in 2015. The relationship to the painting's physical substruc-
ture also exerts itself in stretched pieces where the motion of making the image
is revealed in the shadow images of the stretcher bars. Now we see the faint grid,
and in this revealed grid we see the underpinnings of one of the principal formats
of minimalism.

Role and repetition

A clambering struggle of building and destroying, Sirbiladze's arsenal of imagery
stretches across the canvas: eyes, heart icons, perhaps a pomegranate, a leaf,
a swirl. All of this is rapidly emerging in the oil stick work *Andre's Breton* (2015; p. 24);
the nagging grid below, a reminder of the complex engagement Sirbiladze had with
her subjects. Here the founder of surrealism, André Breton, is paired with (if only
faintly) the inescapable art historical stand-in for male hegemony, the grid. John
Berger wrote that "one looks at paintings hoping to find some secret," and this
sentiment perpetuates the mythic smoke-and-mirrors effect of being *the artist*.
Sirbiladze escaped the persona of being an artist by making all paintings as *the
painting* and moving on. It is the liberation from sentimentality in these paintings
that sets each free.

Installation views
and collaborations

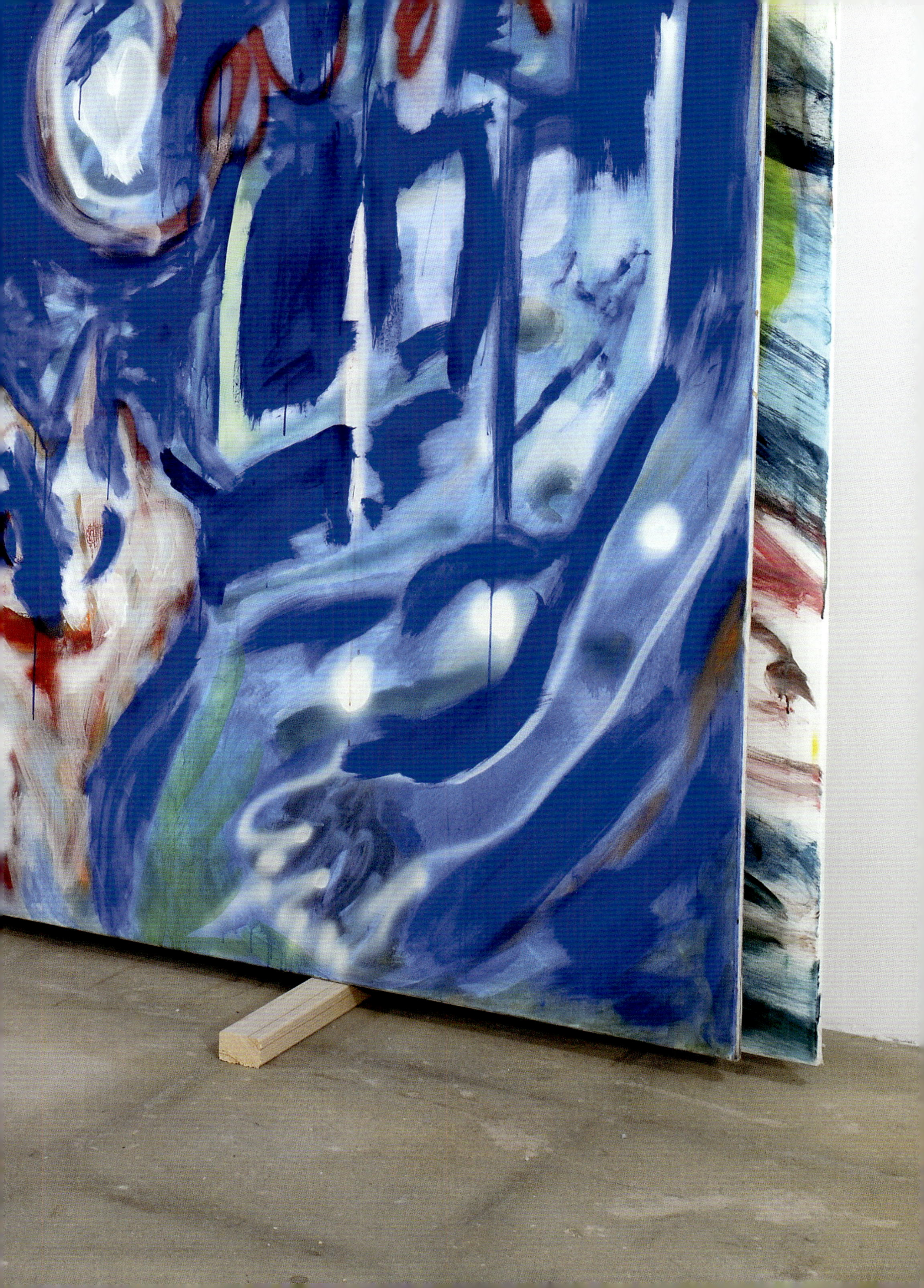

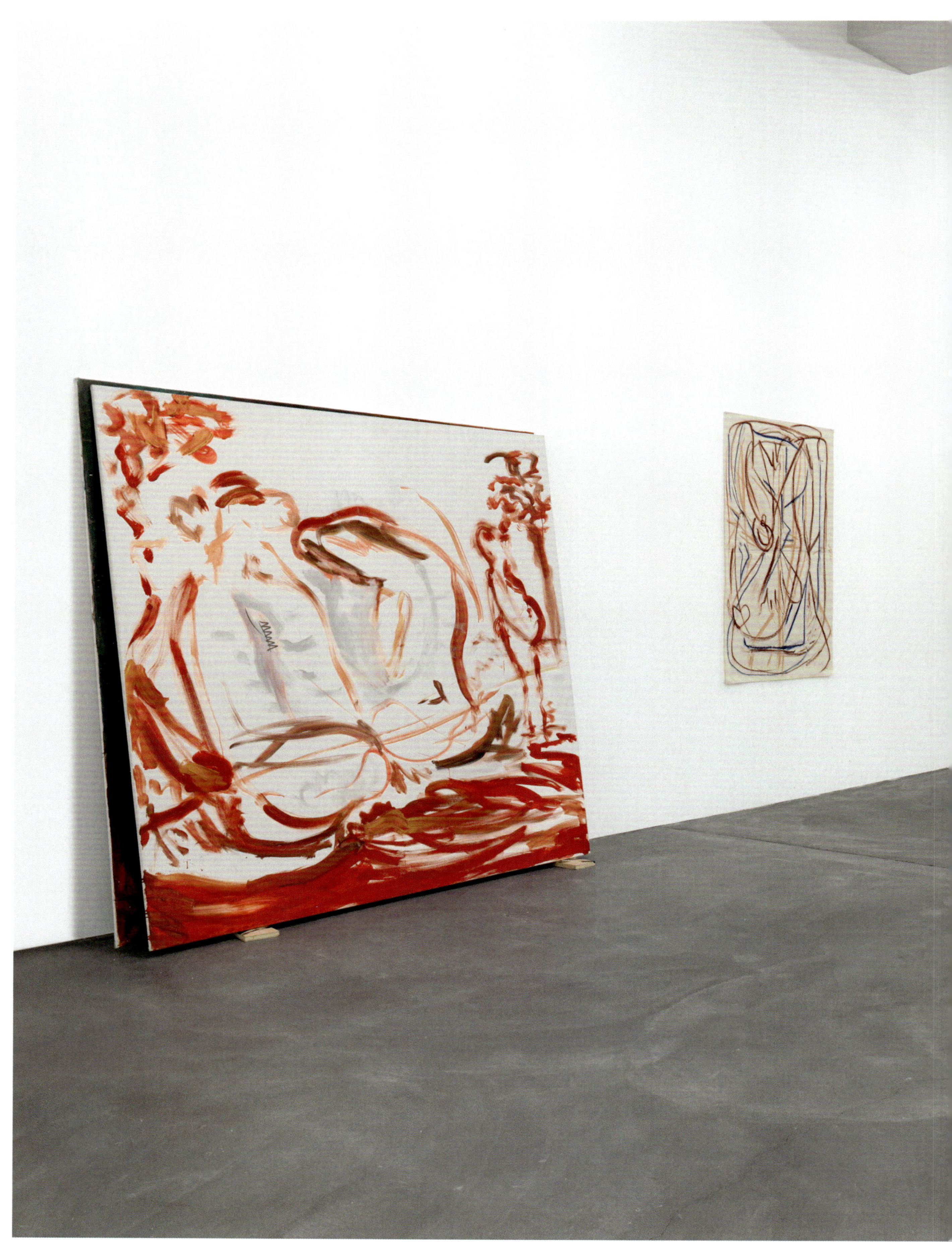

Pages 94–102
installation views: *Traces of Life*

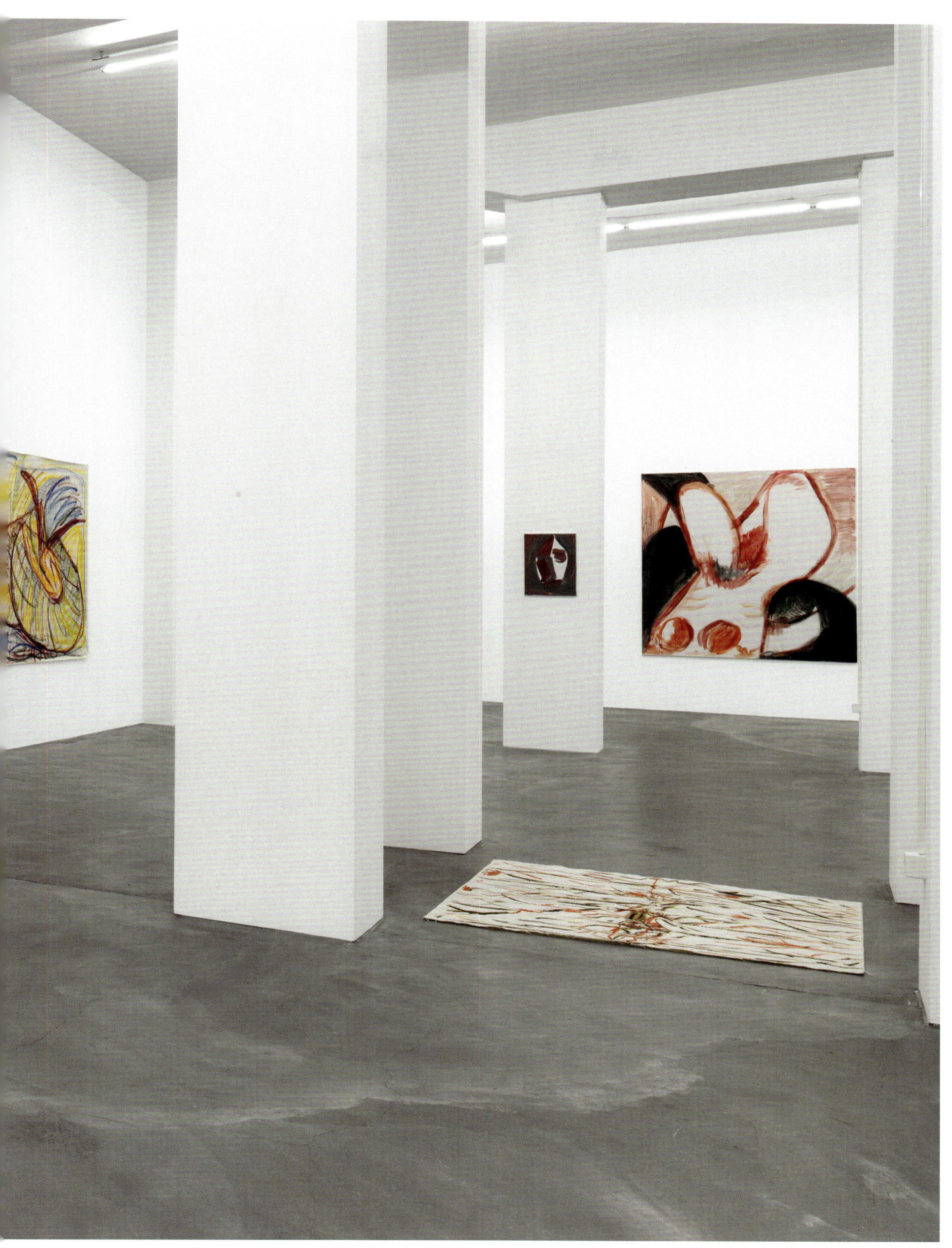

Galerie Eva Presenhuber, Zurich
April 8—May 27, 2017

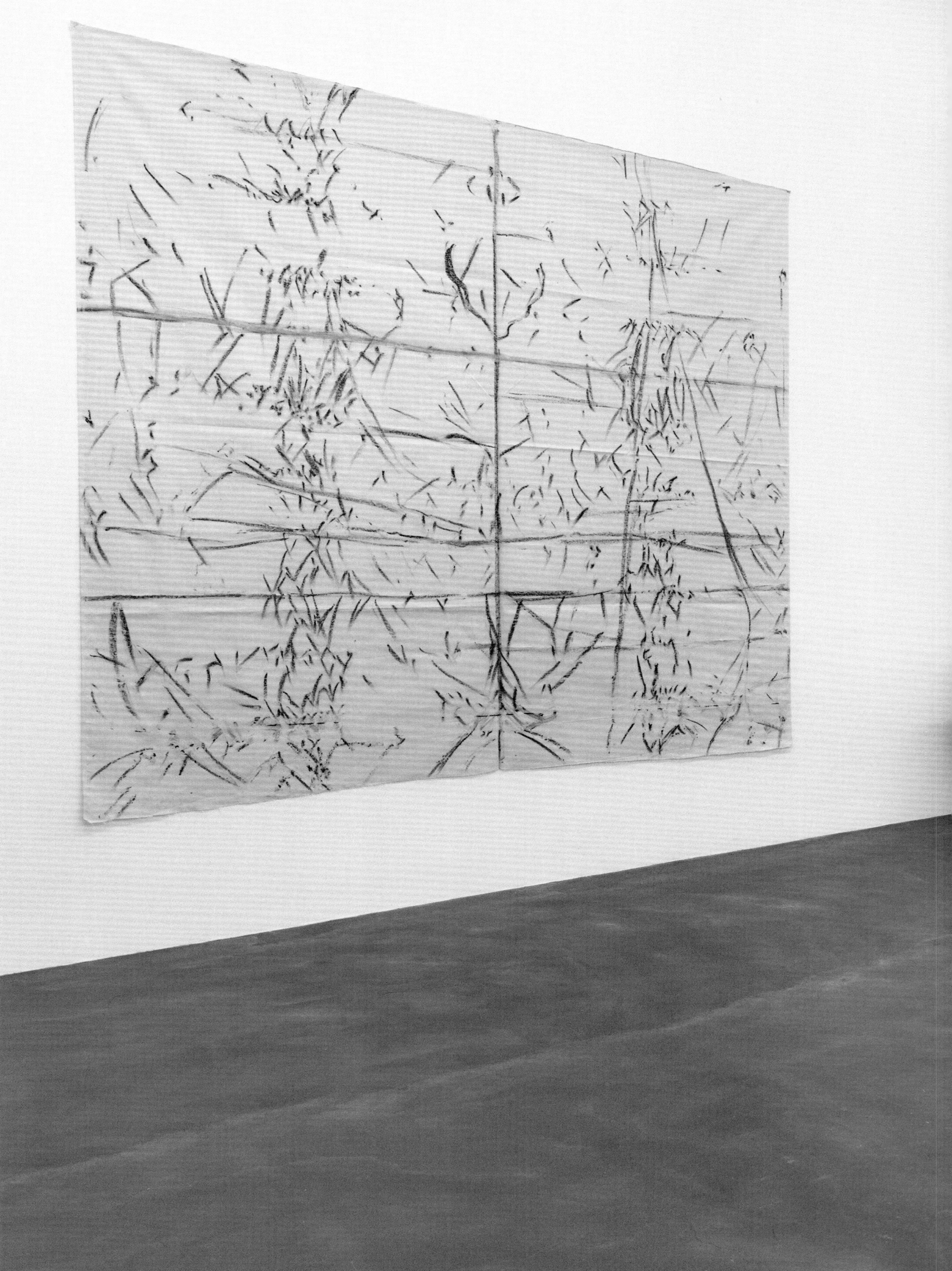

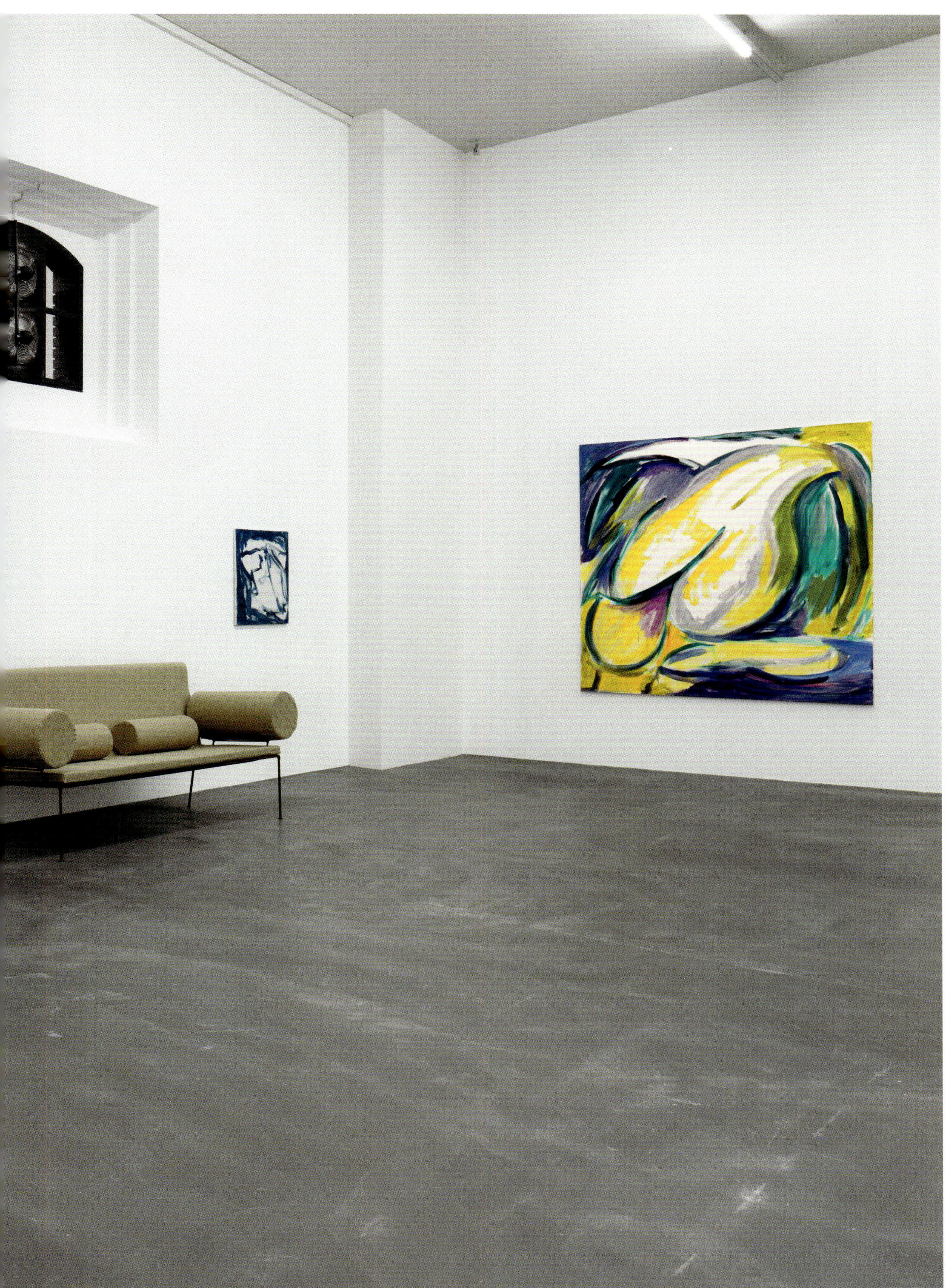

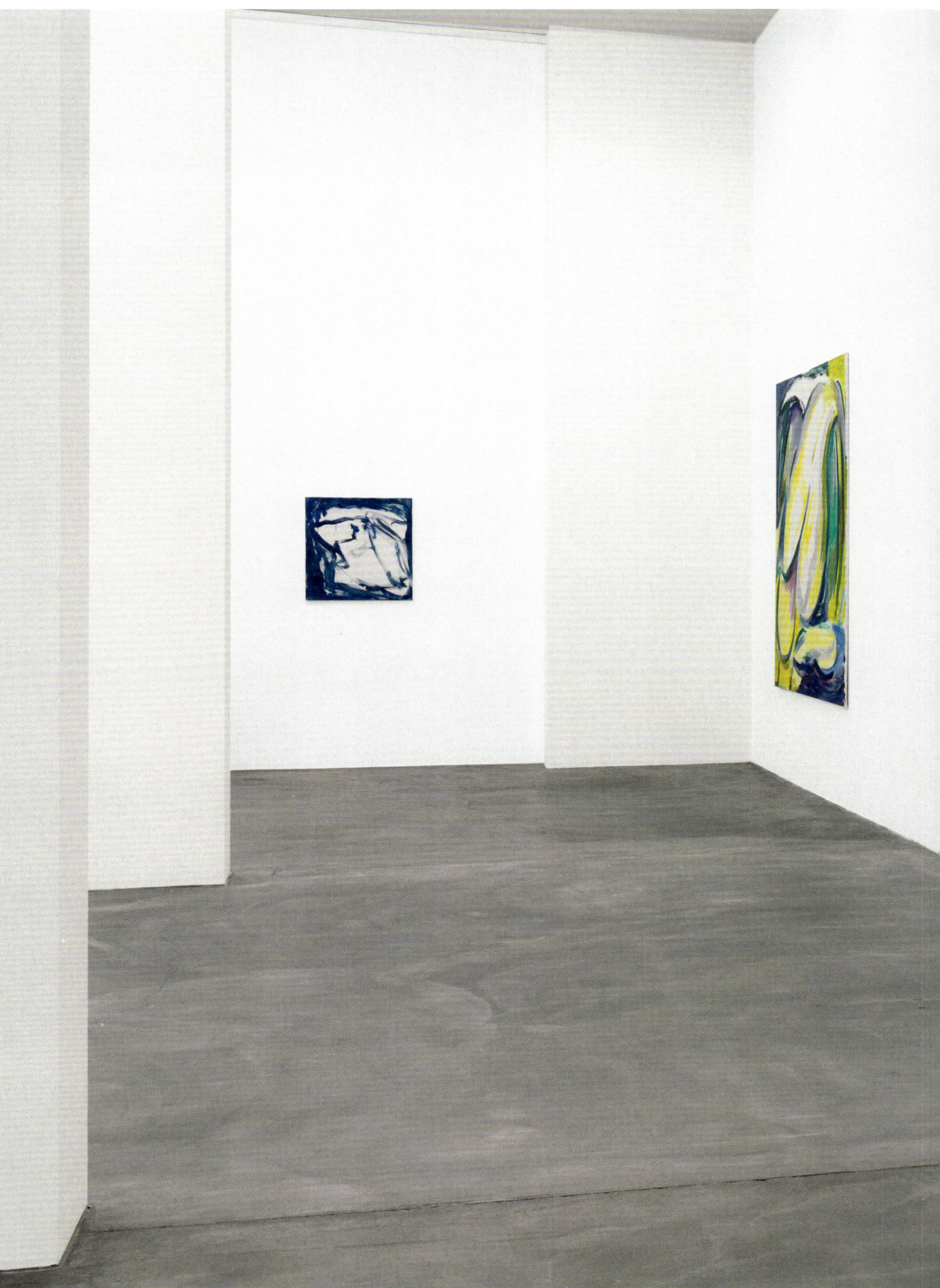

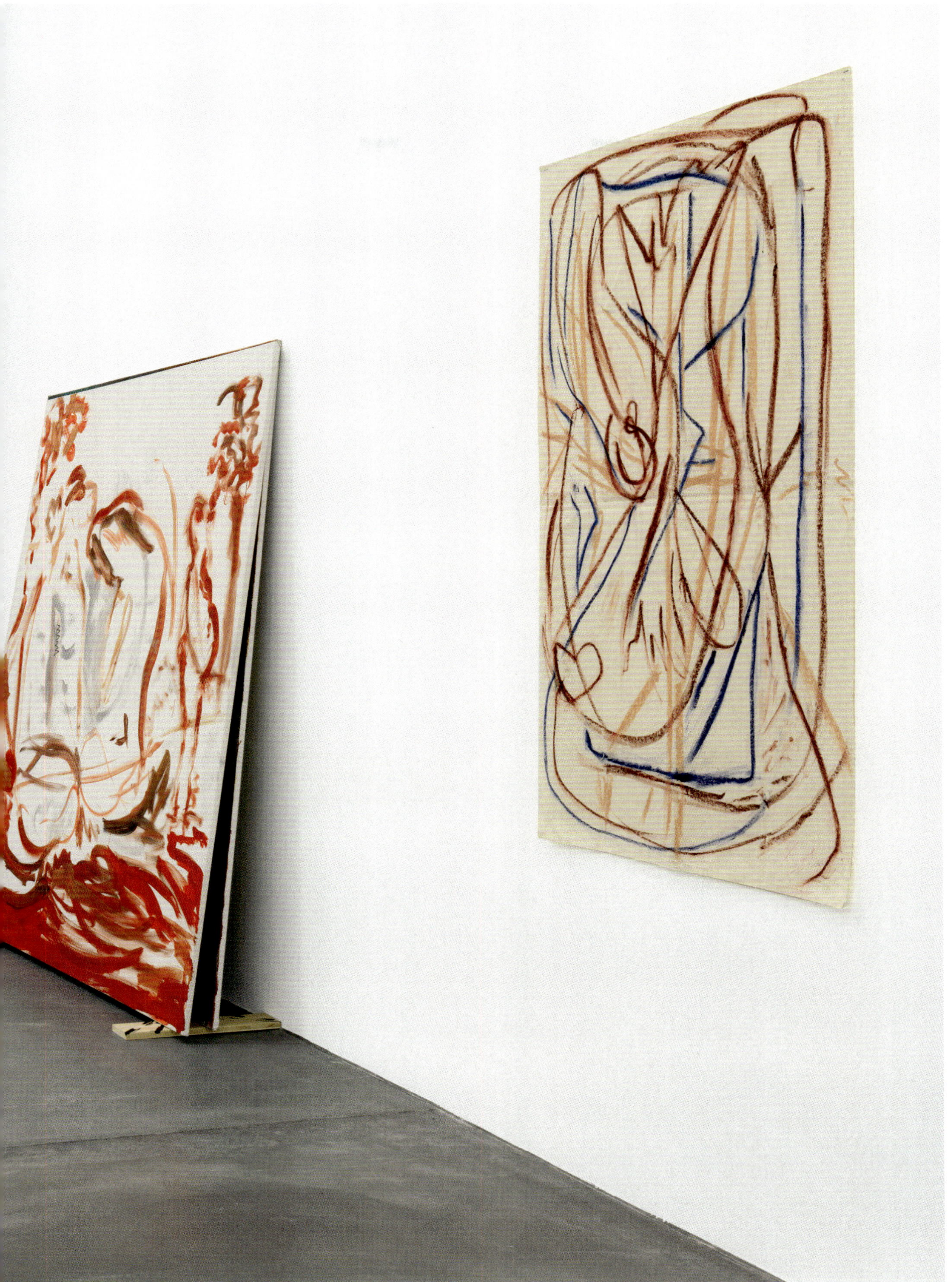

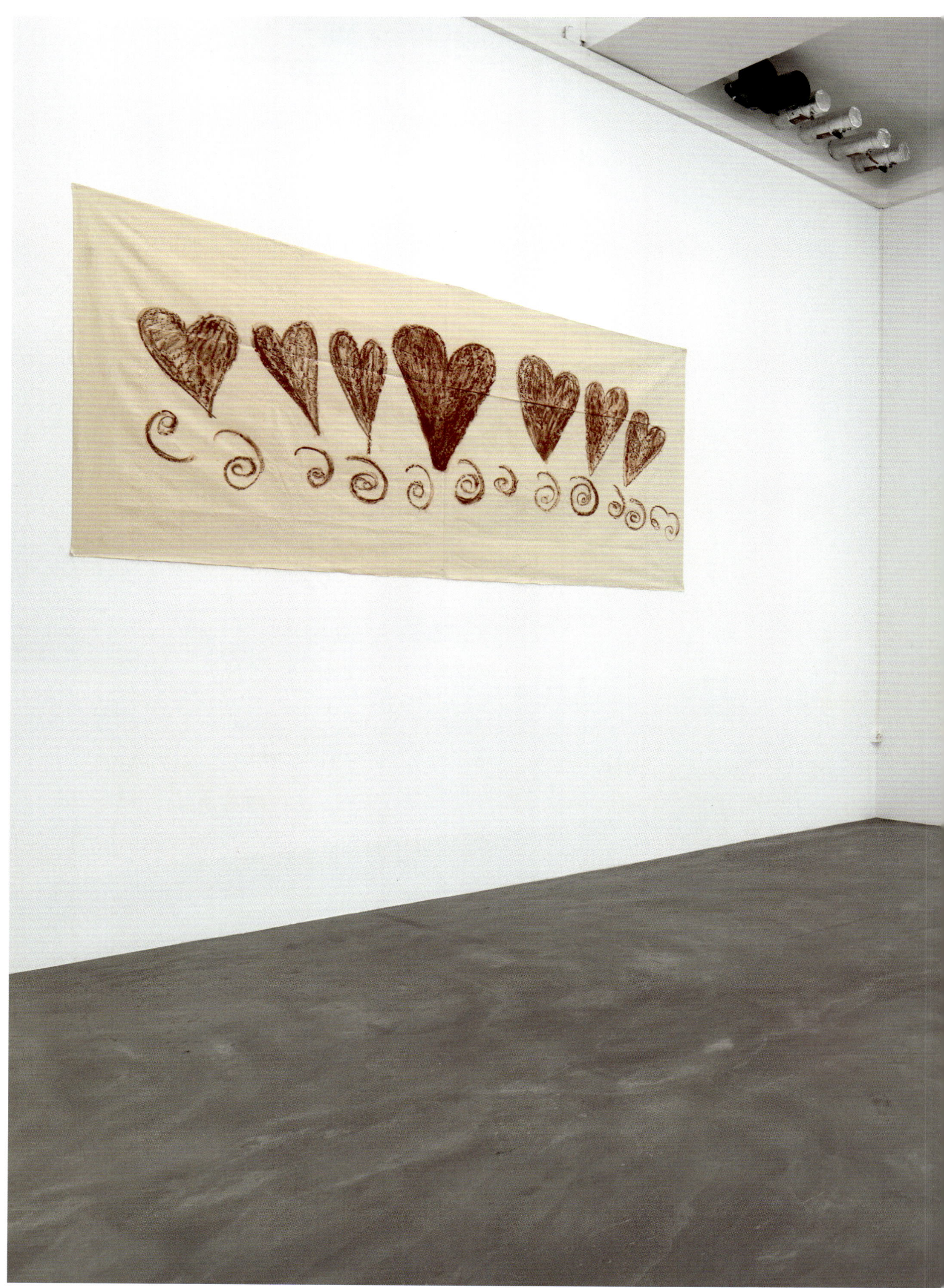

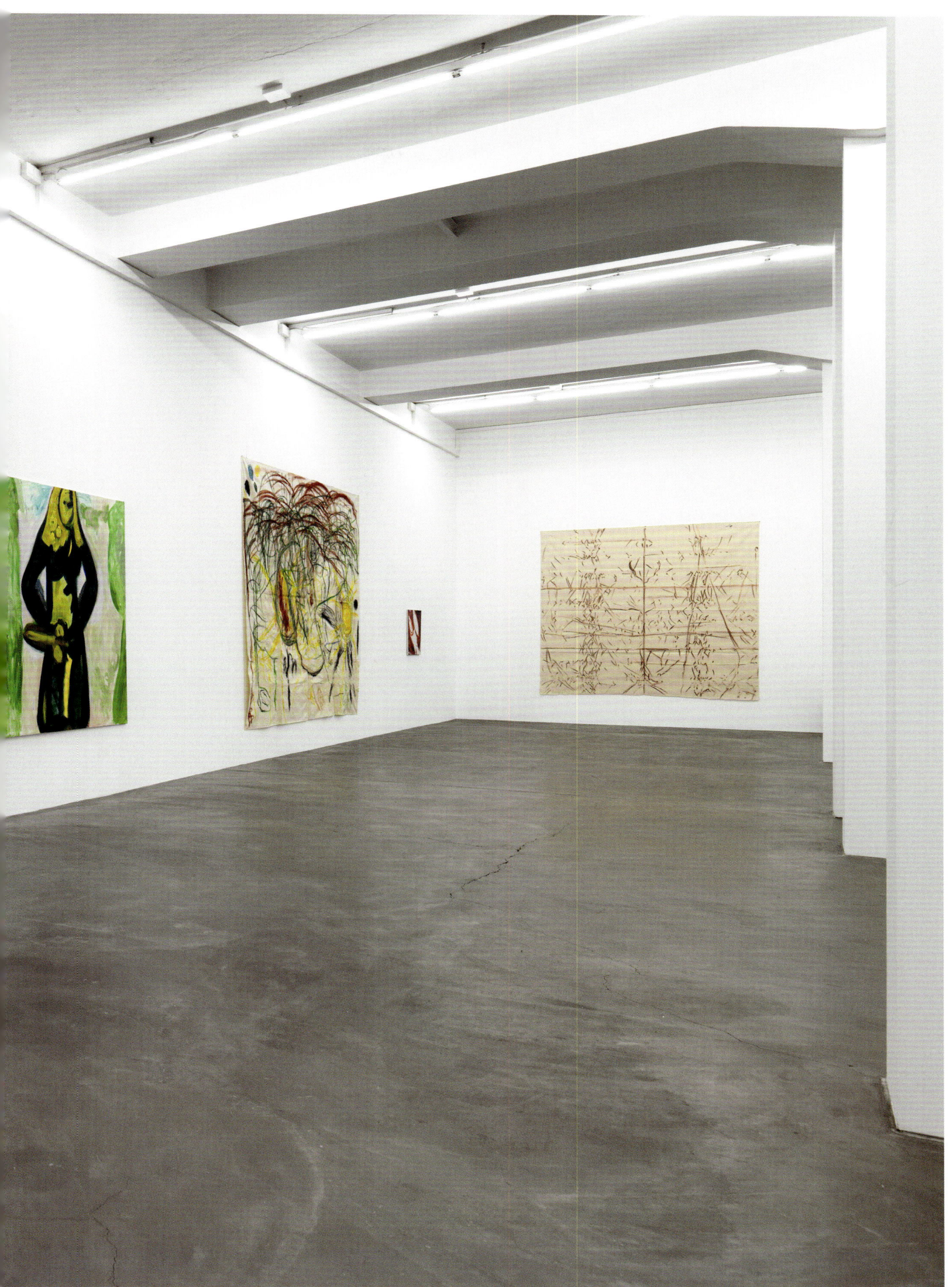

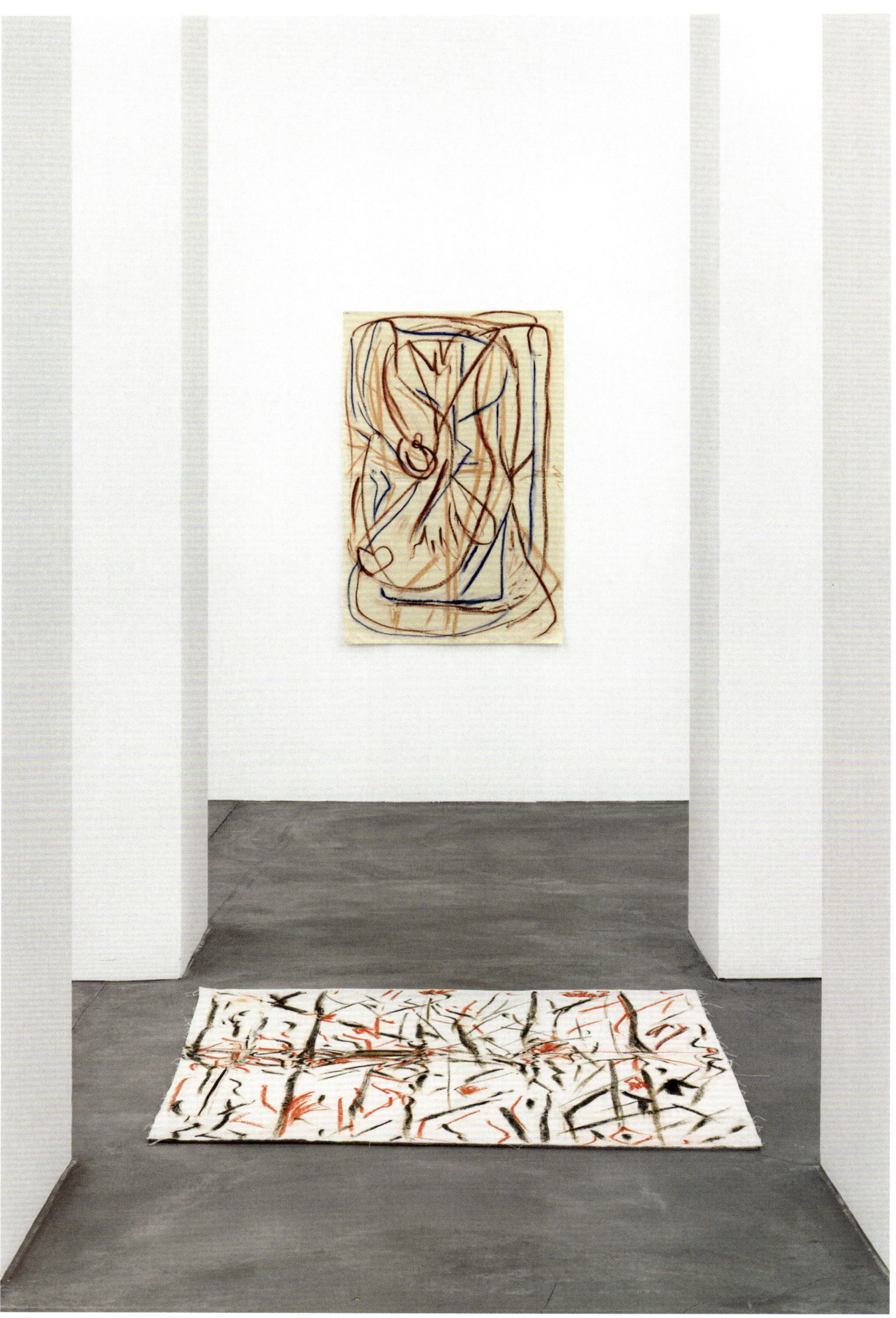

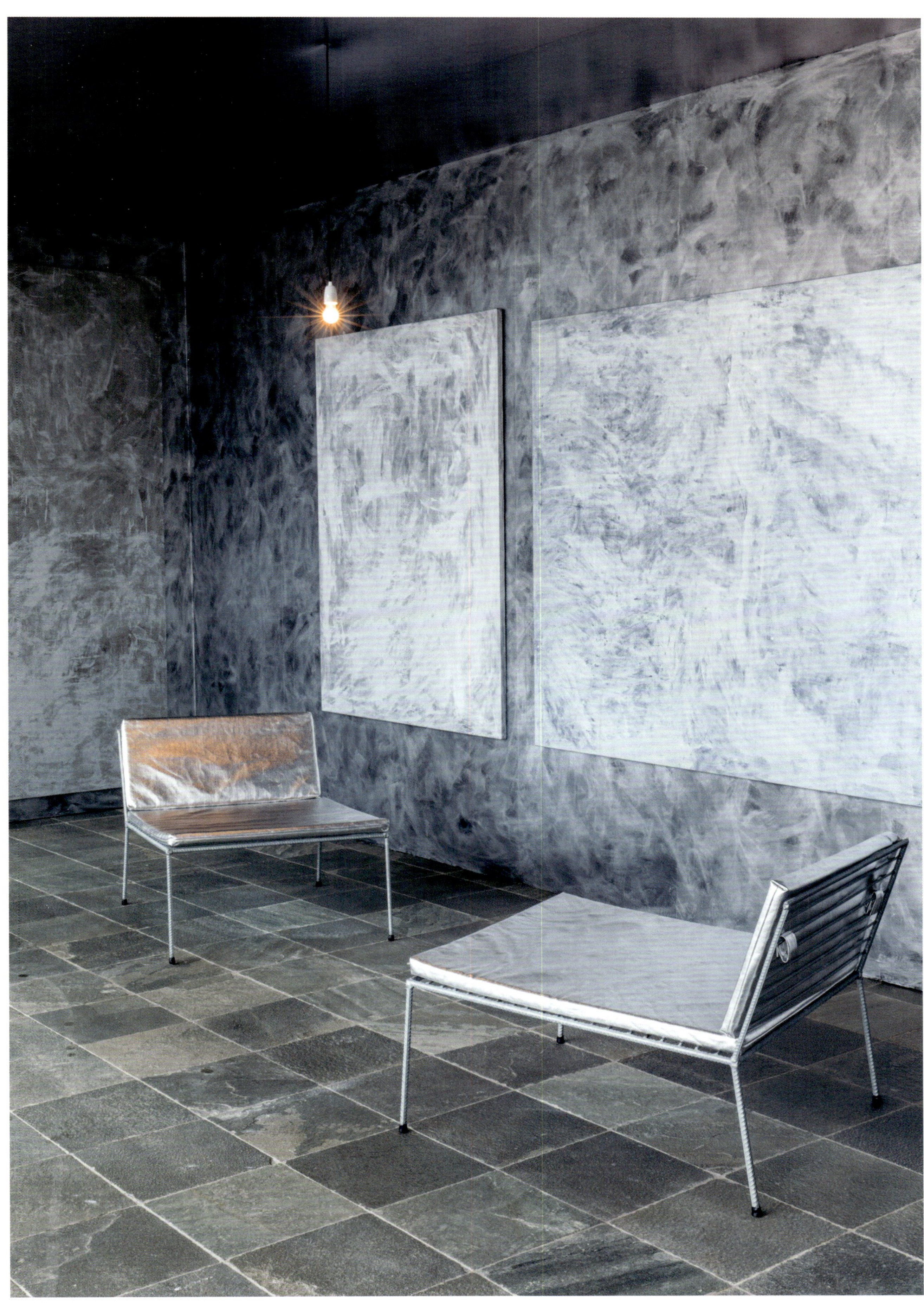

21er Haus, Belvedere, Vienna
December 14, 2016–April 23, 2017

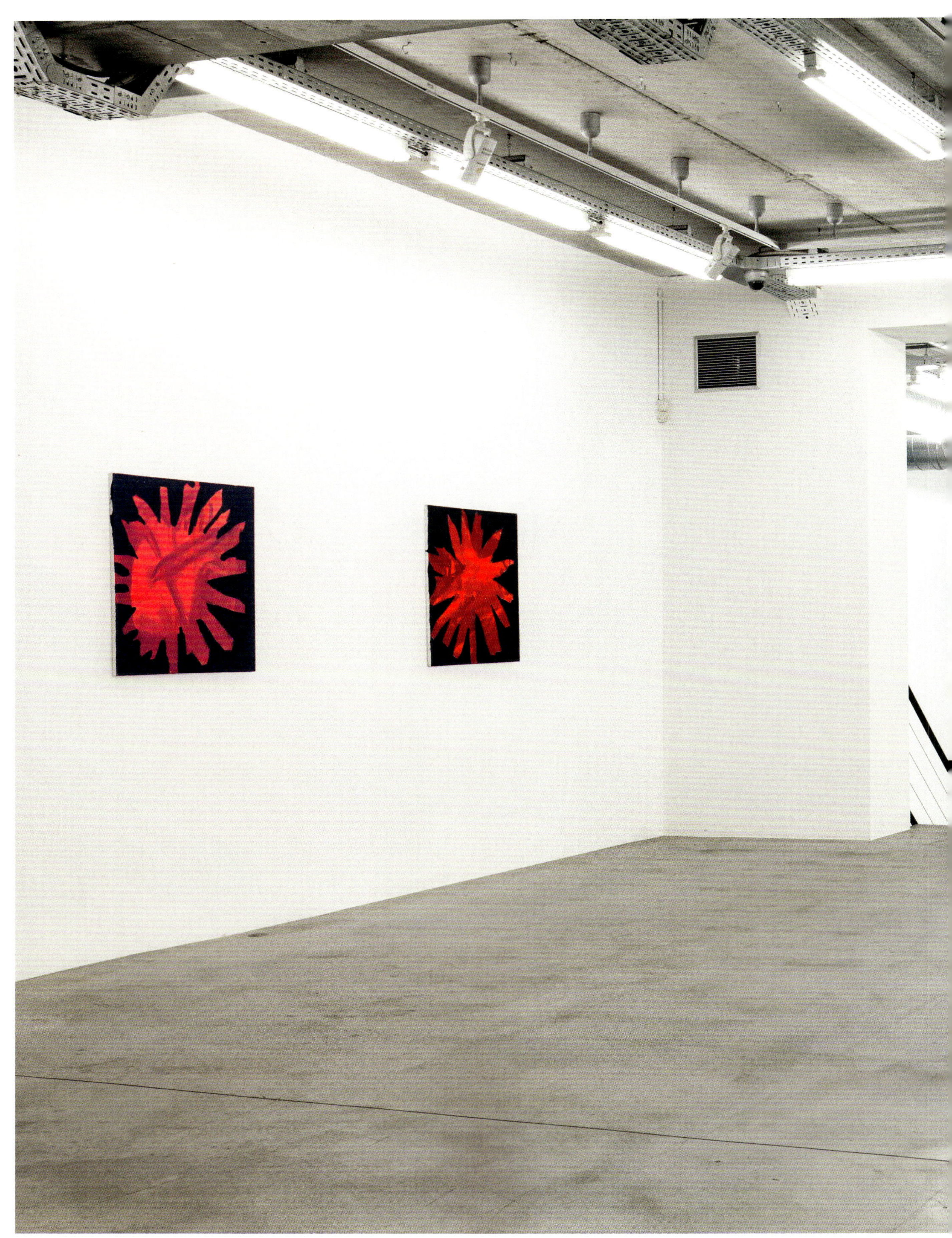

Pages 106–117
installation views: *Tamuna Sirbiladze*

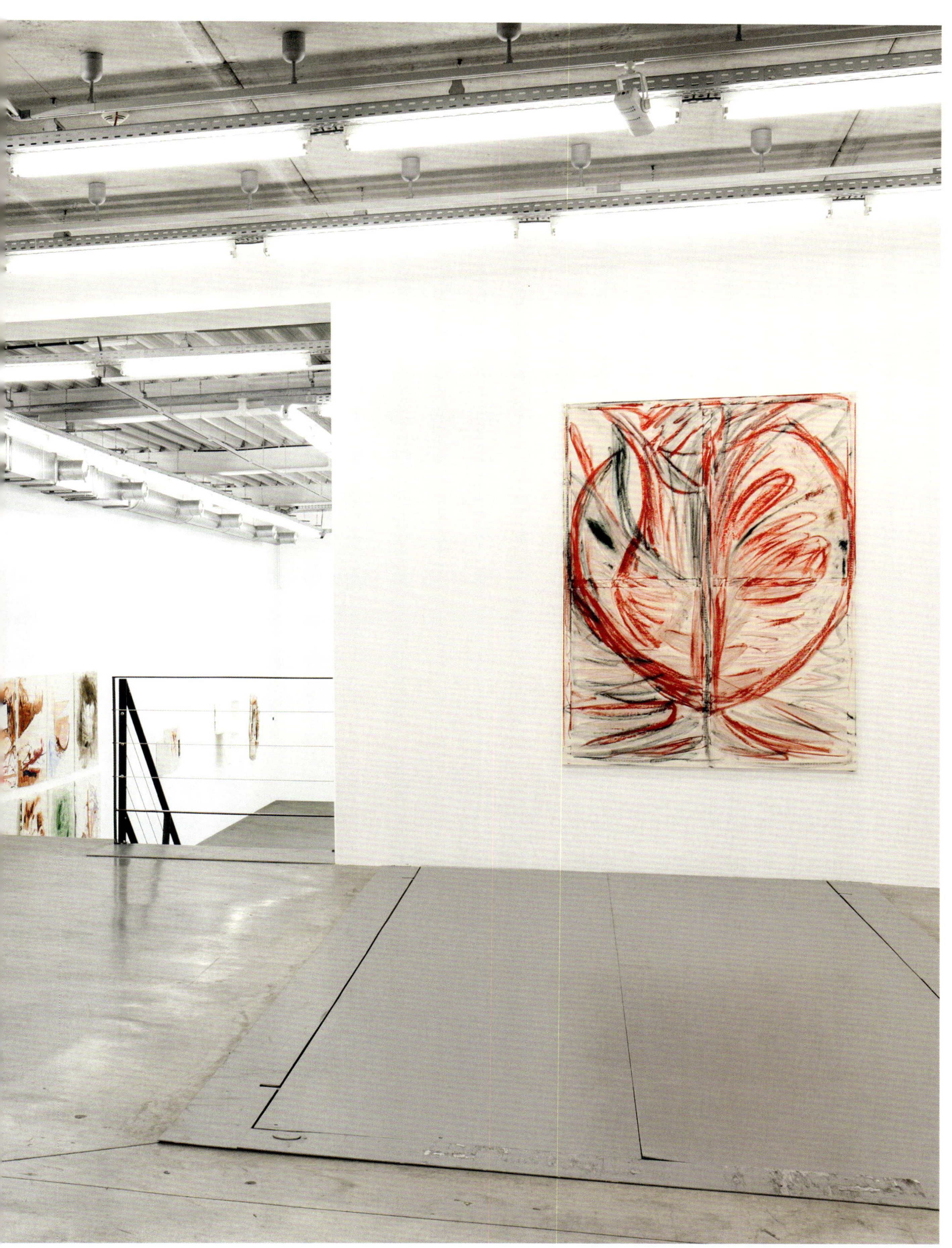

Almine Rech Gallery, Brussels
January 14—April 14, 2016

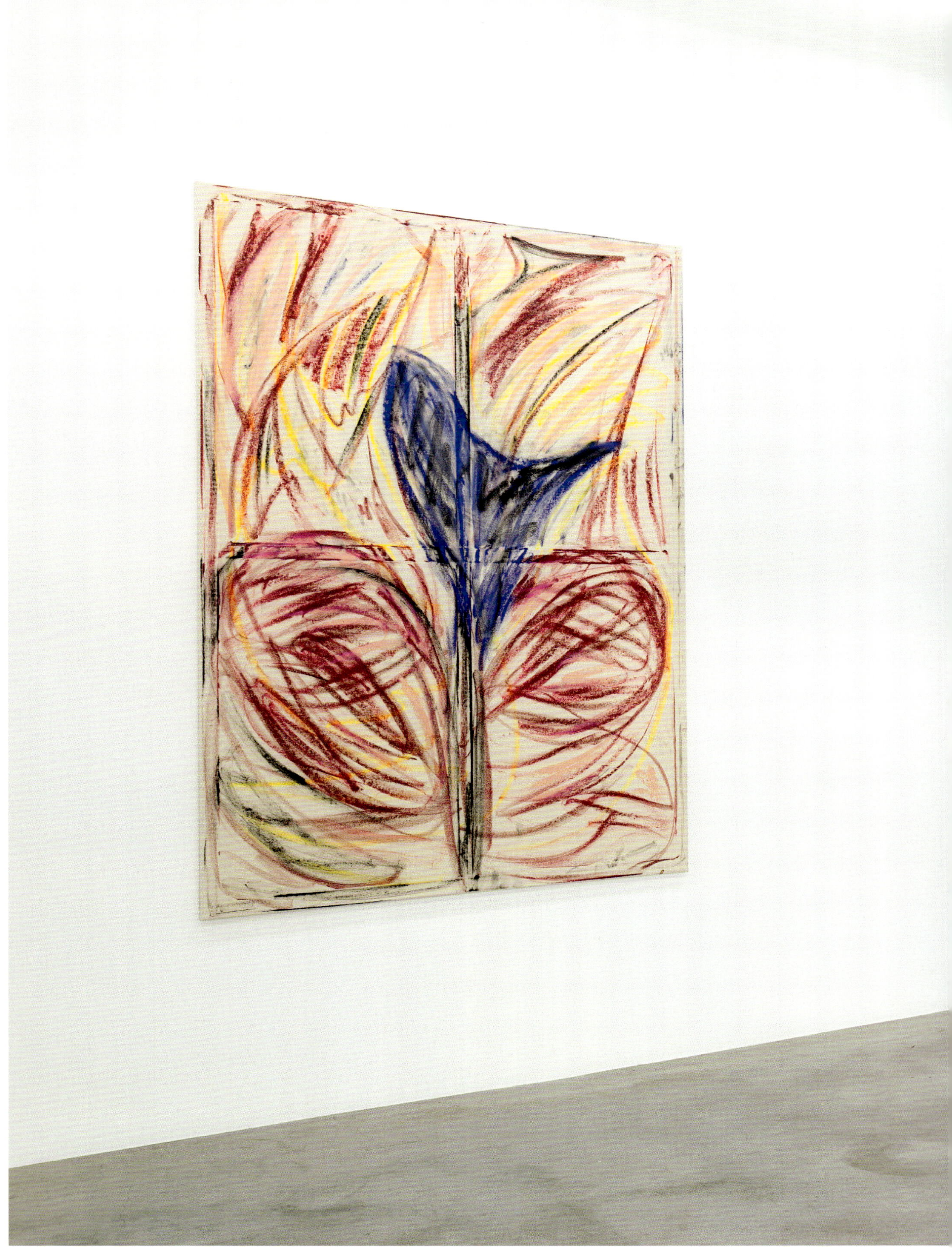

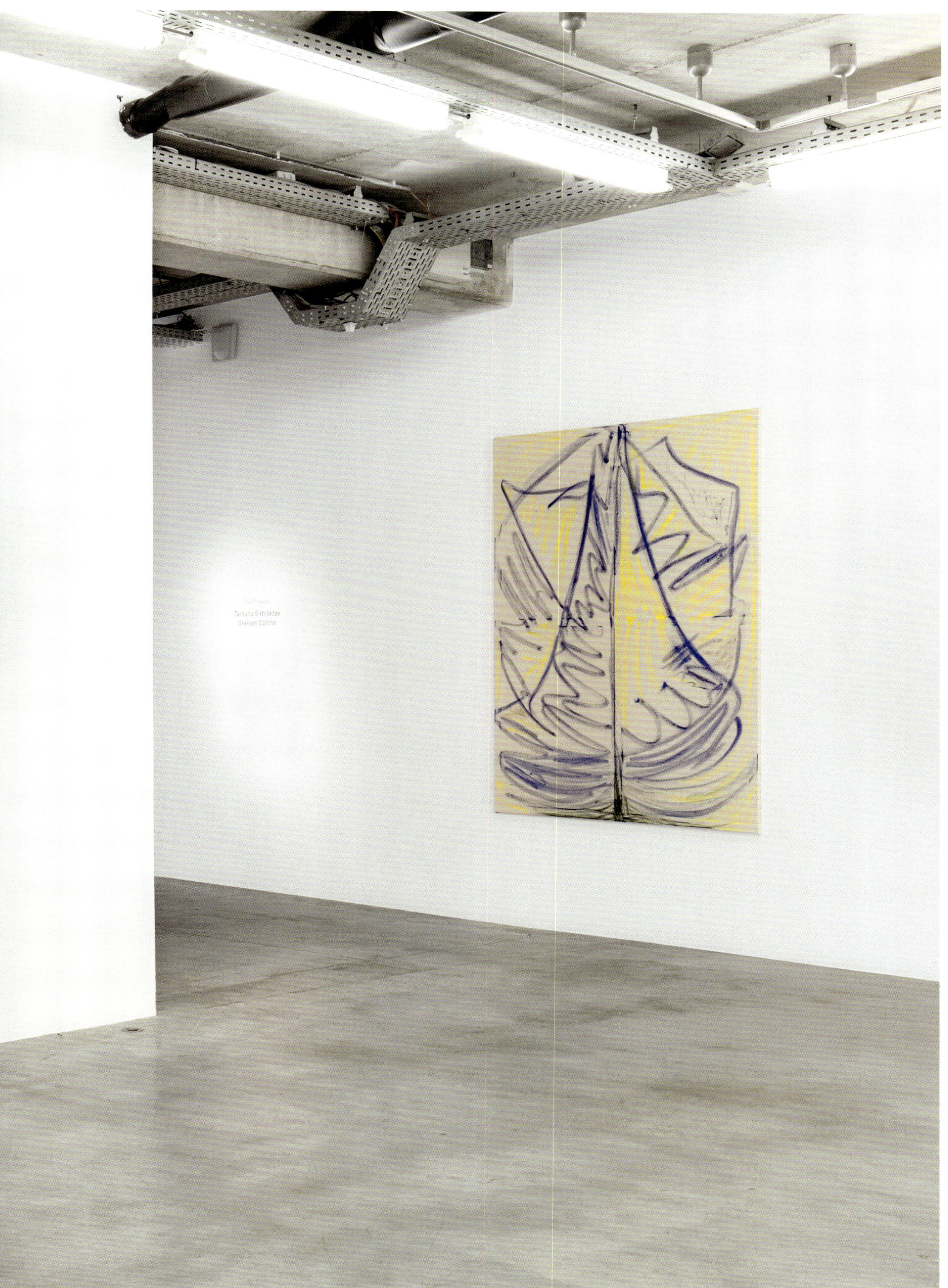

Two Projects
Tamuna Sirbiladze
Graham Collins

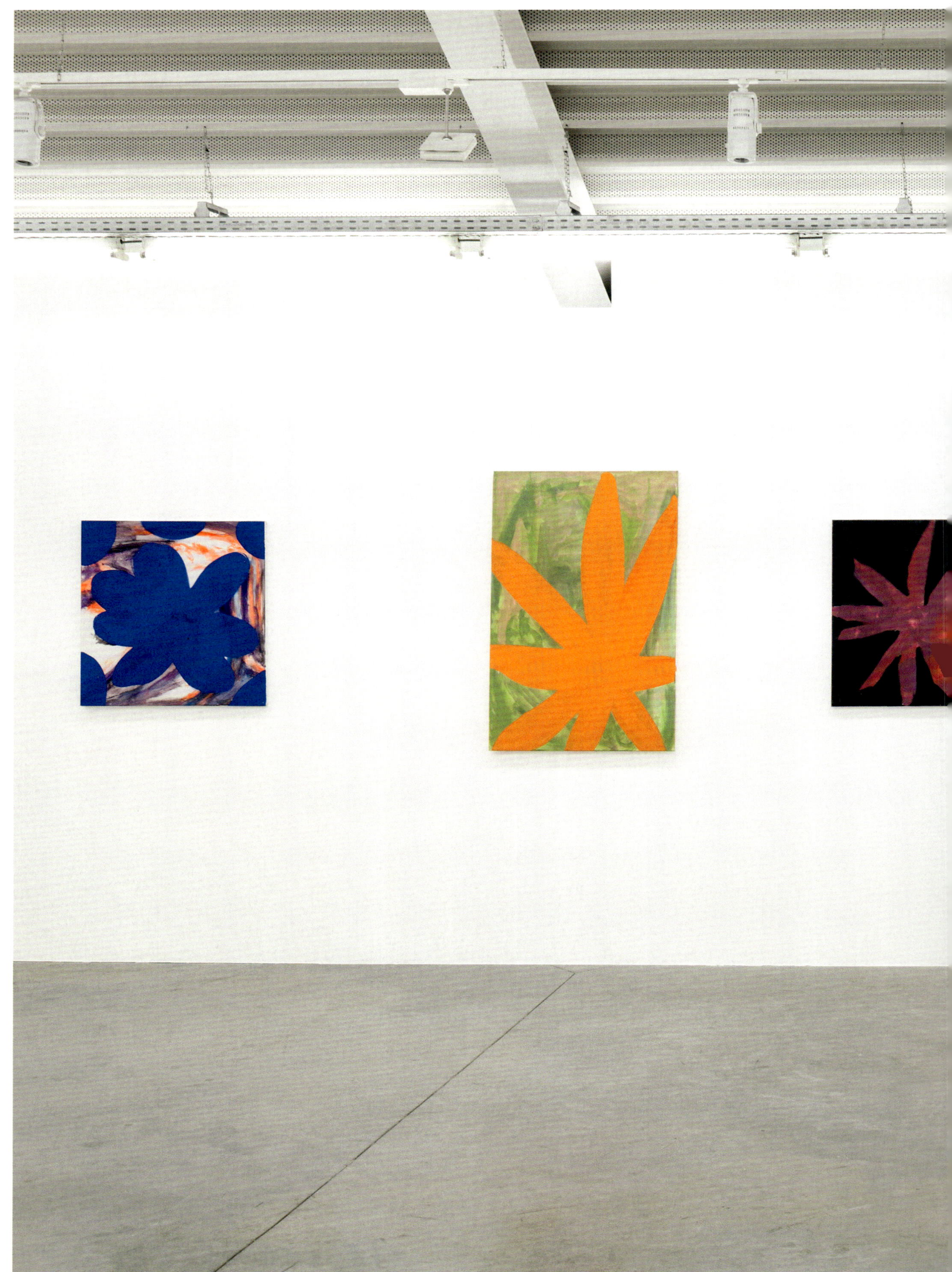

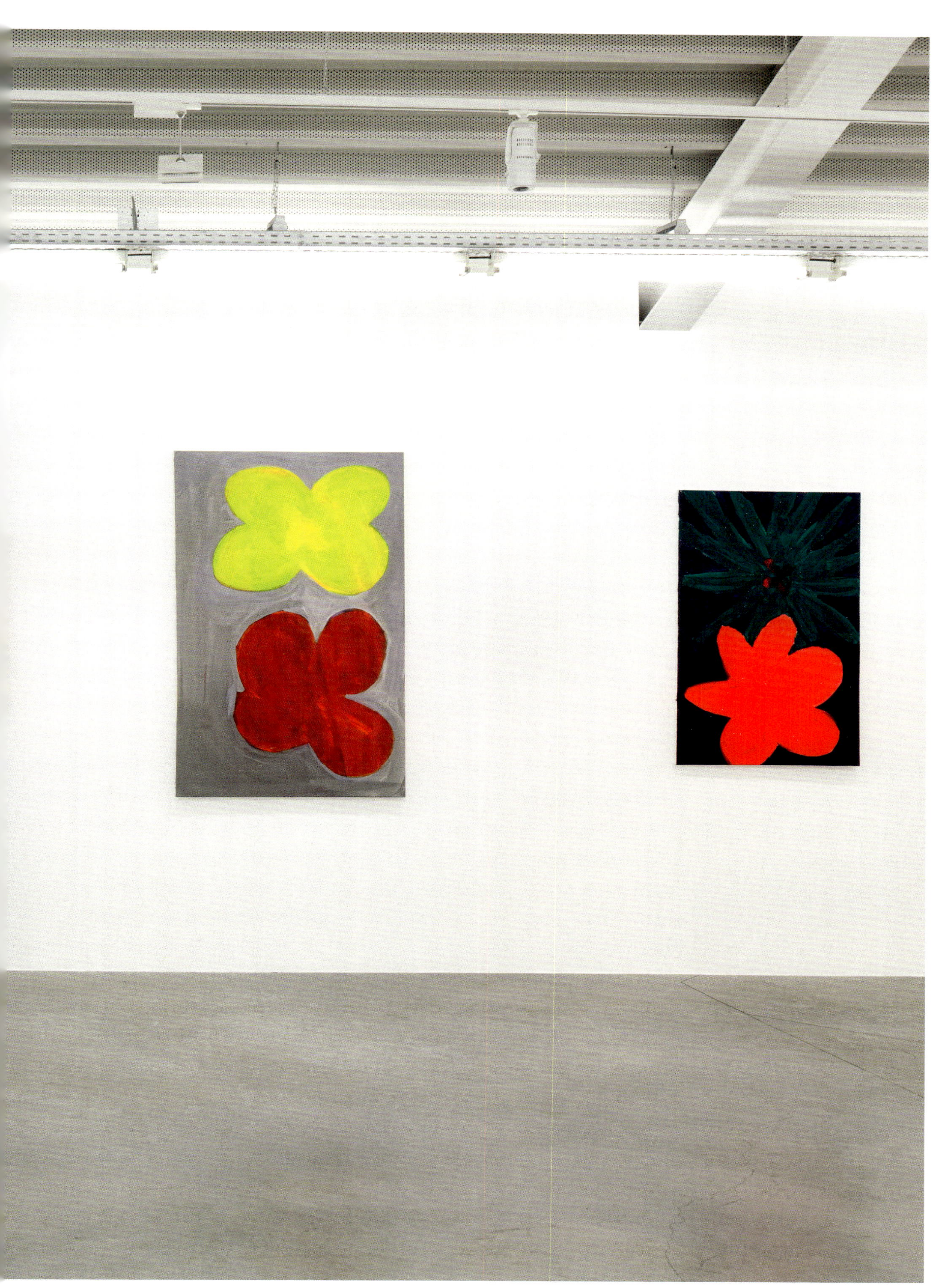

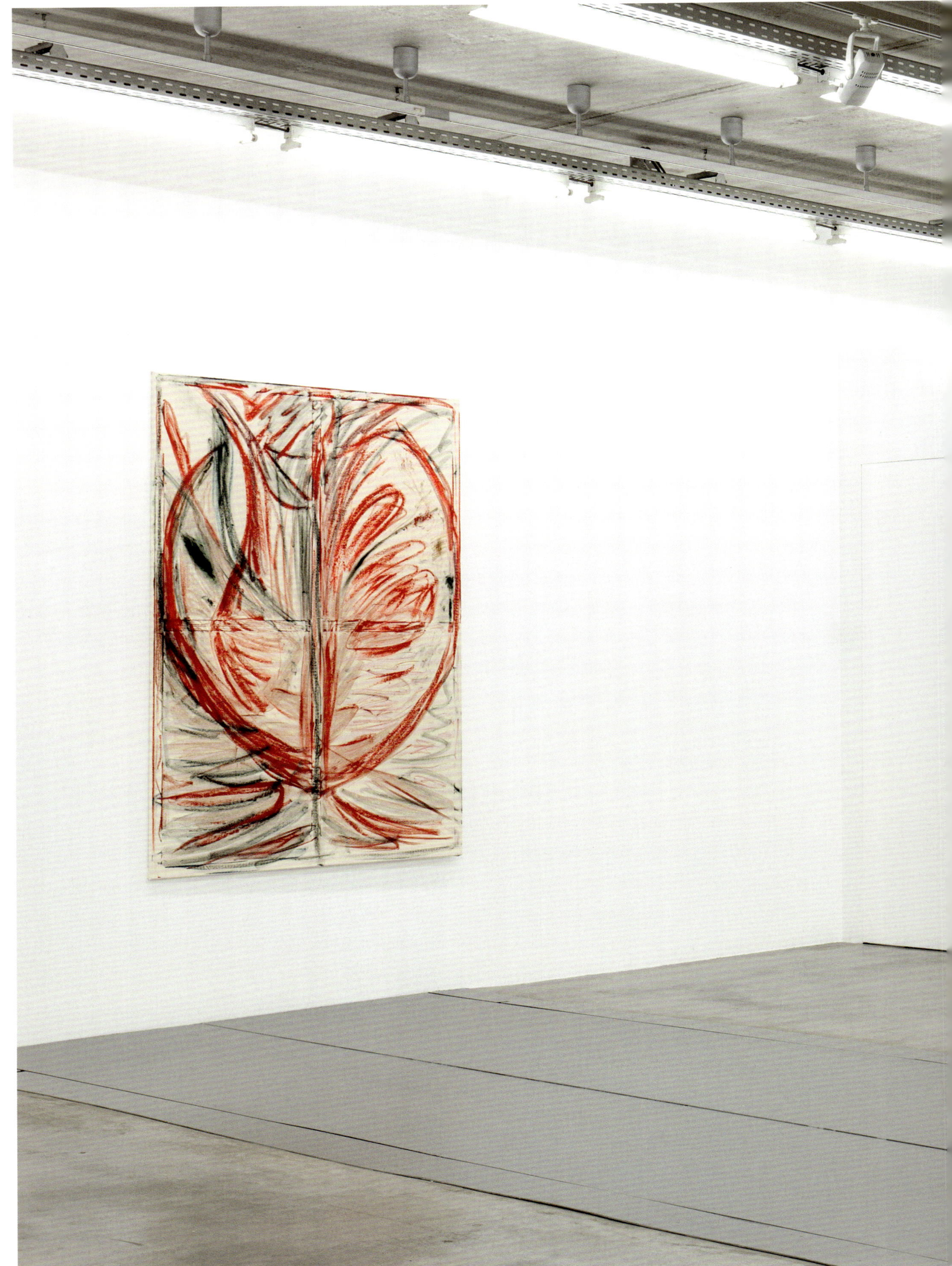

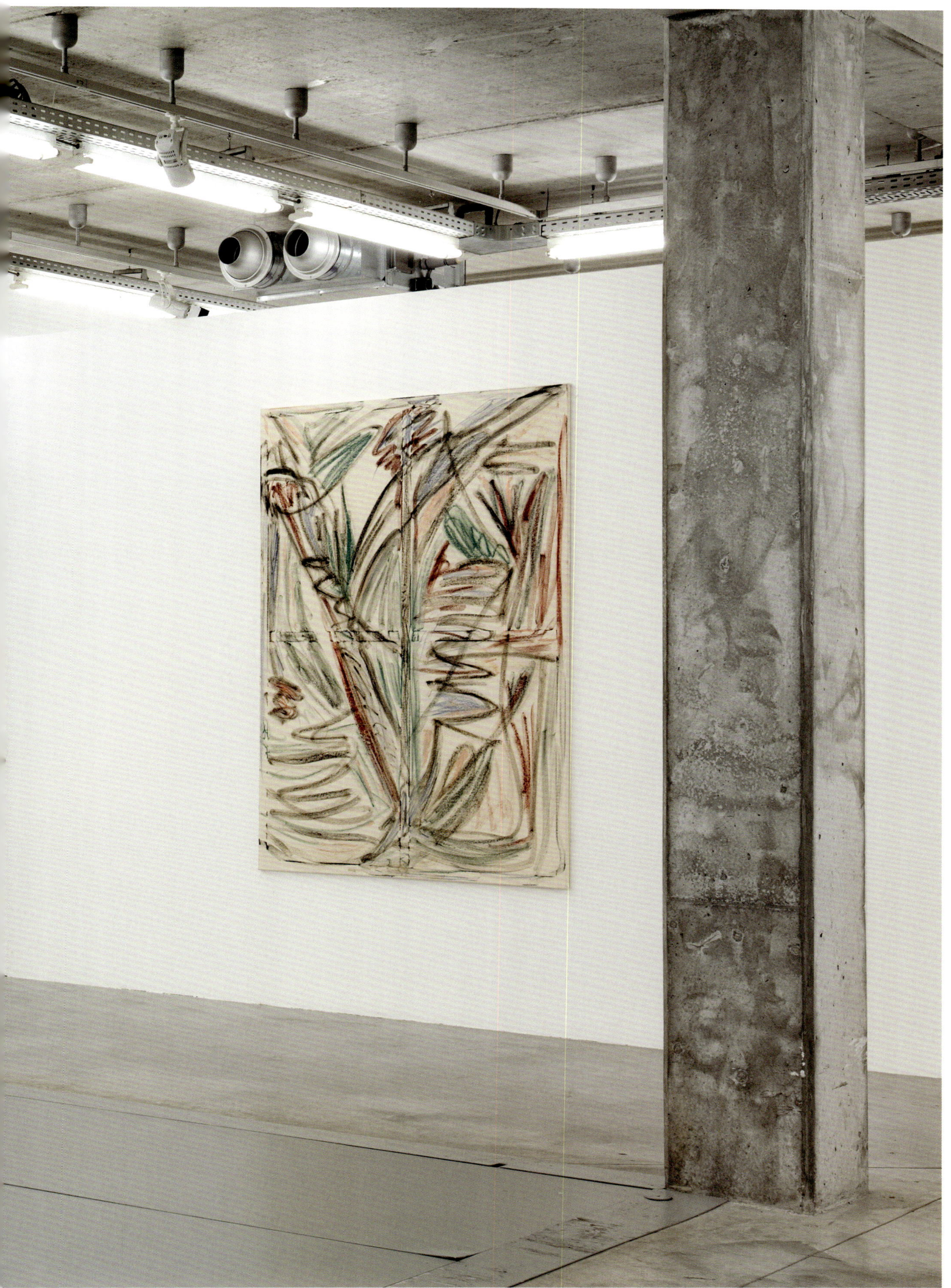

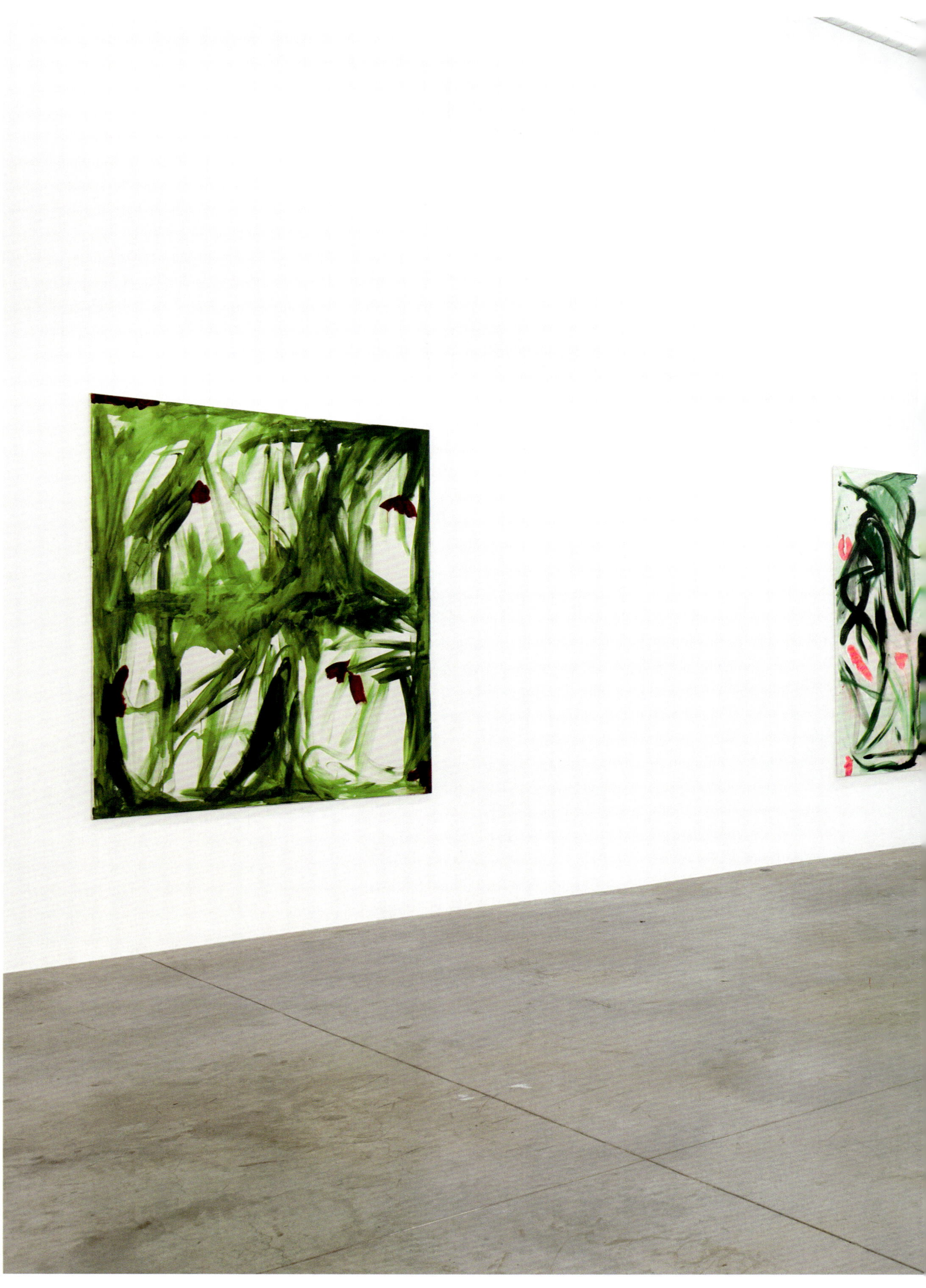

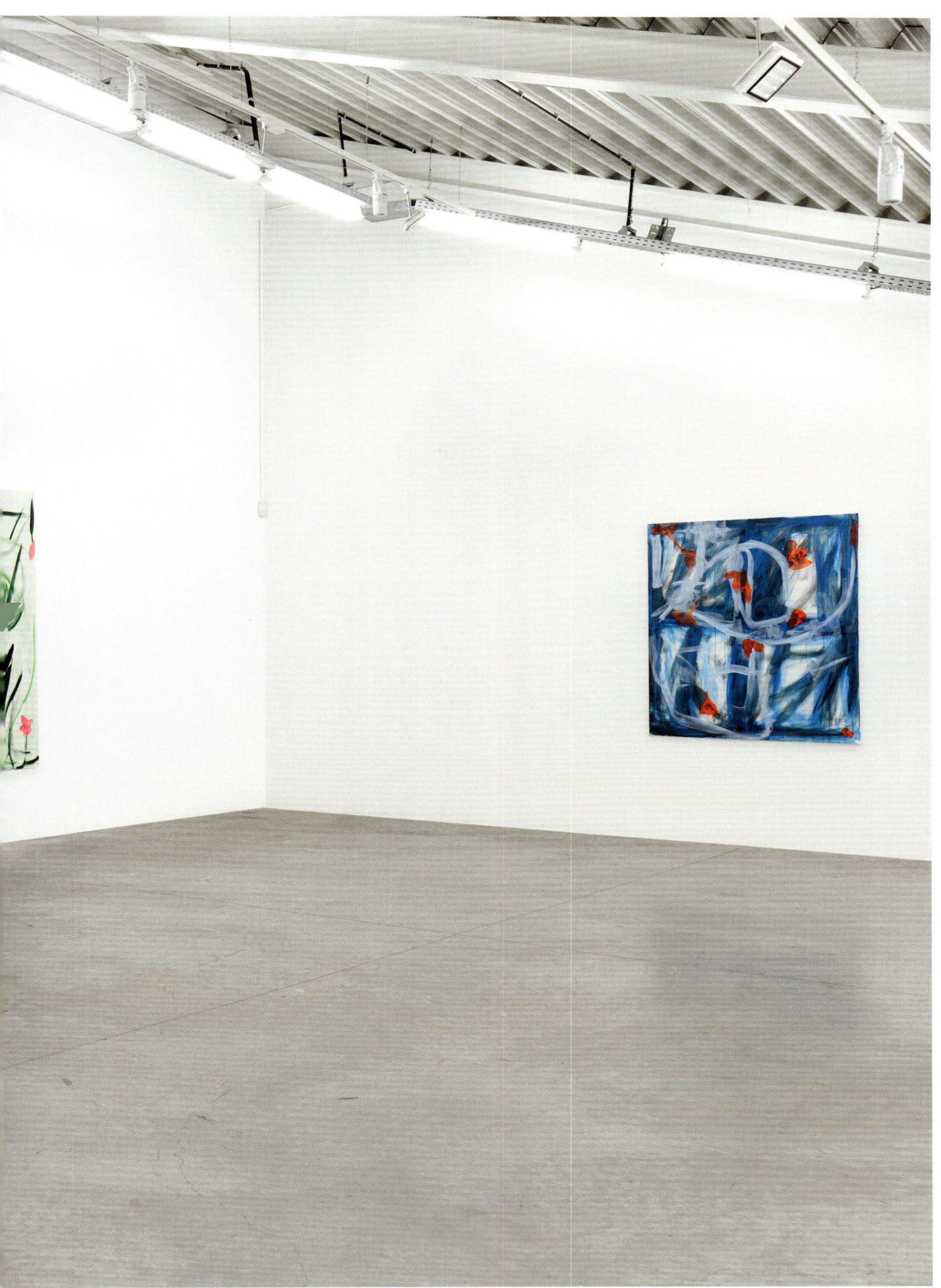

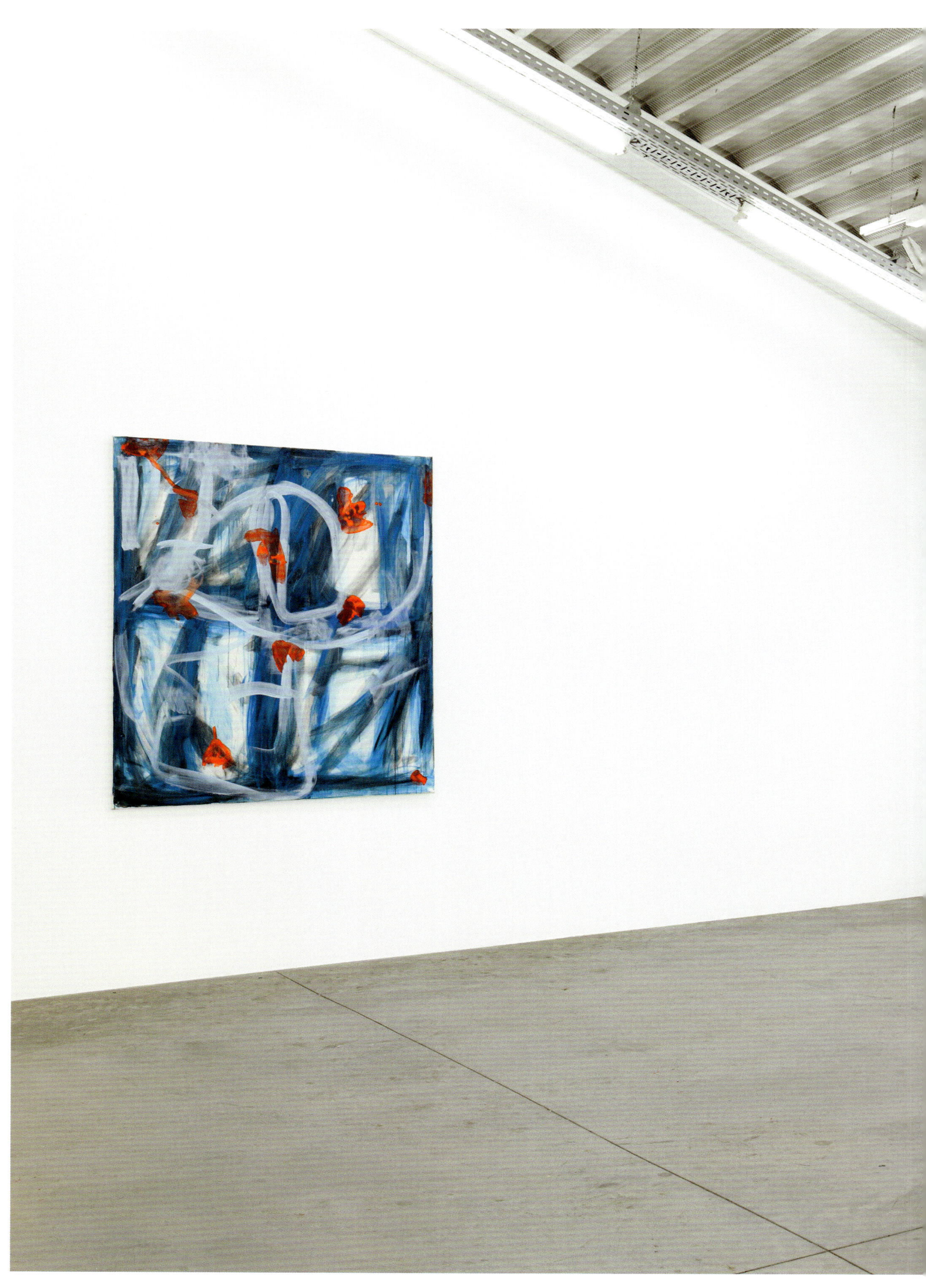

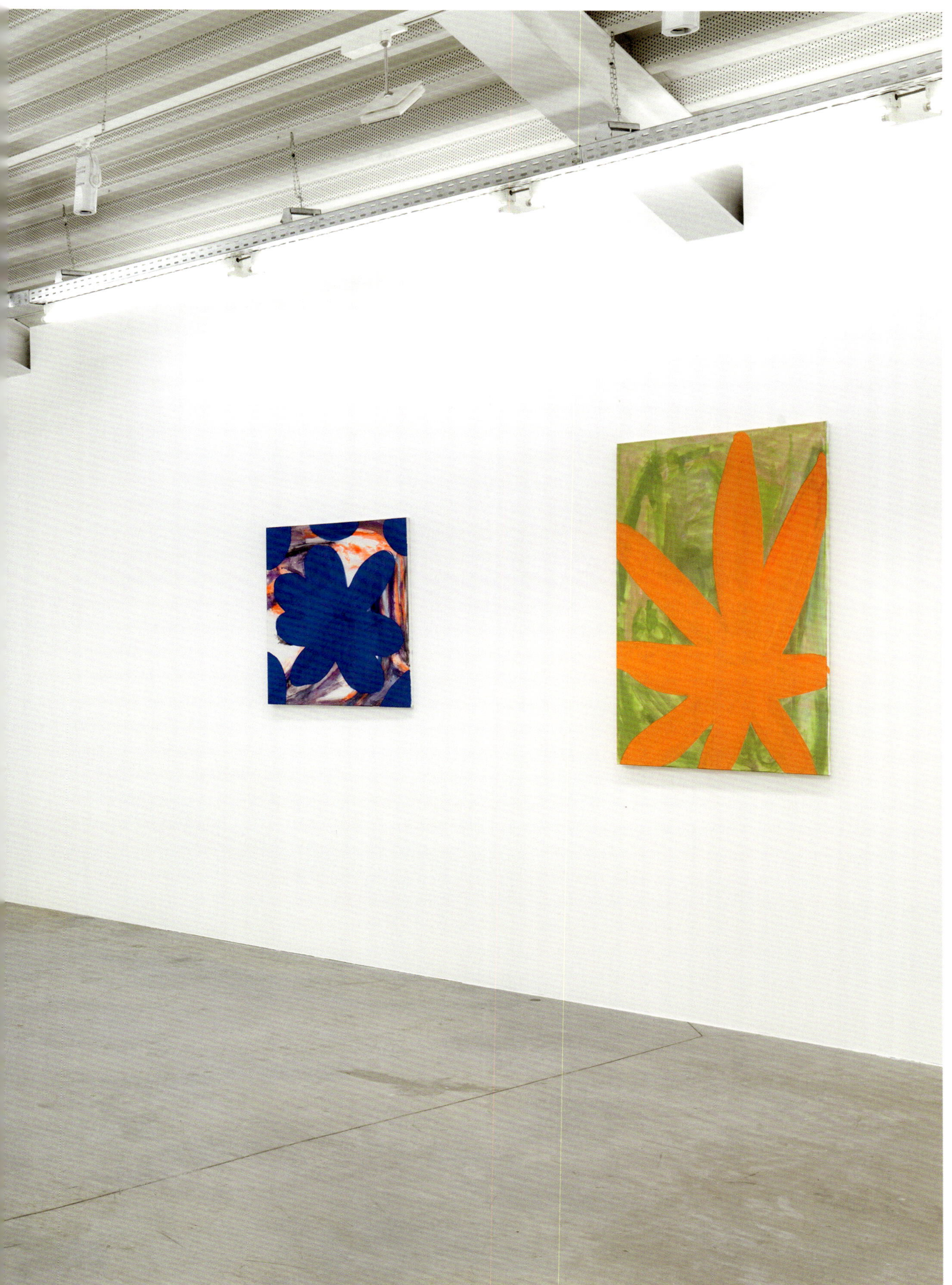

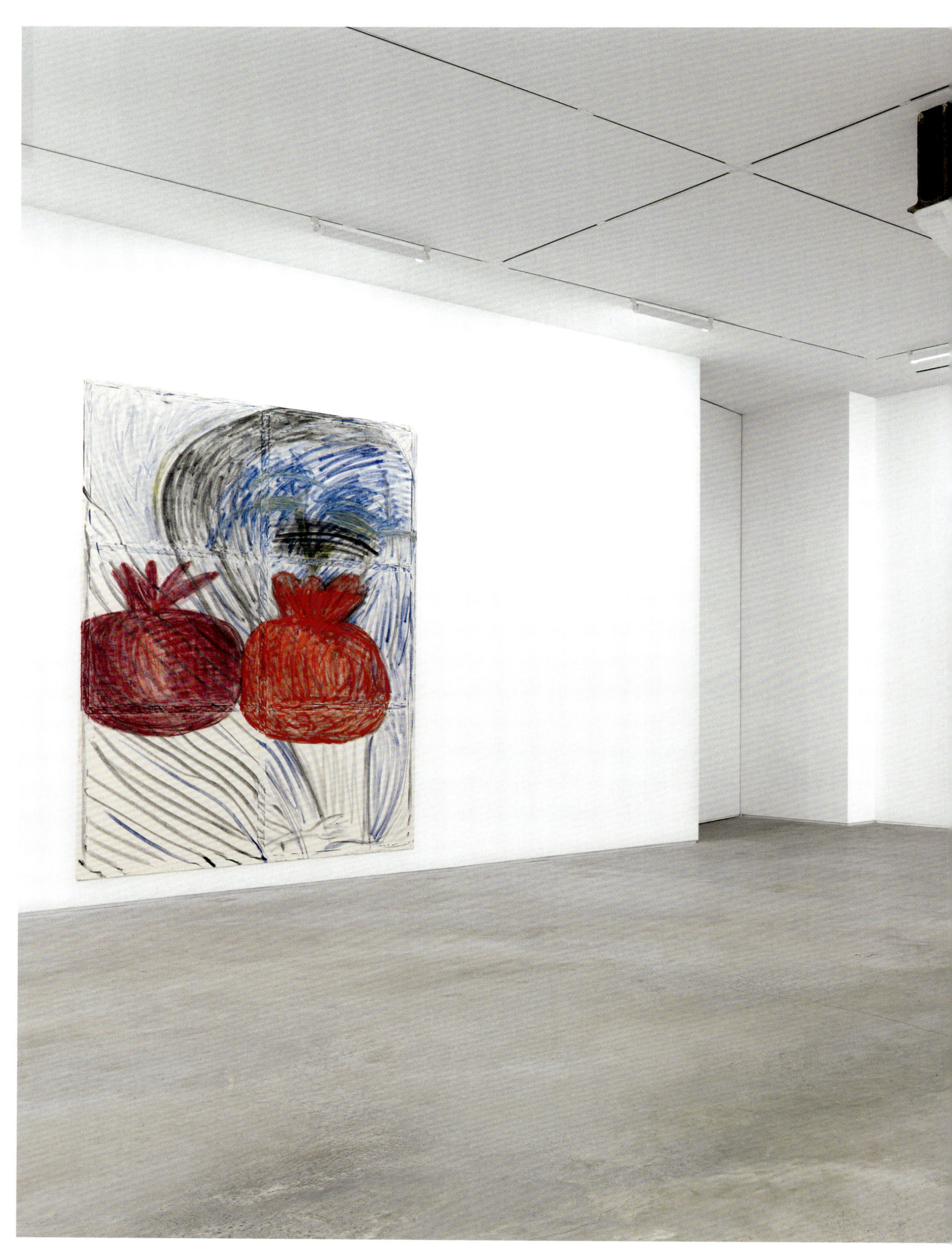

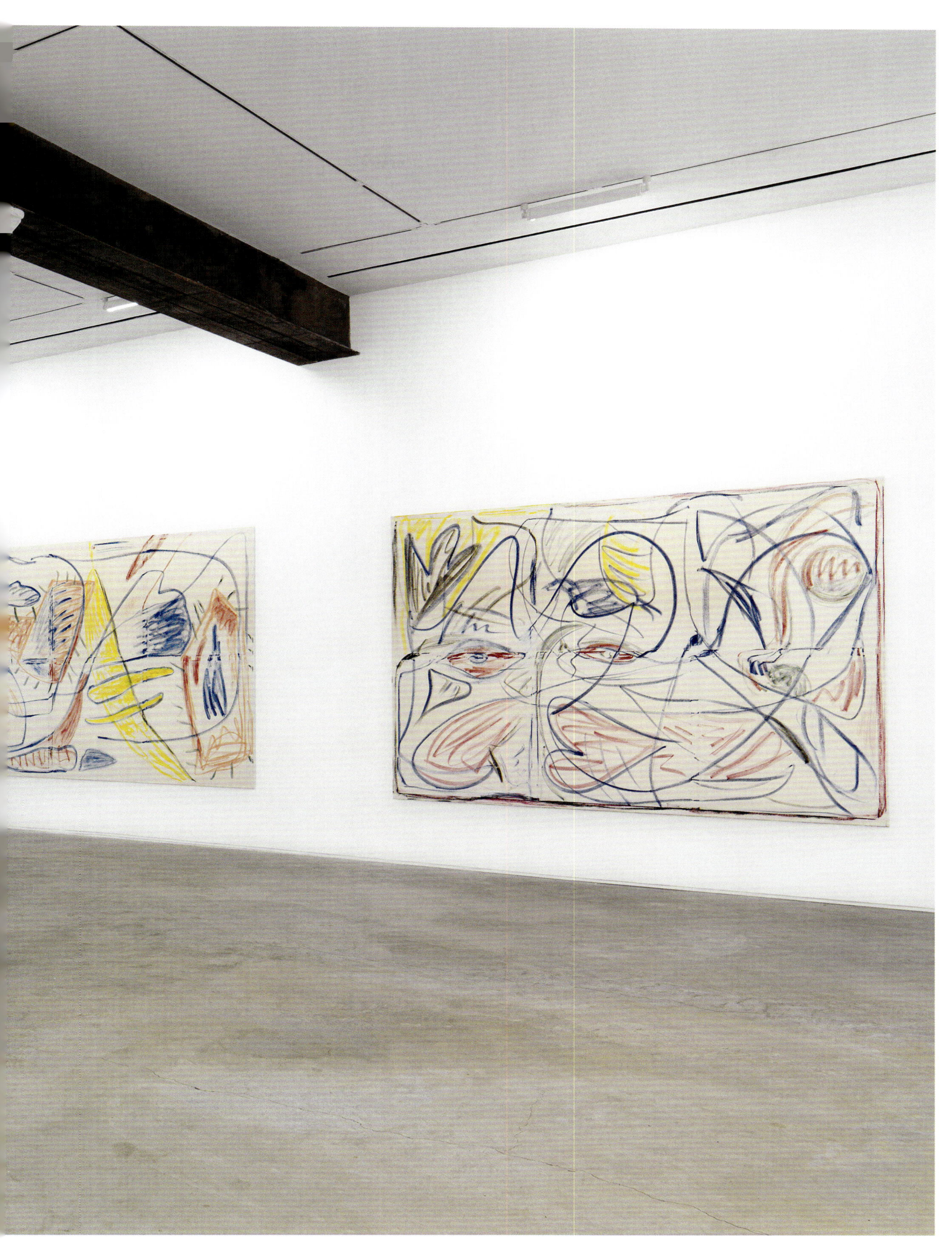

James Fuentes, New York
October 13—November 8, 2015

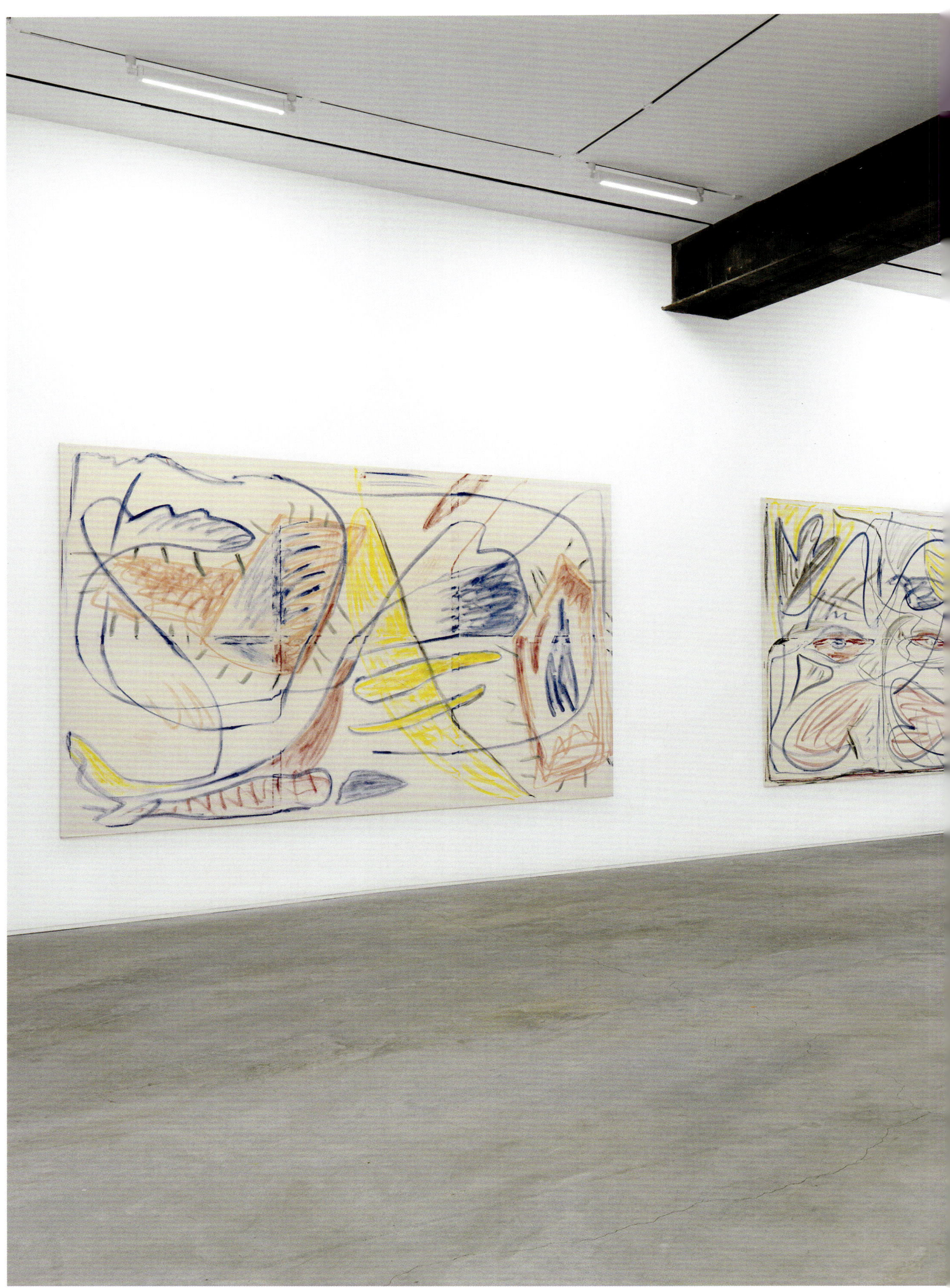

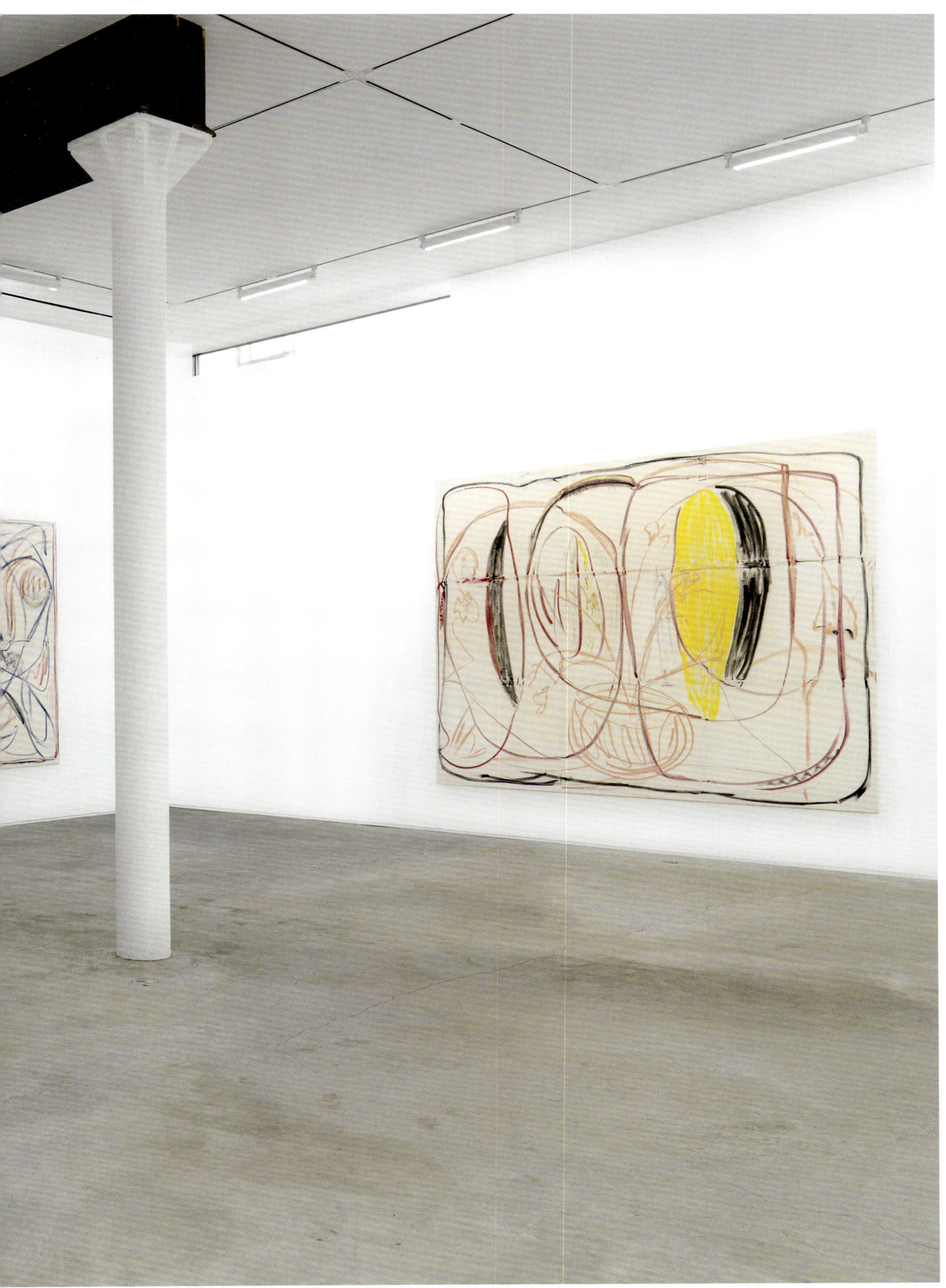

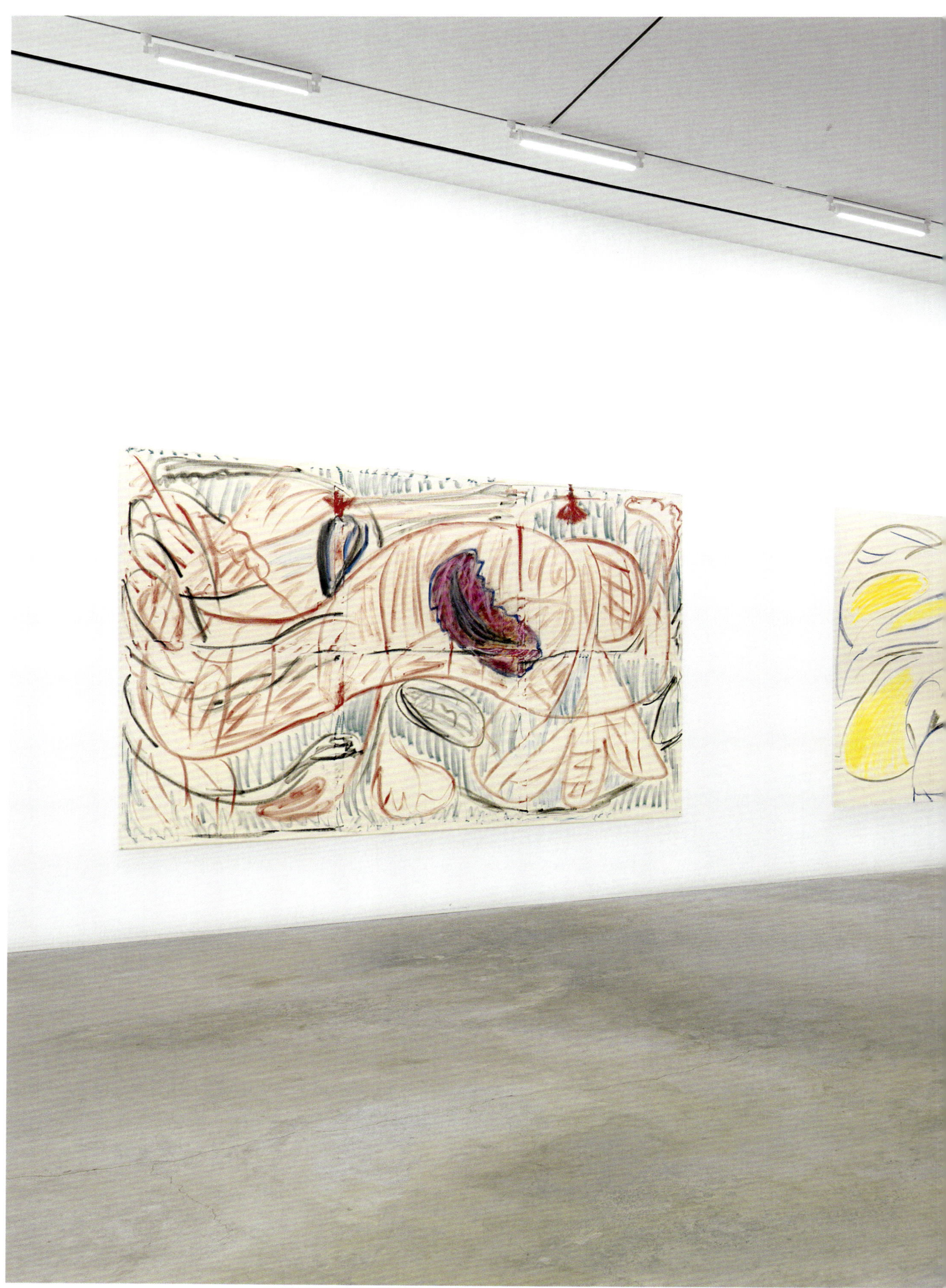

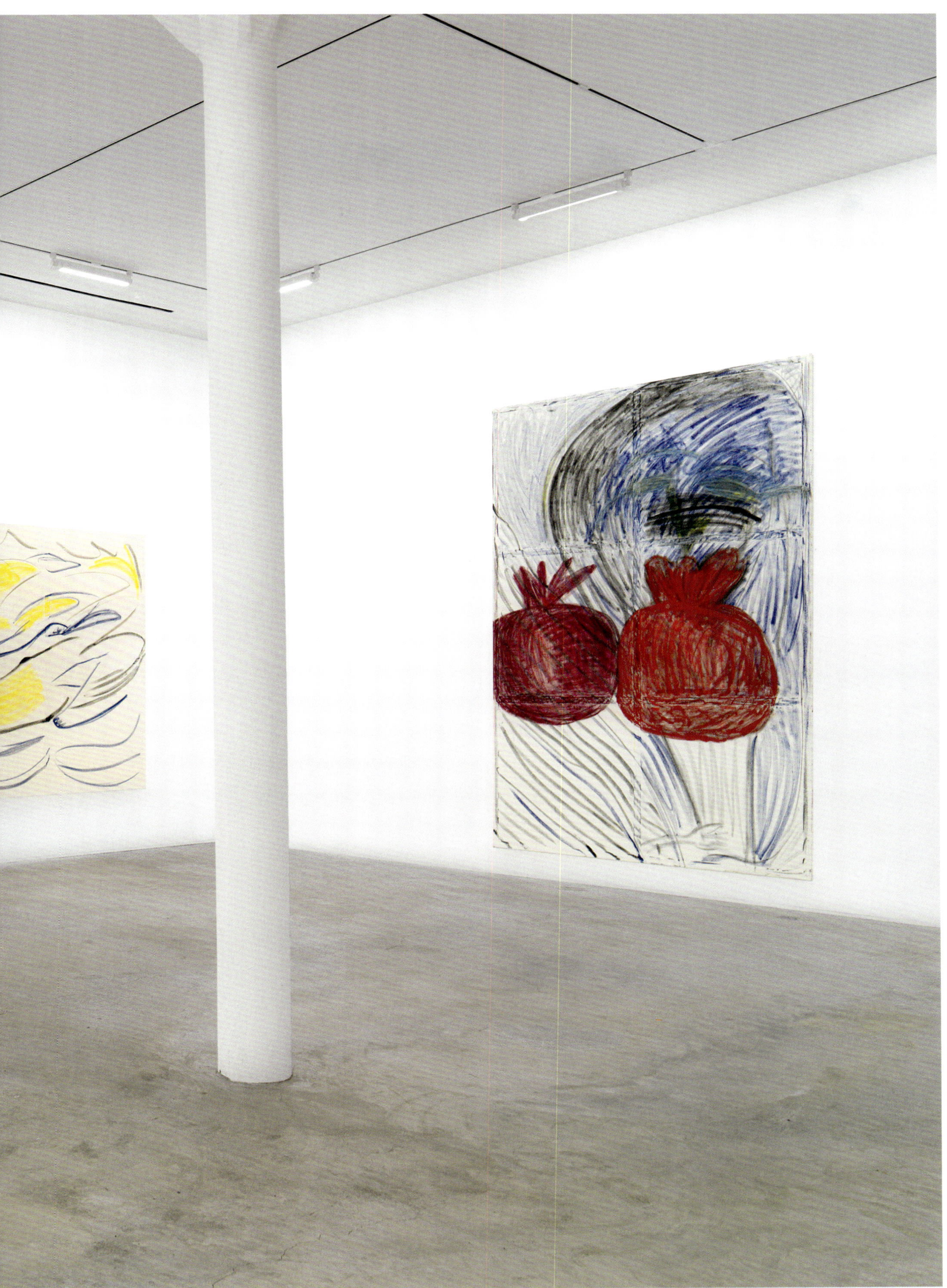

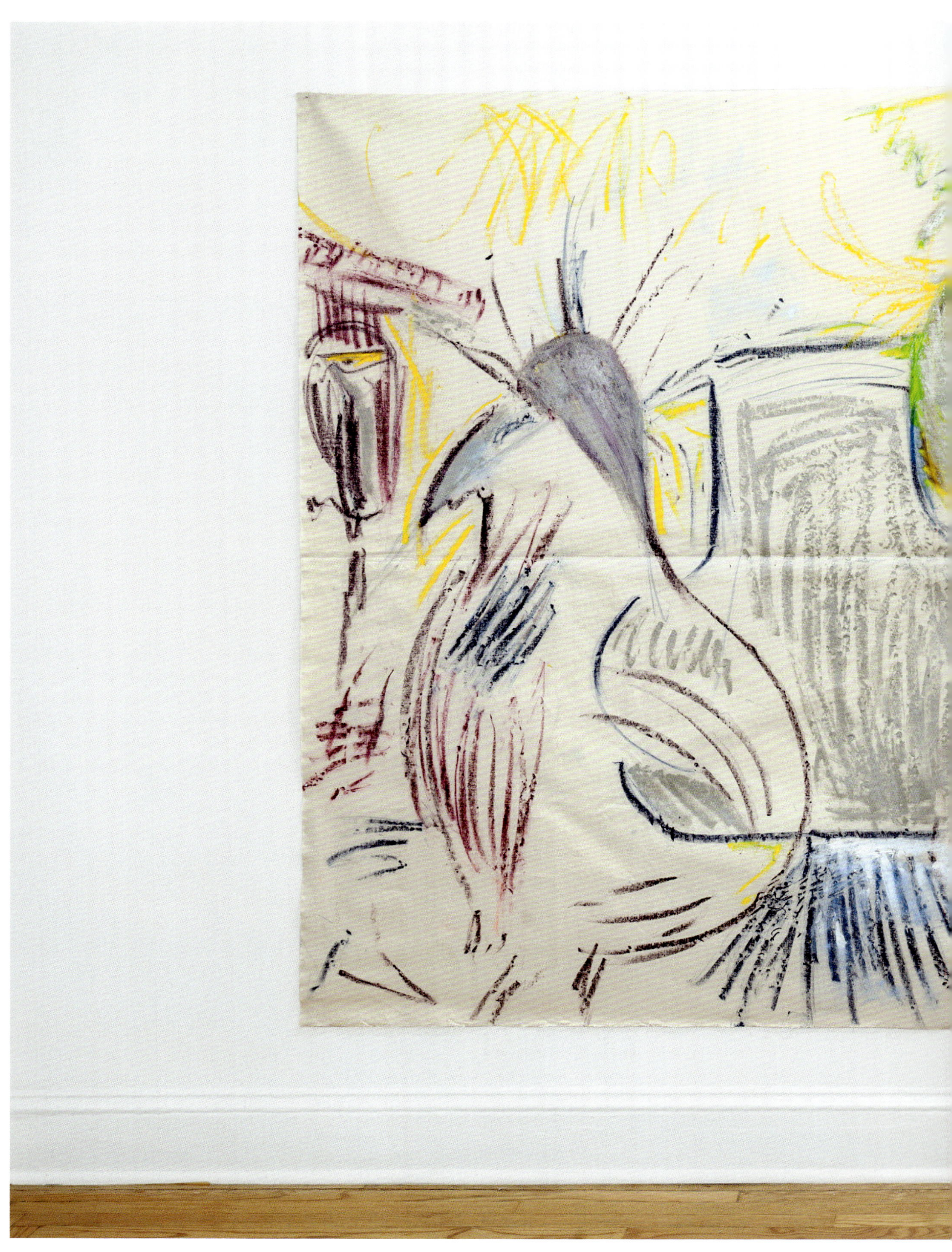

Pages 124–131
installation views: *Take it easy*

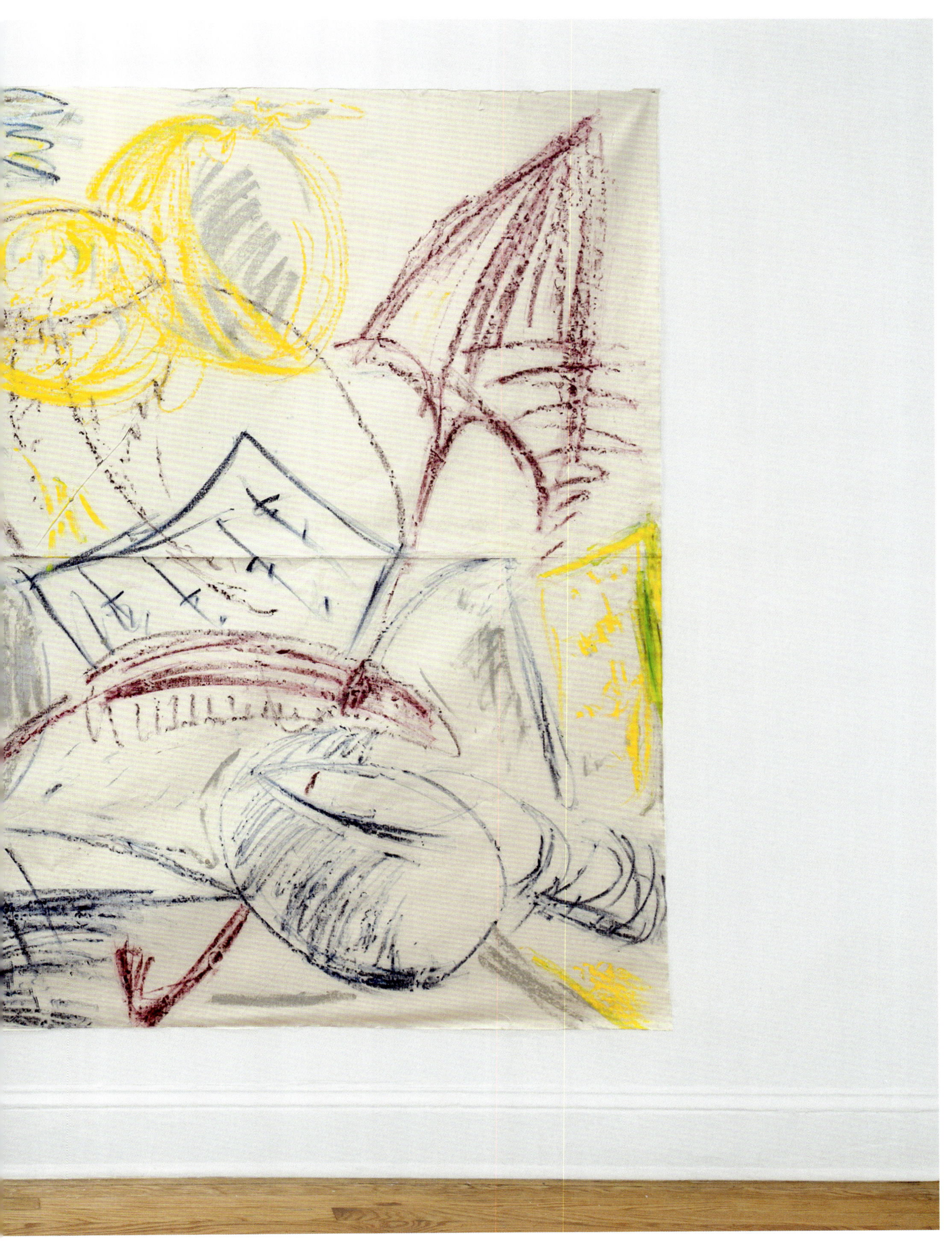

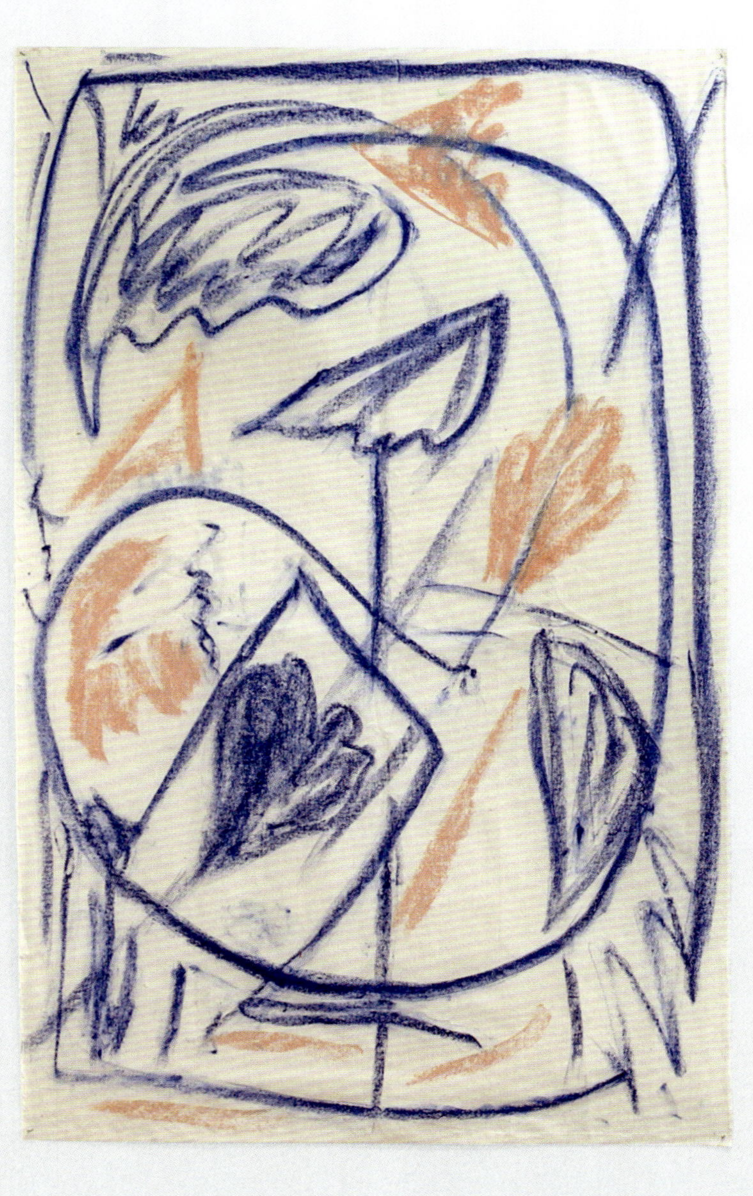
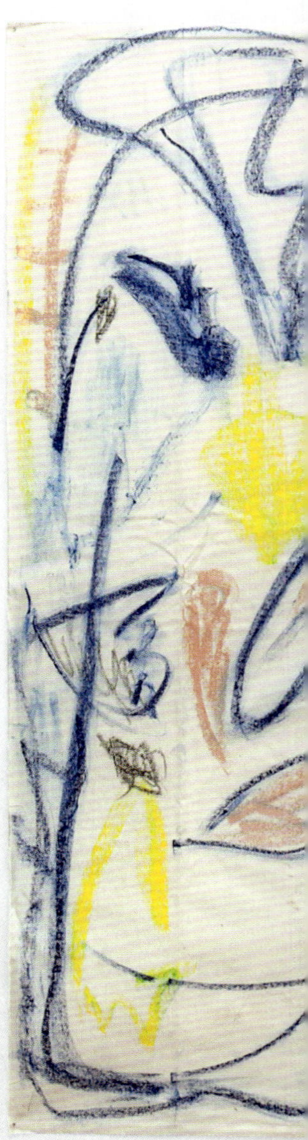

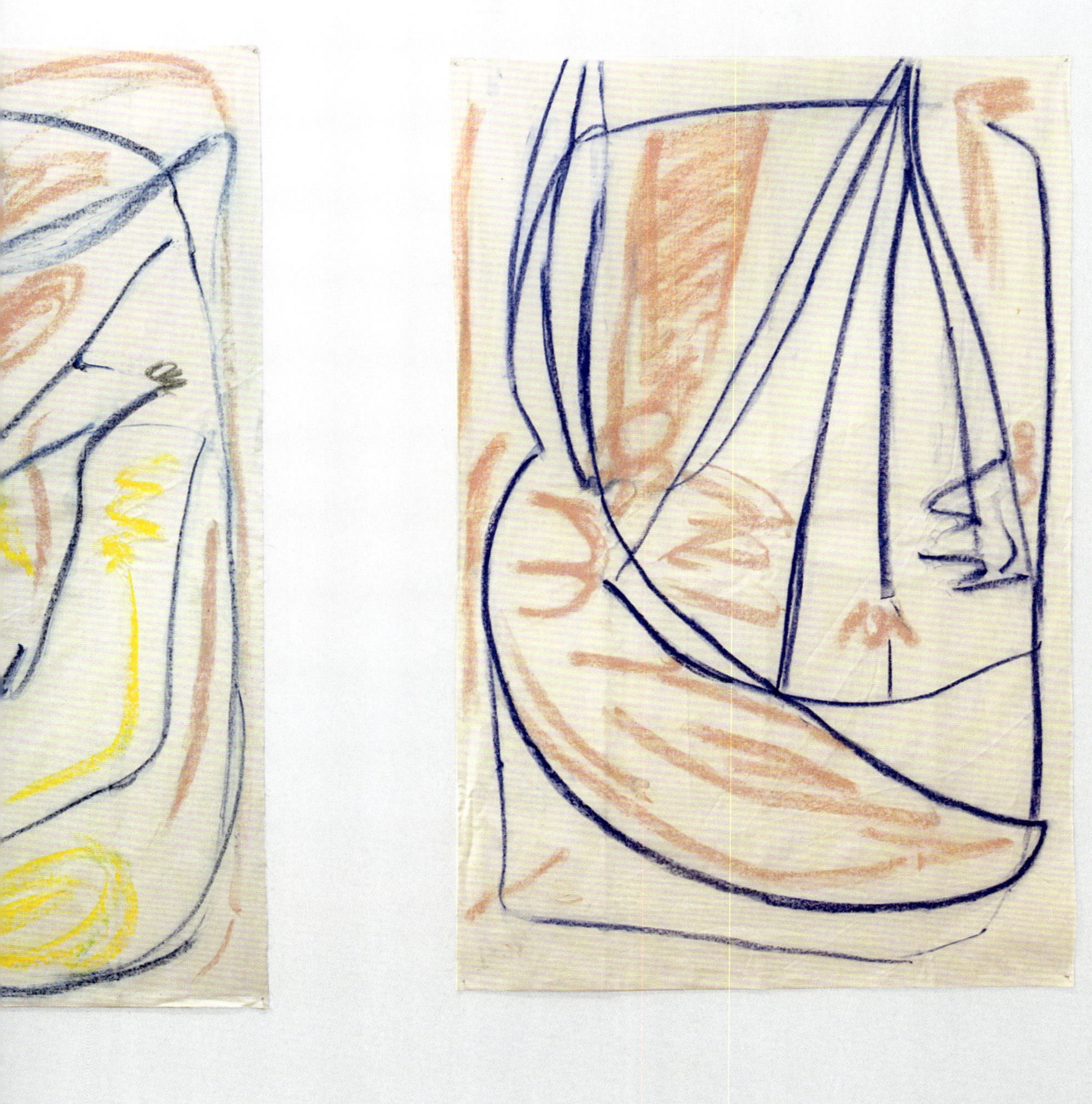

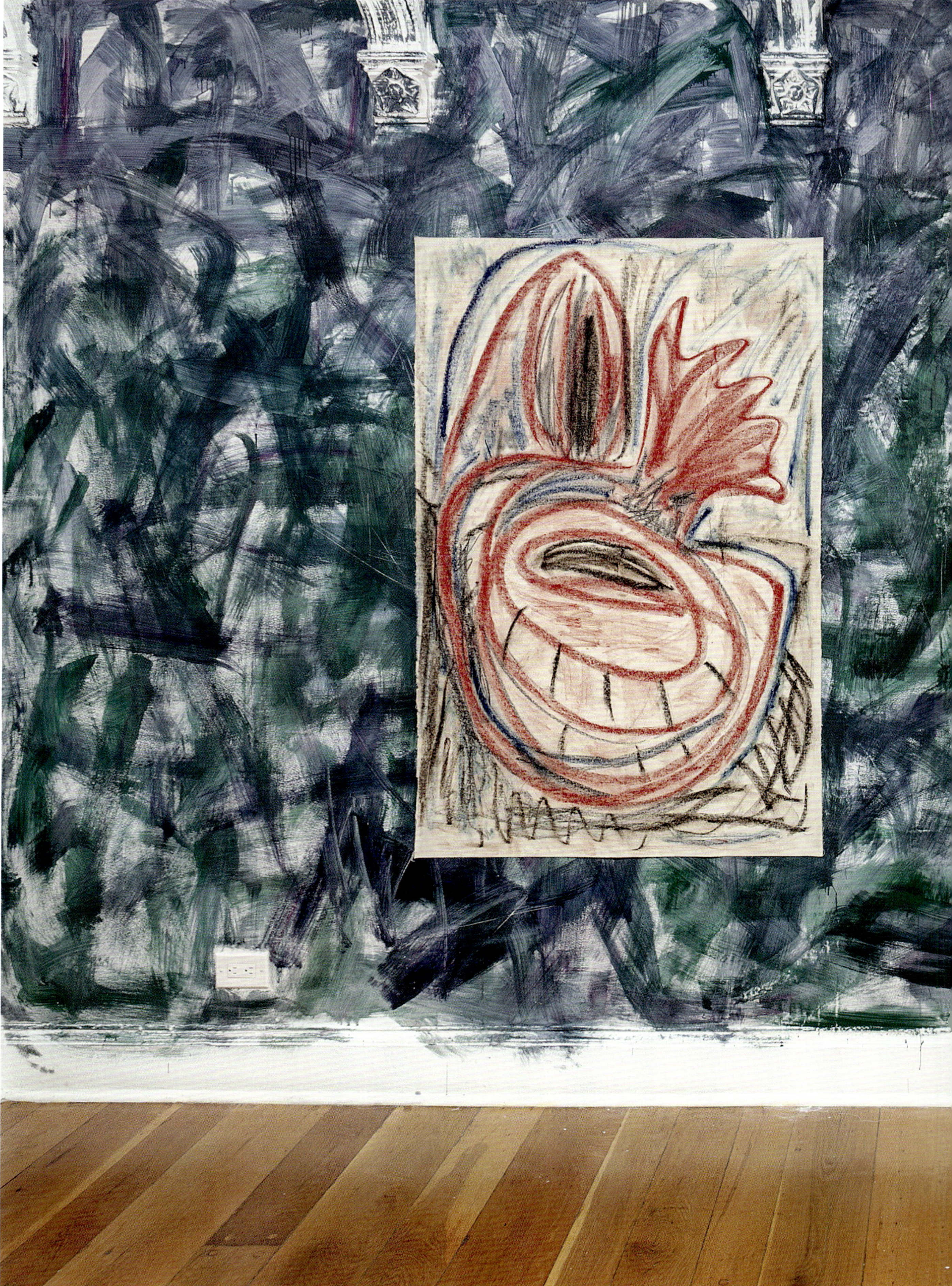

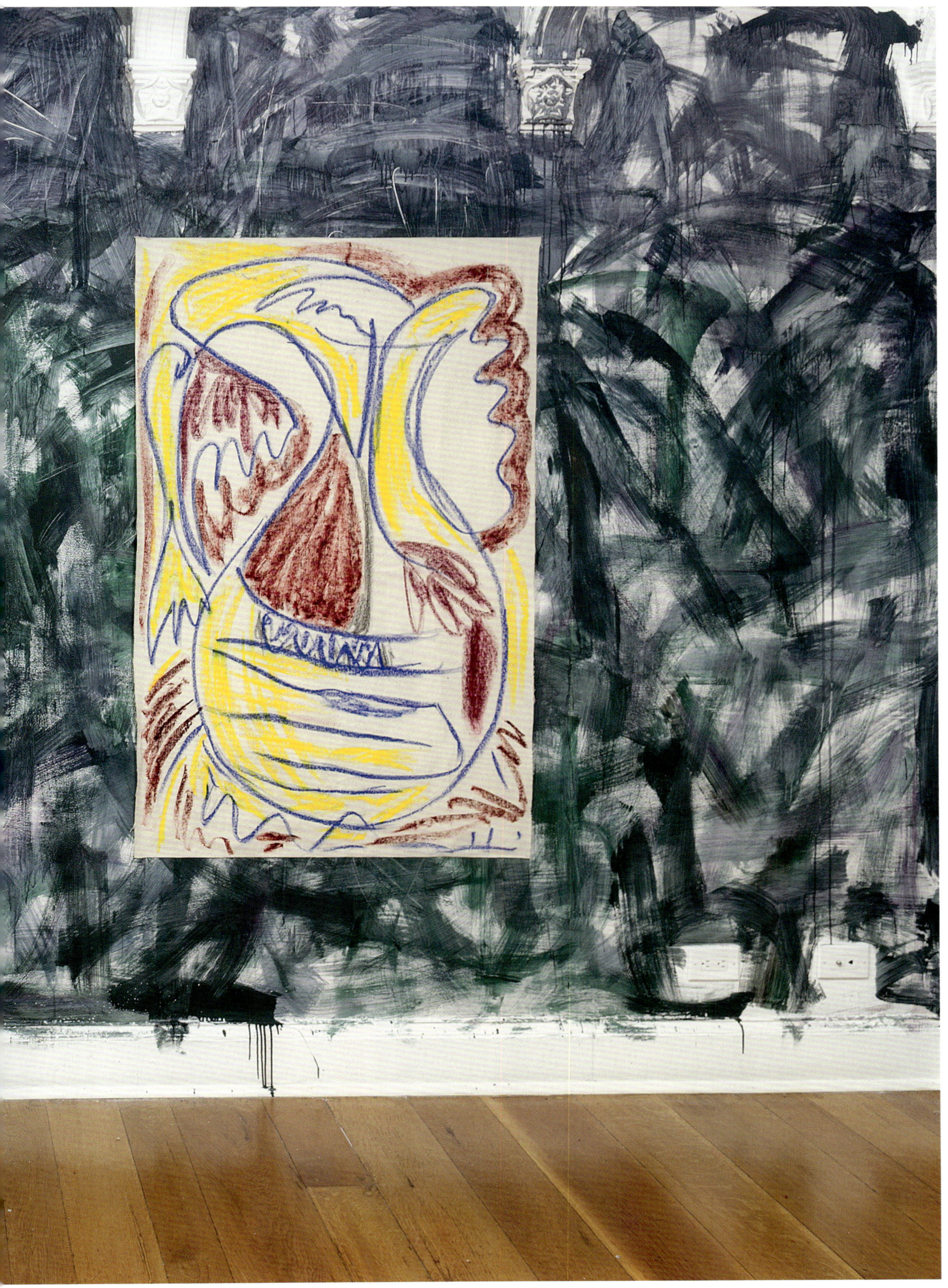

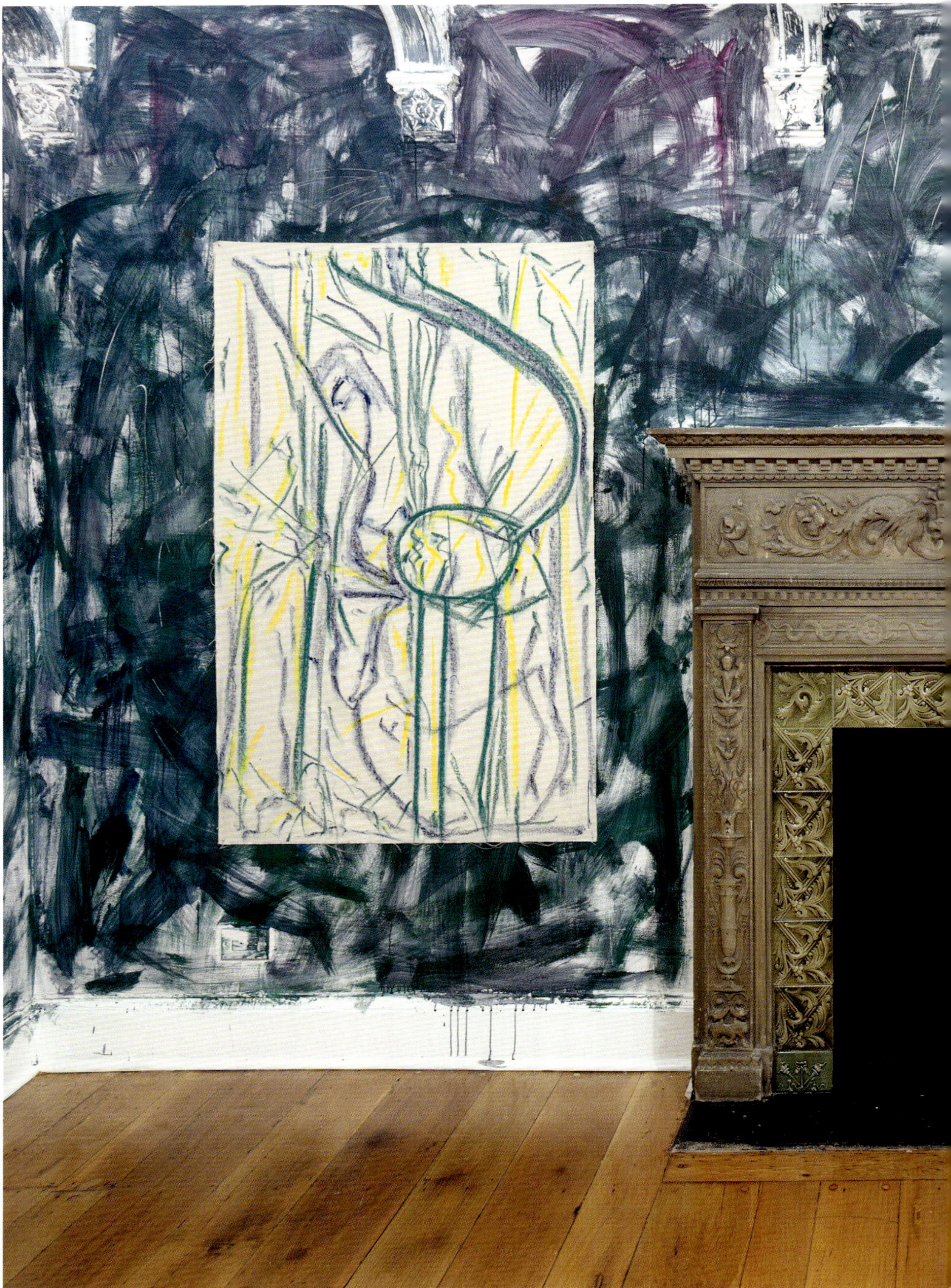

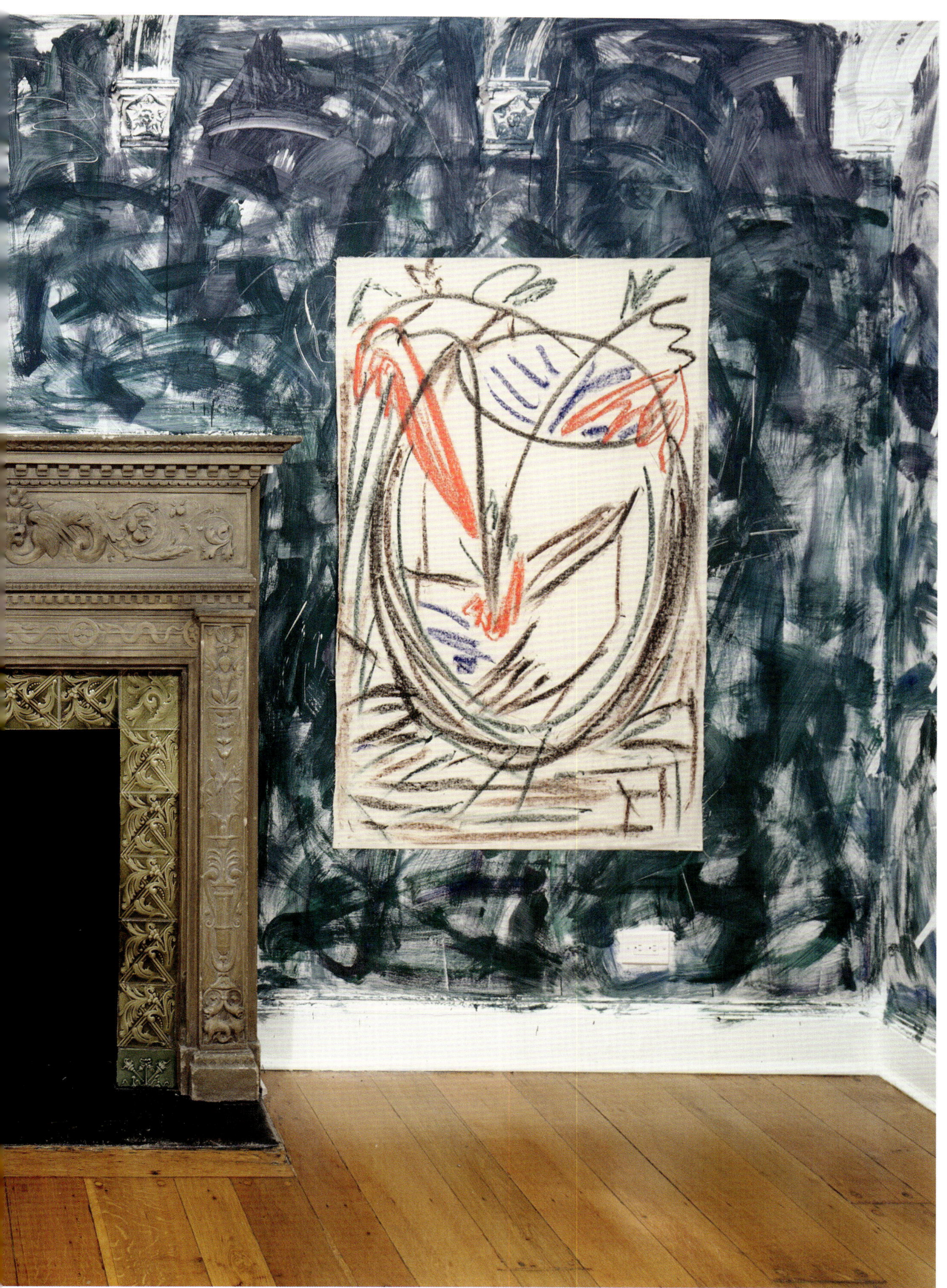

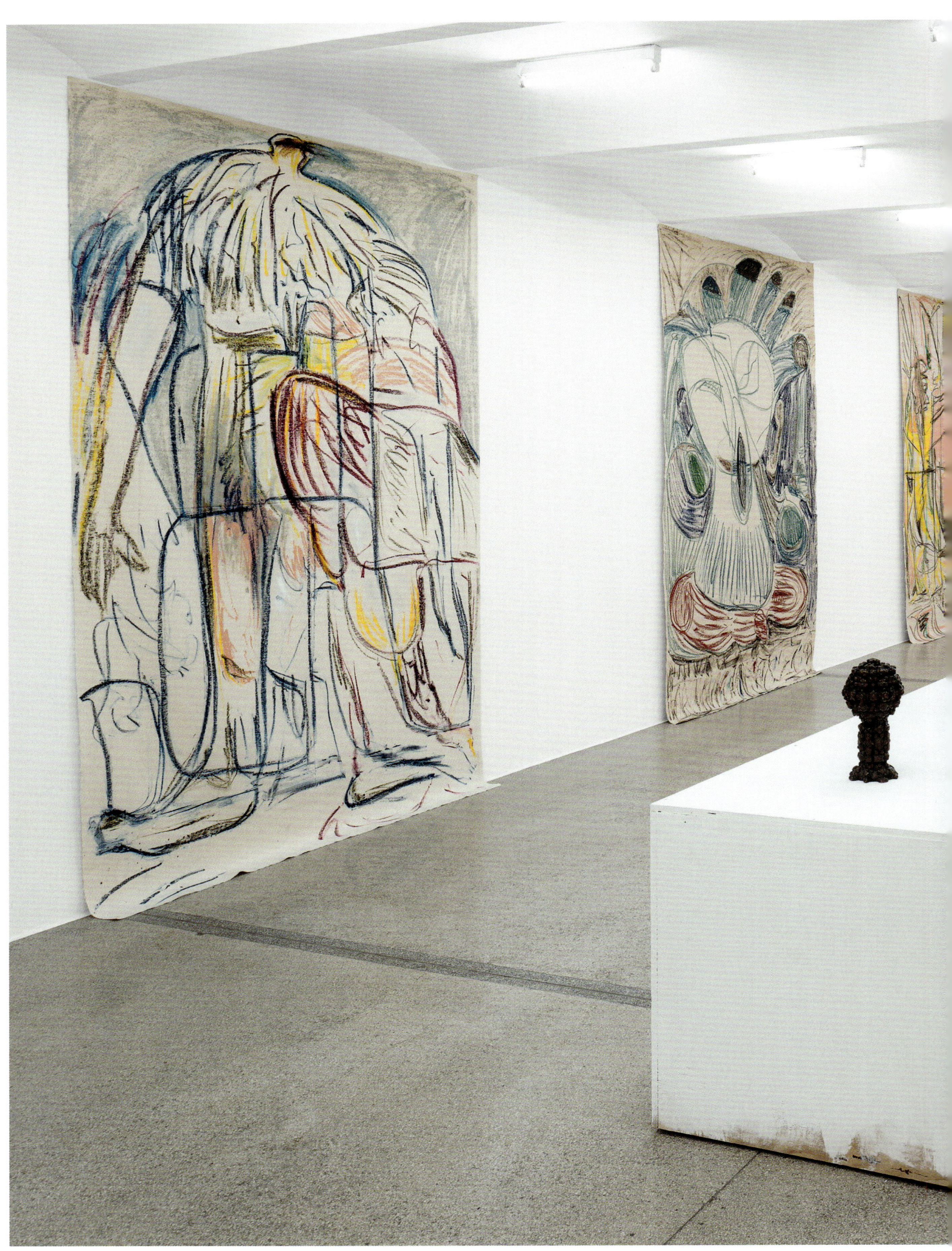

installation view: *artists and poets*   132

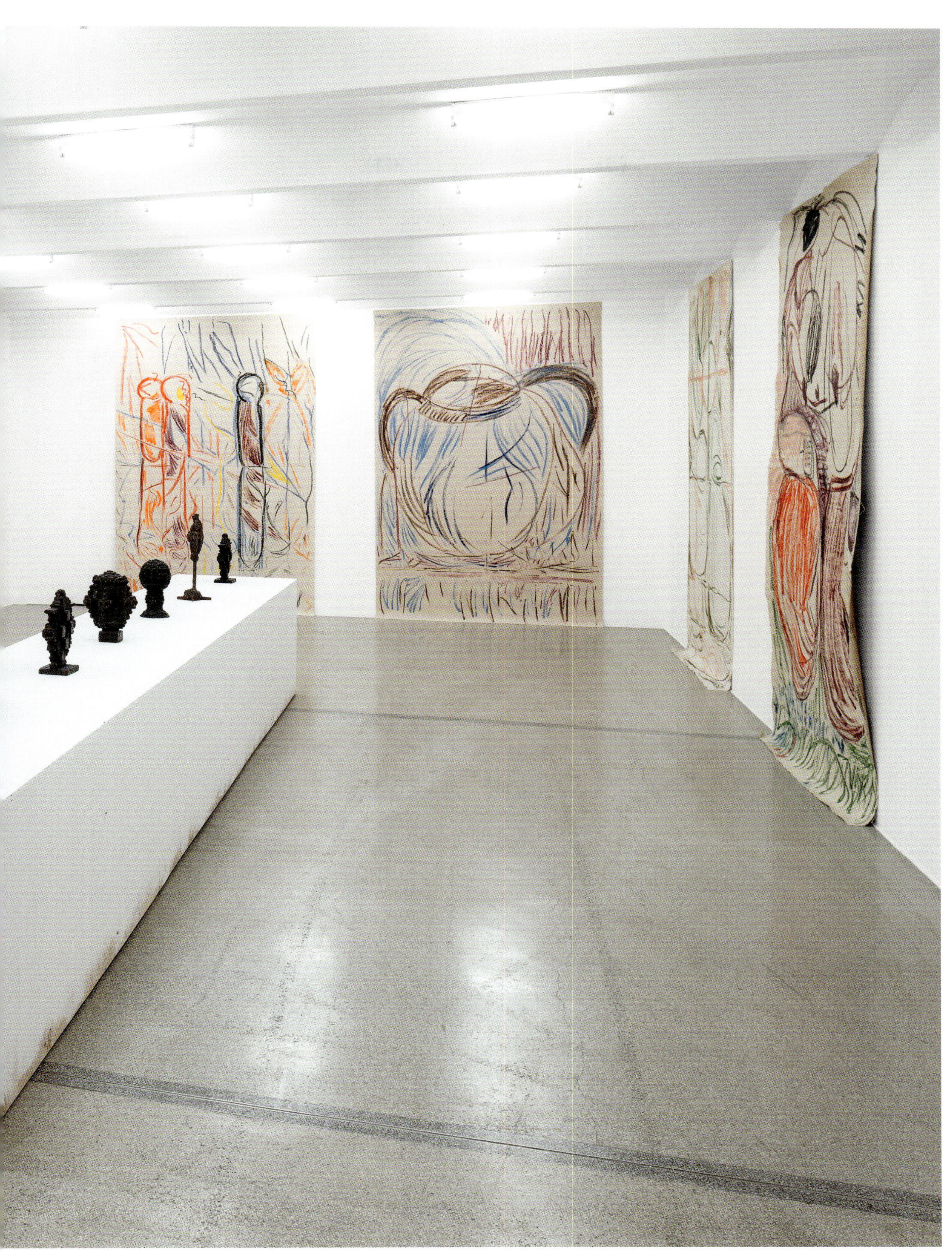

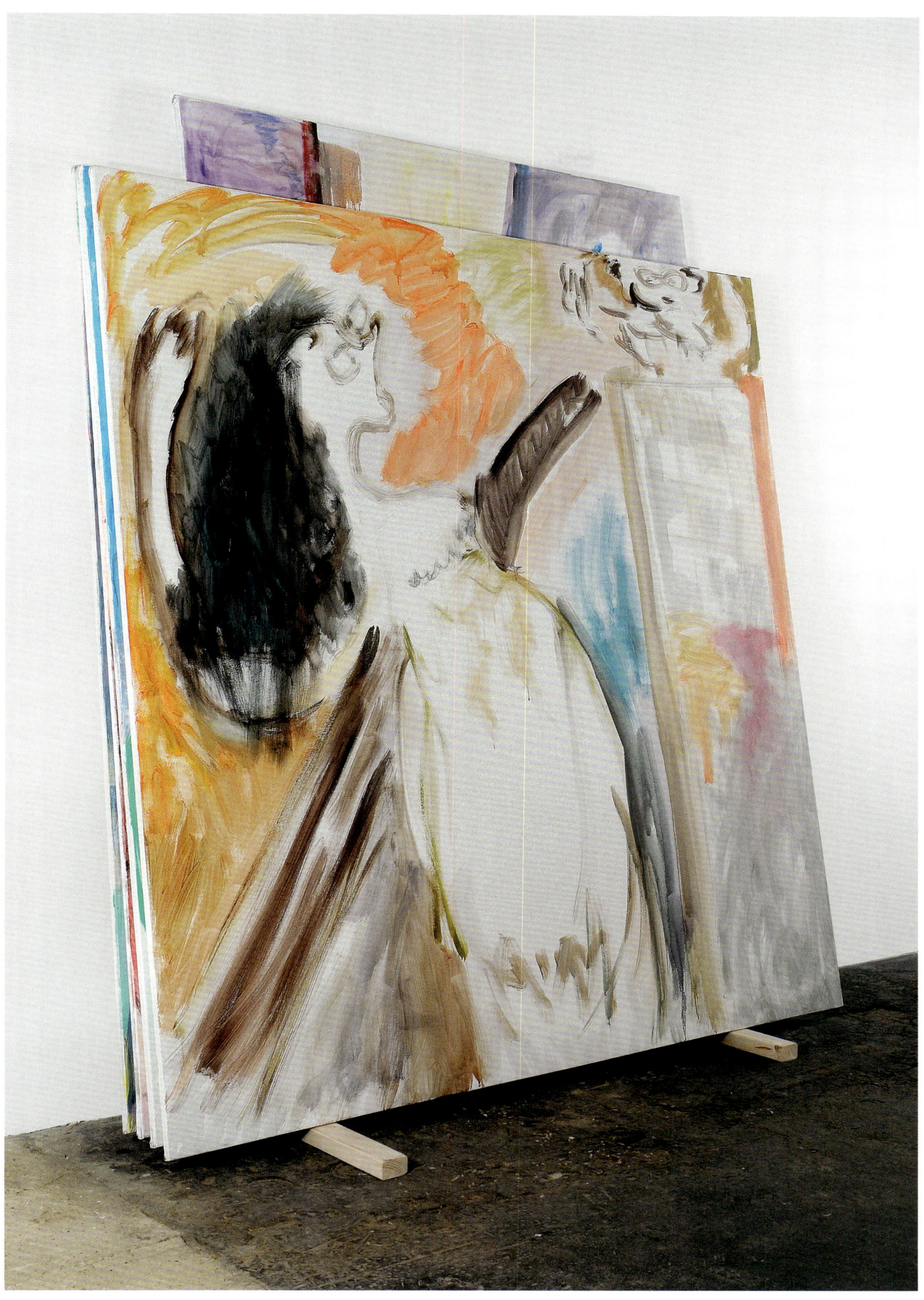

Saatchi Gallery, London
November 21, 2012—May 5, 2013

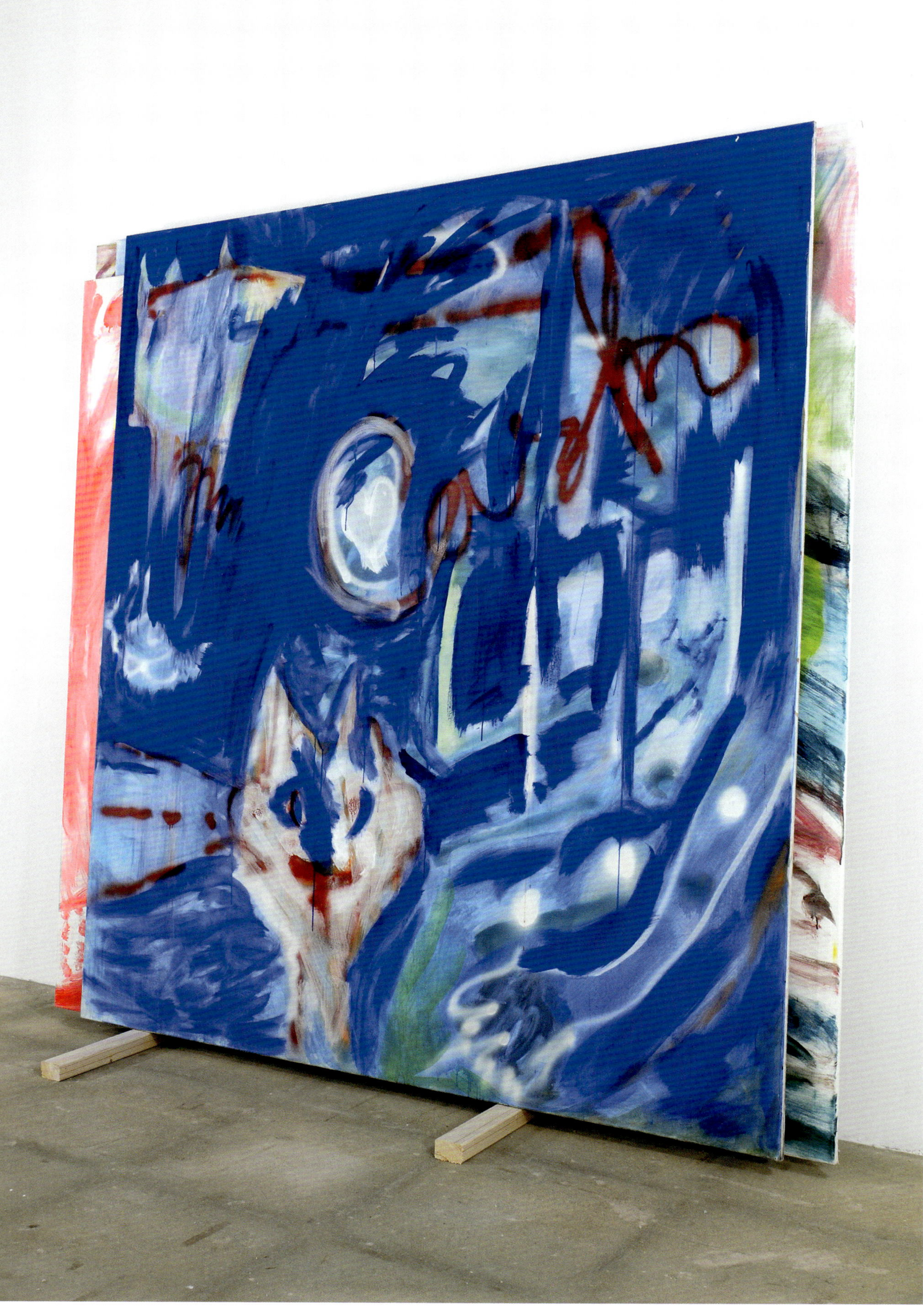

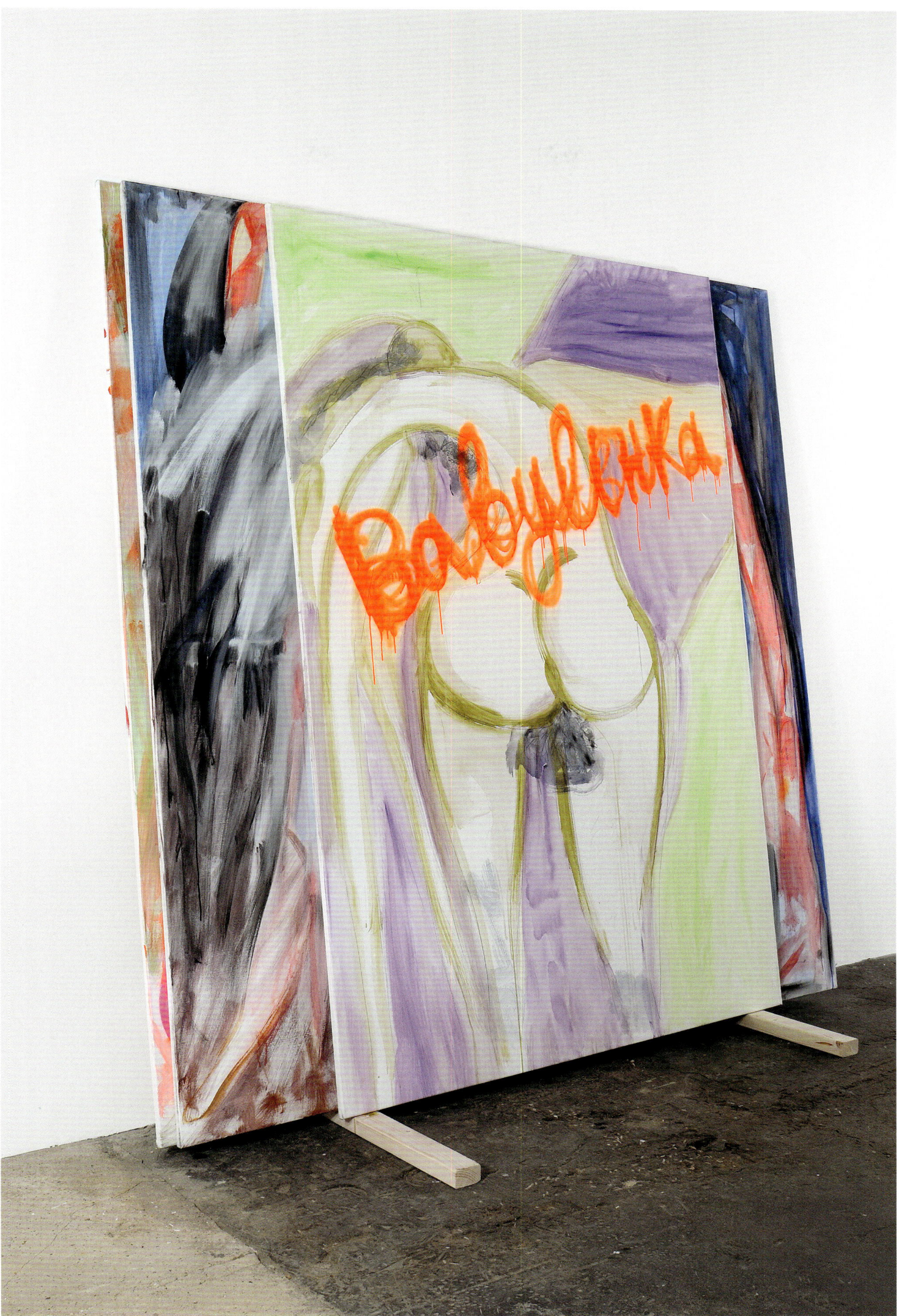

Бабушка

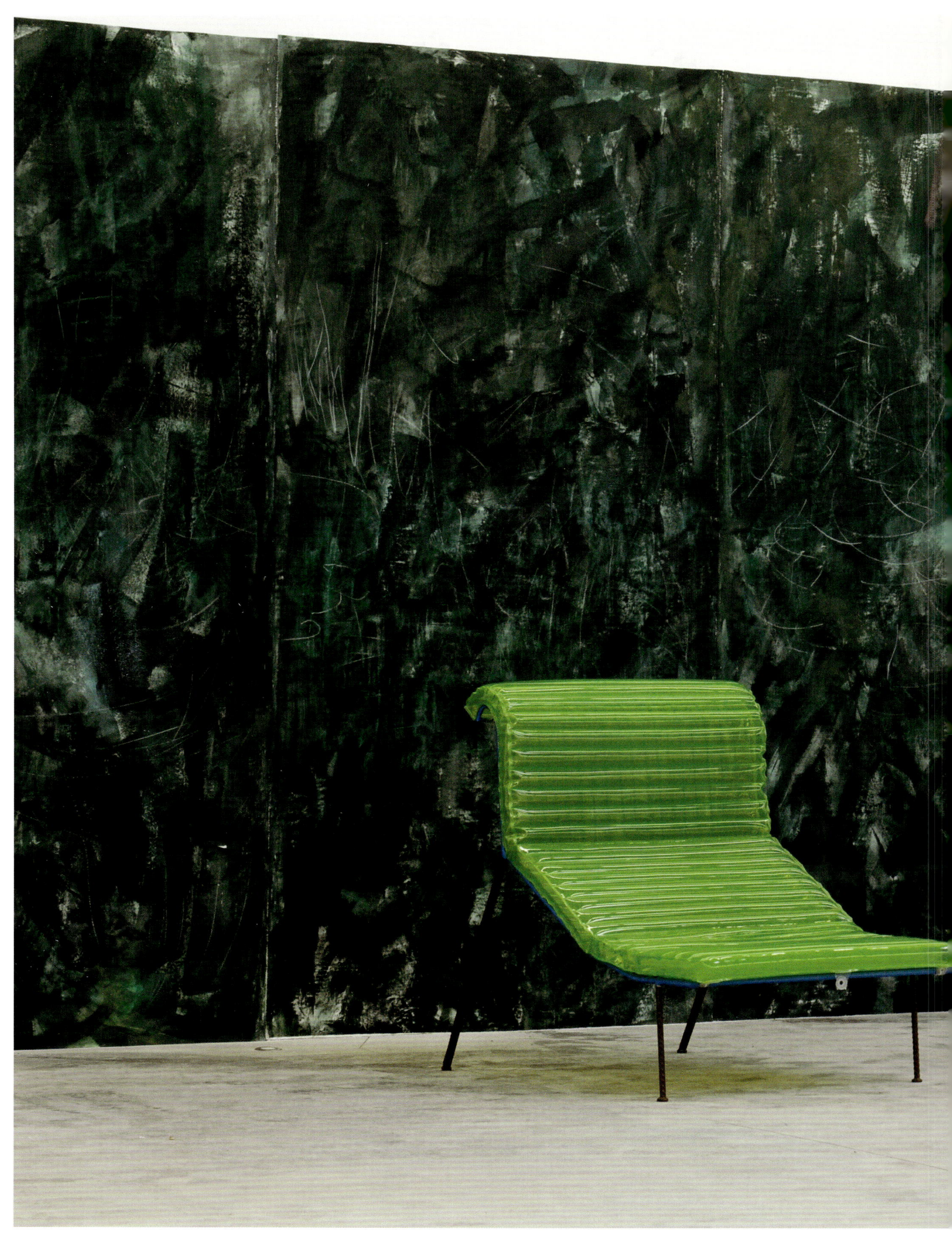

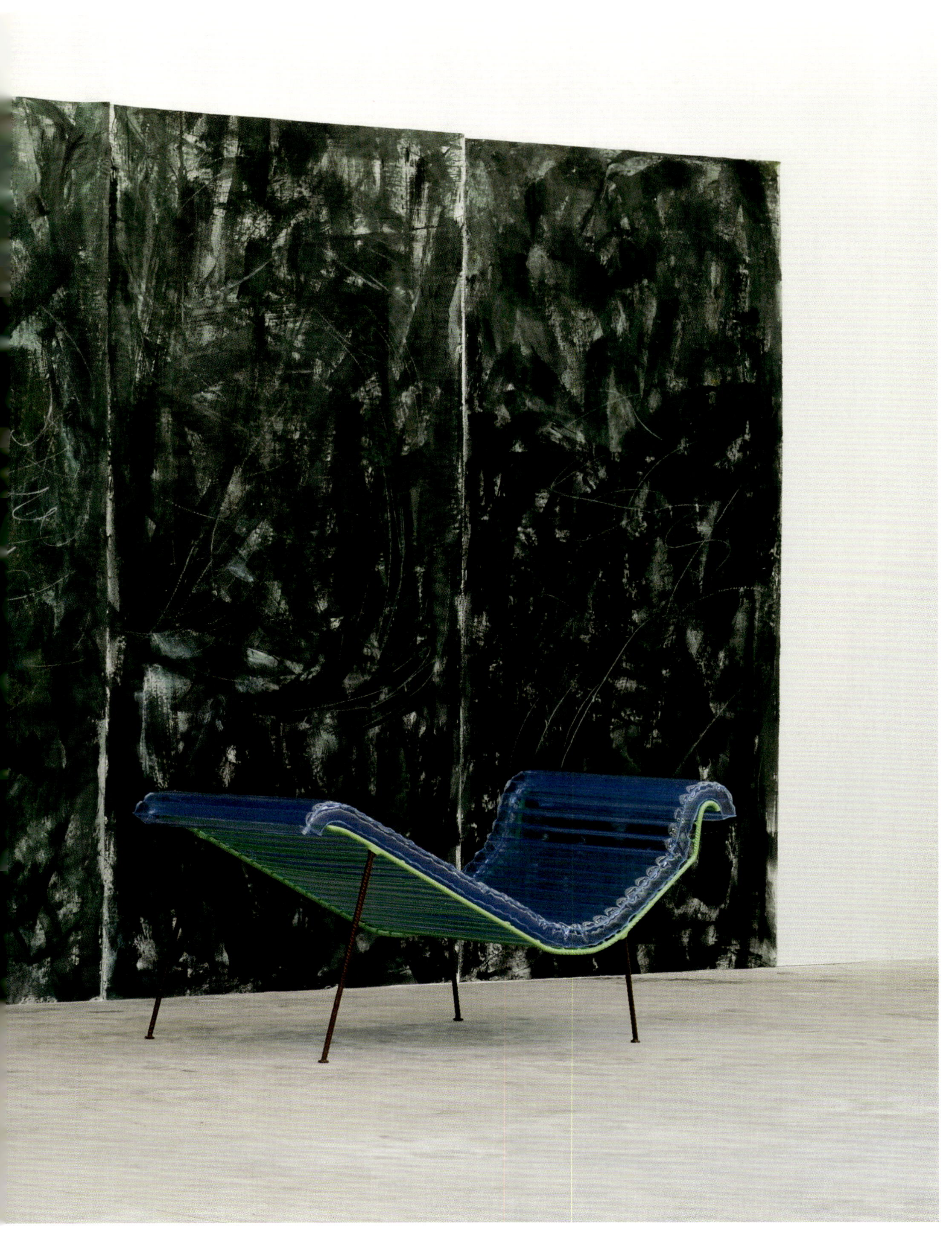

Almine Rech Gallery, Brussels
2010

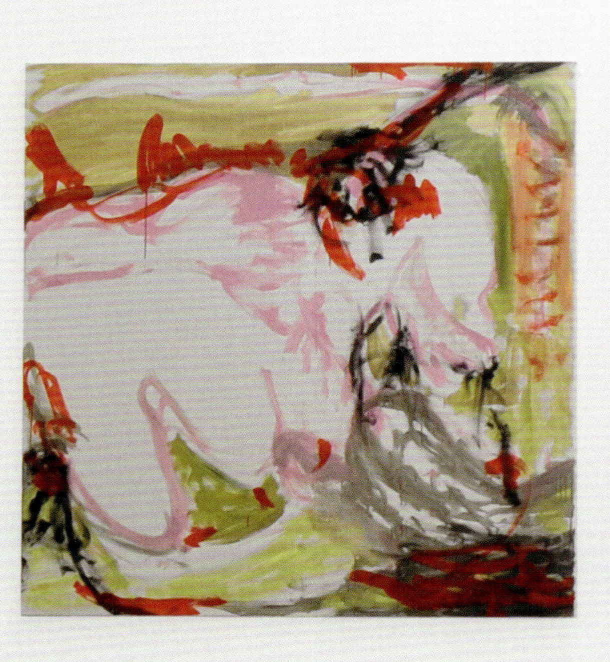
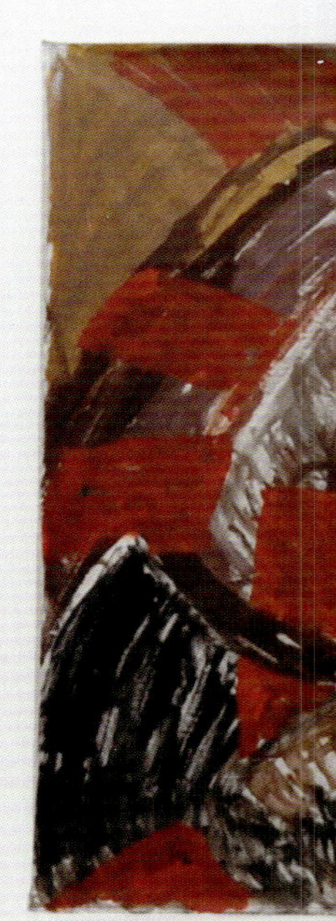

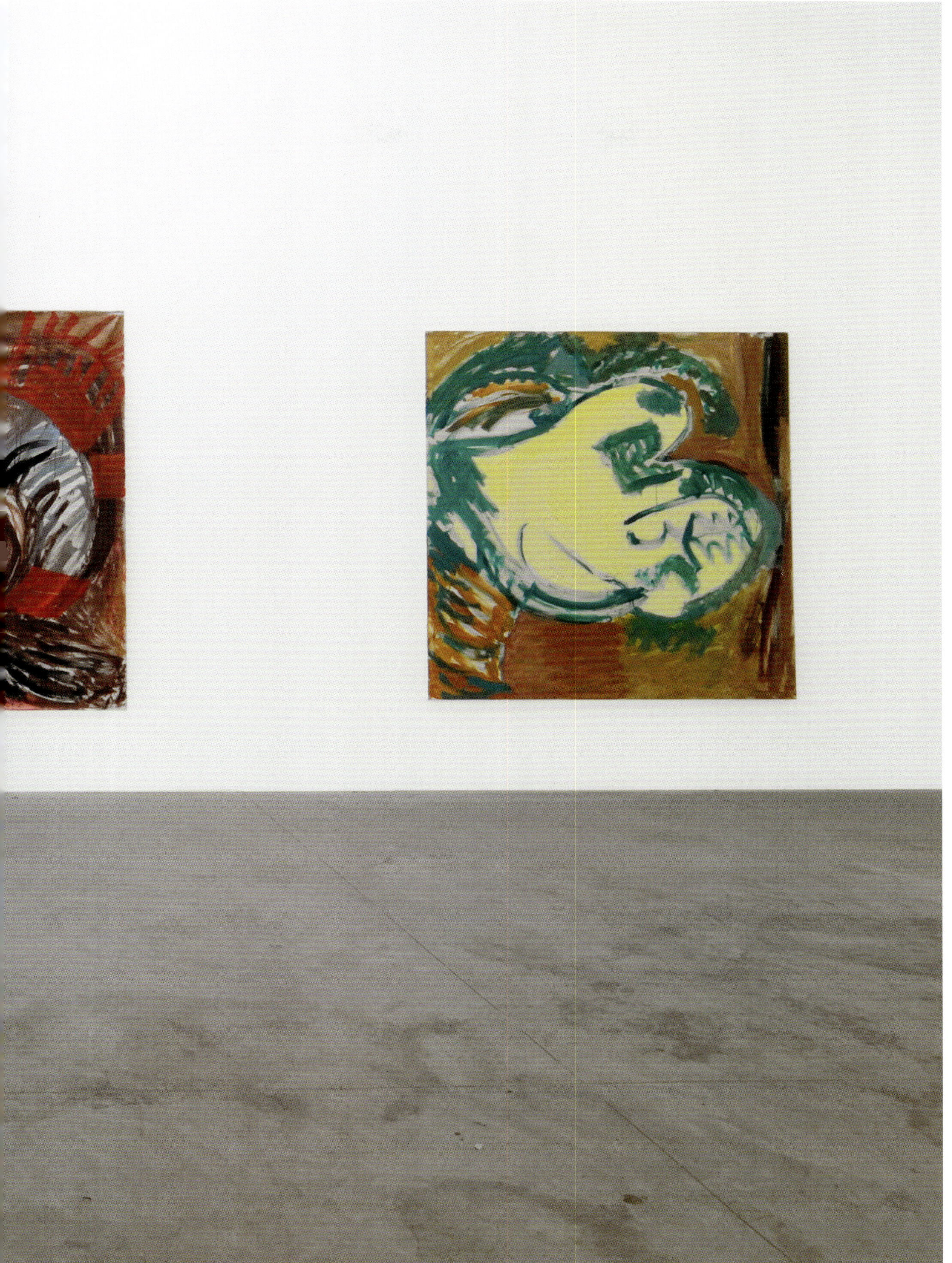

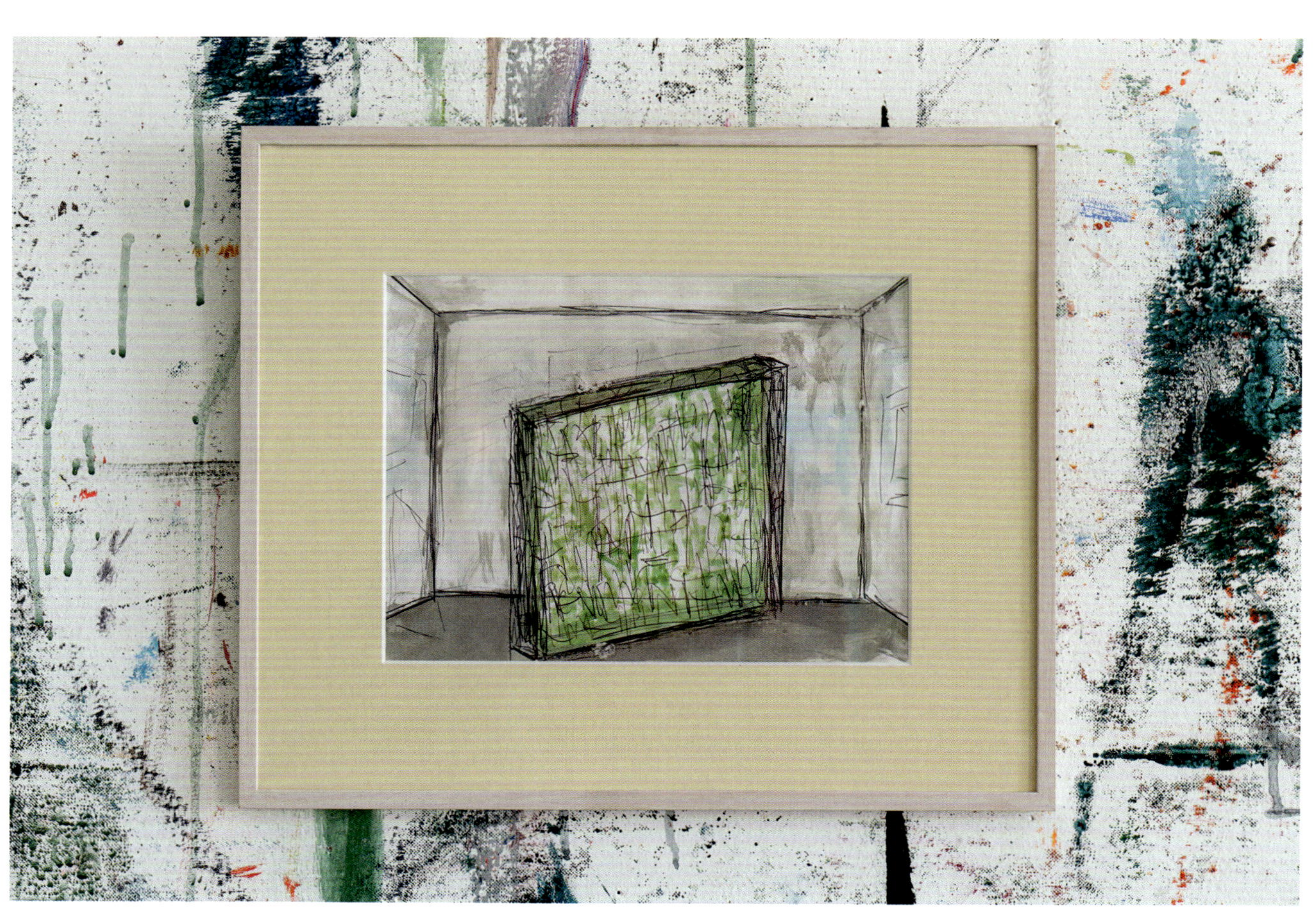

installation views: *Tamuna Sirbiladze—Paintings and Elements*   *The husband is no wall,* 2007

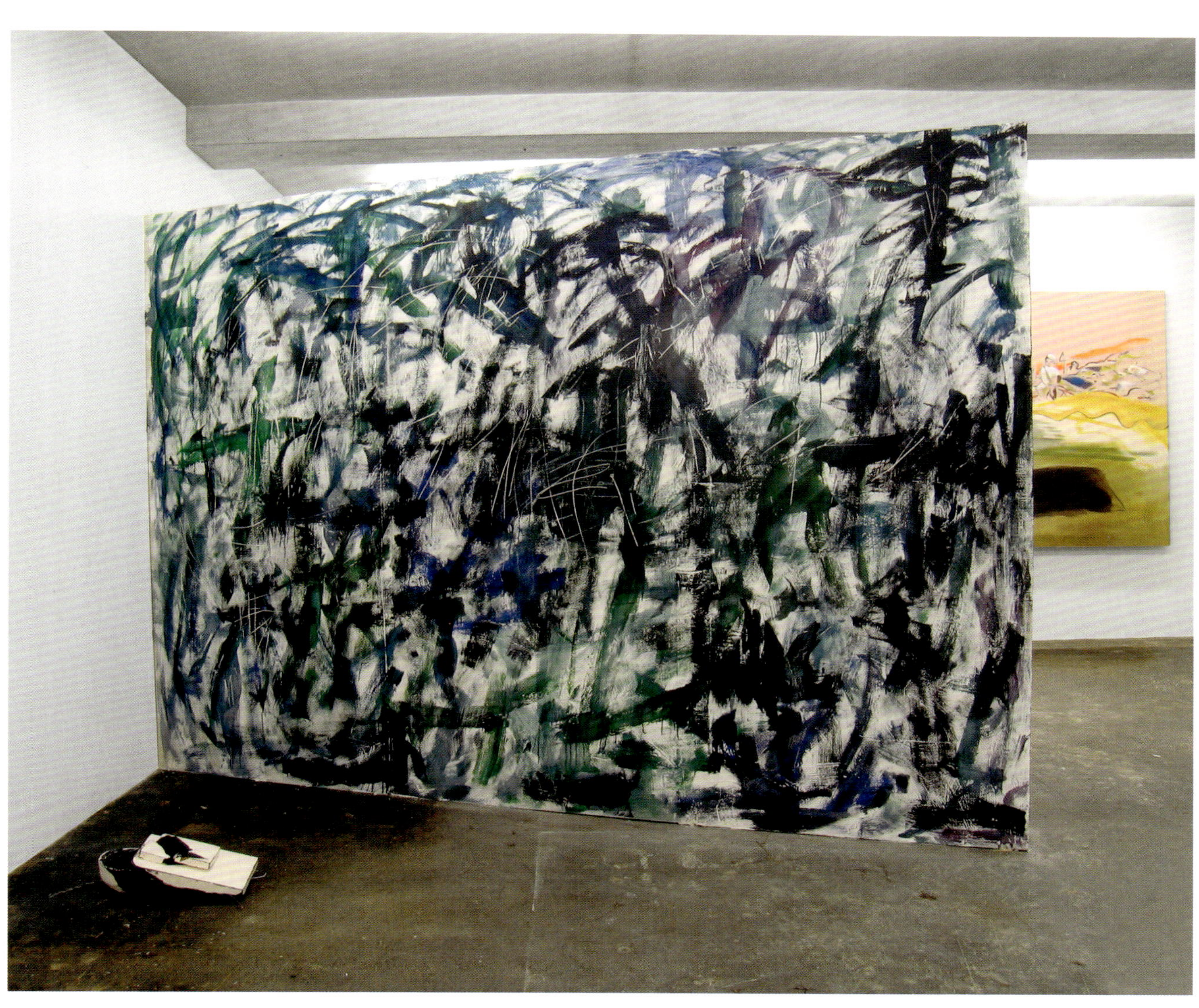

Jonathan Viner Gallery, London
2008

Windmühle
Ein Sonettenkranz
für Tamuna Sirbiladze
Benedikt Ledebur

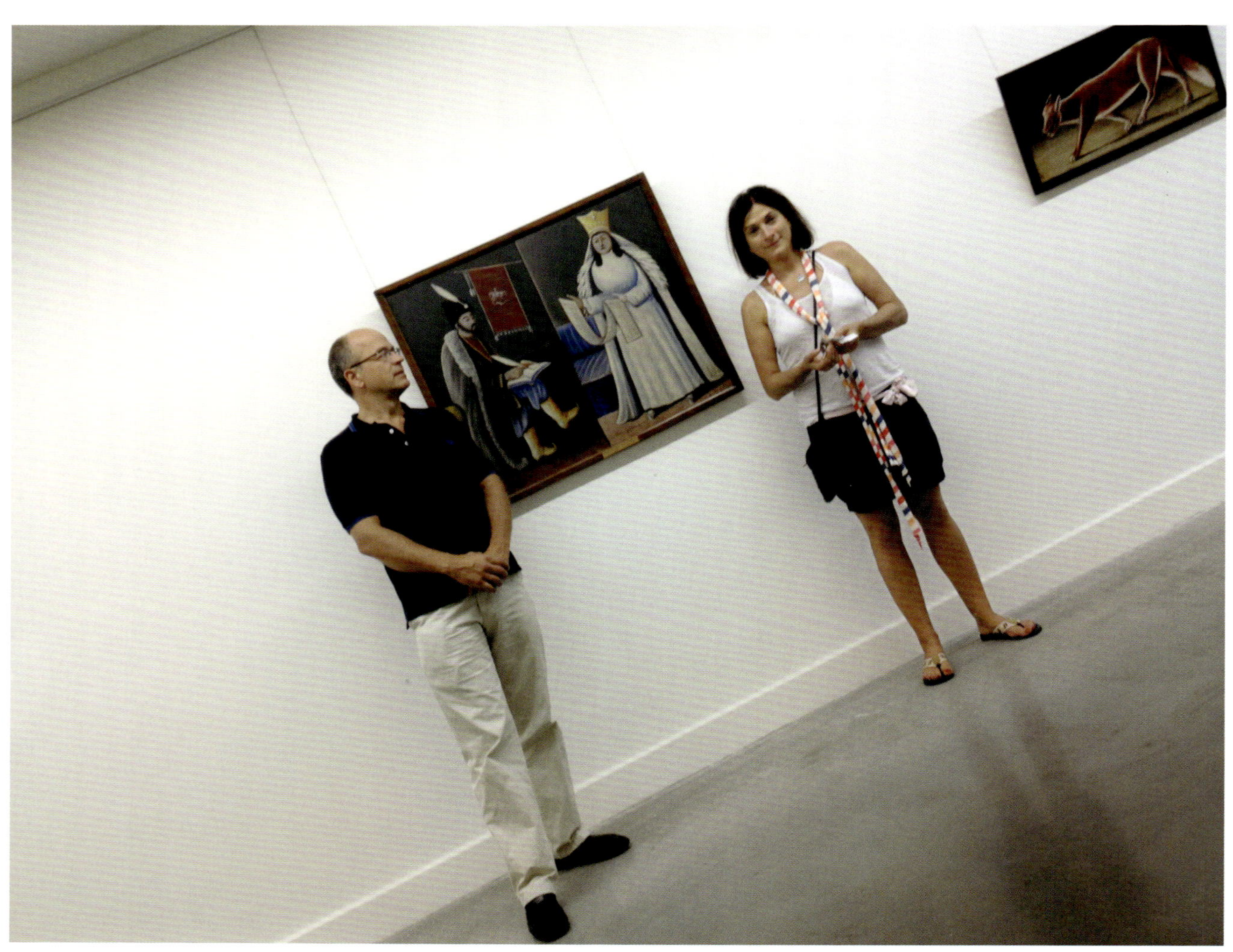

Benedikt Ledebur and Tamuna Sirbiladze
at the National Gallery, Tbilisi, 2013

Windmill
A wreath of sonnets
for Tamuna Sirbiladze

Benedikt Ledebur

Translated by Matthias Goldmann

sie als vergangenes im jetzt zu schildern,
bricht in mir auf, was von ihr nicht geblieben,
lässt im entzweit sein nach momenten sieben,
sucht ihrem fehlen trotz nicht zu verwildern.

was gibt noch acht, wenn ihre blicke fehlen?
auf allen vieren kriecht, was innen sinnt,
wenn jede vorstellung von ihr verrinnt,
statt ihrem strich im licht ein ich zu stehlen.

ich weiss, der farben schillern kennt den dreh,
im scheiden jeder braue, ihrer züge
verbannt gewesenes, das ich versteh,

jeden versuch, den ich zu ihr mir füge,
den punkt im jetzt, auf den ich reglos starr.
am rad zu drehen, stellt es eher dar.

they are the past but speak of her today
with images of her rushing my mind,
i sift the spaces she has left behind
for moments, staring her distance away.

her eyes have closed, unseen her rooms look still.
brooding and down on all fours i can feel
my vision losing hold. sure, i could steal
from her brushstrokes light, a self, and will.

the shimmering of her colors points the way.
but her brows in the ironclad distance,
and her features, i understand their play.

any attempt to invoke their presence,
they frown upon. from time we're now unbound.
just call it a wheel that i'm turning round.

am rad zu drehen, stellt es eher dar,
als sich auf übertragung zu verlassen.
wie weder TAt noch MUt den NAmen fassen,
der auf mir wirbelt, wie ihr braunes haar,

gefärbt in stufen, nächtens mich berührte,
klingt jedes wort im nächsten nach und leer,
und jeder witz, den gegen mich ich kehr,
rauht ihre stimme auf nicht, die verführte

mich in dem raum in hall. die andern lagen
berauscht in ihren federn, während wir
die flügel spreizten, kannten nur noch hier

und jetzt. was andere darüber sagen
dann werden, war egal. wir ratlos schufen,
statt uns auf, was sie sprechen, zu berufen.

just call it a wheel that i'm turning round,
don't read too much into vague translations
of all that's in a name, and all the spirit
i saw in the swirling of her brown hair,

dyed in steps, swirling over me at night;
words' hollow echo in those that follow,
and all the jokes i turn against myself
can't mimic that raspy voice, the seduction

that lit up the room in hall. the others
asleep in their beds, intoxicated.
perched on a wing, high in the here and now,

we gave no mind to what others would say.
puzzled, lost for words we watched the turning
of the wheel, not its spokes and their movement.

3

statt sich auf, was sie sprechen, zu berufen,
die frage, die nicht tief in sie gesunken,
entleert doch nur, wie sinnlos sie getrunken,
die hosen voll gestolpert über stufen,

gestottert und gestopft, die ganze blase.
warum denn etwas und nicht nichts sei, zeichen,
gedanken, loses bild, nichts wird erreichen,
was sie entstellte. keinem hilft die phrase

von tiefem blicken, wenn konkret nicht werden
die eigenschaften klingender gestalt,
der wendungen erinnerter gebärden.

wie finden farben im gedächtnis halt,
wenn wesen streiten, die ich nie gerufen,
wie schellen tönen auf ganz hohlen stufen?

it was not about spokes and their movement.
in our eyes they never saw the empty
depths of the questions they bellowed as they
tripped drunkenly down the stairs, in jitters,

stammering. they called a wing a bubble.
why was there something and not nothing, signs,
helplessly linked thoughts, images, phrases?
there are no words for her disfeatured state,

no insights if features do not mingle
to form resounding figures, of speech, colors,
gestures i remember, places she'd been.

how do colors attach to remembrance,
does the screeching sound of arguments seem
always more hollow the higher its notes?

4

die, schnellen sie hinauf zu hohen stufen,
das gleich als wahn bestürzt, gewicht verlieren,
und sinn verweben, ich bewegt aufführen,
was brust vom korb absprengt, bestückt mit hufen,

berücken meine lage, galoppieren
die fabeln ab, dass etwas von ihr bleibe,
in kindern, zeichnungen, was ich hier schreibe,
in aufgelösten formen, die verzieren,

was längst verlebt. wie könnte denn ein satz
nur irgendetwas von dem treiben fassen,
das bunt uns einte, hinter sich gelassen

sie hat im zwang. gemein, die hier noch platz
sich schaffen wollen, wie sie früher war,
die richtung wechseln, die vorher noch klar.

the flying steps of their highest moment
at the precipice of dismay, shed weight,
are swept into a landslide, so to speak.
i make sense, behooved, chest spilling from cage,

close in on my situation, gallop
up and down fables of lasting. something,
in her children, her drawings, my writing,
disbanded decoration, arrangements,

jaded ornament. could a sentence now
capture just one of the shooting branches
or the colors that brought us together?

left behind, viciously, by sheer force, just
as they had cleared space for her true person
she was taken off her course, outward bound.

5

die richtung wechseln, die vorher noch klar
vorschwebte, fällt mir schwer beim flügel schlagen,
die ganz zerfetzt zu fallen suchen, fragen
nach schnellem drehen, wenden ihrer schar

in mir die schwärme fliehender gedanken.
gefallen stört den rückfall, den die zeilen
beflügeln sollen, wehen riss zu heilen,
der mir entriss sie. mit ihr die versanken,

die nie zur sonne streben mehr, versuche,
die glieder zu ersetzen, die zu spüren
mein alles war. was klage mir verbuche,

glanz ihrer augen, blicke zu verlieren
für immer, statt was sie mir im versenken
gewesen, in lebendiges zu lenken.

taken off their soaring course, outward bound,
a flapping of wings that now seemed burdened,
feathers torn, forcing descent. my questions
as to turning, landing flutter about,

a swarm of fleeing thoughts hungry for shores.
their falling, relapsing, disrupted lines
a thicket of directions; there's no cure,
there's no coming home. the light in her eyes

has receded, as mine still remember
how hers were drawn to the sun, touched bodies.
i can still see it all, but my lament

cannot bring about the blink of an eye
that has closed. still her gaze sinks into mine,
lifewards, my mind is still looking that way.

6

gewesen, in lebendiges zu lenken,
sind gang und anmut, all die vielen stunden
von ihrer hand geführt, zum bild gebunden,
auch wild geschminkt, den trieb nicht zu bedenken,

den tanz der gesten, leiber, die uns trennten,
bis sich die augen, hände, münder fanden,
uns zu dem einen in dem abort banden,
bis morgen graute, diese nacht zu schänden.

wozu es nacheinander auf hier zählen,
will farben der vergleiche nicht entrinnen,
was lässig hingepinselt nicht befehlen

die sätze können. sollen sie nicht innen
die sicht abschminken? niemand kann sie sehen,
erinnerung, die jetzt erst im erstehen.

lifewards, my mind is still looking that way,
recalling her walk, her grace, and hours
led by her hand, bound into images;
some of her face, wild makeup, urging

a dance of gestures, bodies, separation.
we felt the life of eyes, hands, mouths converge,
binding each other, forgetting where or when,
violating the still of night until dawn.

these stories leave no traces. i still feel
some colors that defy comparison.
there is no brush, no paint, no camera

or sentence that can hold a candle to them.
how to get it out of my head? i'm still seeing
and only now forming remembrances.

7

erinnerung, die jetzt erst im erstehen,
versetzt mich in lebendigere tage,
wo jeder streit und ausichtslose lage
sich mit dem glück verbanden, sie zu sehen.

das sagt sich einfach, klappert ab die mühlen,
statt gegen vorstellungen zu erheben,
was tiefer schürft, geschärft durch mein erleben.
was durch die form gedrängt nicht mehr dem fühlen,

nur noch als reim unsinn entsprechen kann,
verstellt den duft, die äderung der haut
am halsansatz. getroffen durch den bann,

der es benennt, bleibt tot, was ich geschaut,
trübt sich das bild, der blick, der sie gesehen,
sieht nichts vorher, wie wesen, die vergehen.

i am only now forming remembrances
that take me back to days filled with life,
when arguments and desperate situations
were linked to happiness and grateful eyes.

that's easily said, but i can hear the mills
clapping, drowning out imagination,
depths, blunting edges. my experience,
brought into form and detached from feeling,

is tied to rhymes and the sound of meaning,
nonsense blocks out fragrance, skin, collarbone,
movement of neck. spellbound by names and words

i know i'll awake. what i see will have passed.
dim light of gaze that cannot see itself
in time gone by, at growing distances.

8

so wie gewesen vorher, die vergehen,
sie selbst, hemmen vergleiche, übertragung,
die fäden zu erkennen, die entsagung
der bilder freilegt, formlos zu verstehen,

wie sich verläufe ihrer hand verschlingen,
im tasten in schwarzweiss die finger finden,
den film nur streifen, spürend ganz erblinden
und taub pulsieren folgen. unter dingen,

die leben bloss verlängern, trifft ihr deuten
nackt auf die wunden, die ihr schwinden reisst,
auf ansichten, die sich im hinblick häuten,

den sinn ersticken, der in sie verbeisst
sich. was im bersten soll davon ablenken,
sich im gewirr der wege sie zu denken?

time gone by, growing distances, and those
that left us stand beyond comparison,
translation. stepping back reveals the threads,
connections, shapeless understanding, forms

of the paths of hands, their intertwining,
fumbling in black and white, locking fingers,
passing glances at blinding experience,
a pulse that rises to the ear. among the things

that make life last, their interpretation now
touches the naked wounds their waning caused.
the vision that sheds its skin under this gaze,

stifles significance wound up in them.
yet nothing will make me take my mind off
tracing this maze of roads and shadow play.

9

sich im gewirr der wege sie zu denken,
ihr mienenspiel in allen einzelheiten,
der lippen druck, bewegungen in häuten,
die rauhen töne, die, um mich zu kränken,

sie mit den passenden titeln versah,
hilft nicht, die nackten reize zu entkleiden,
die jeden fetzen wie teuerste seiden
zur wirkung brachten. was von ihr noch nah

mir geht, werden die worte, die ich finde,
zur strecke bringen. fährt mein blick den farben
und linien nach, die ich mit ihr verbinde,

lässt er die formen, die sie schnitt, vernarben.
verdammt, was sich bewegt im allgemeinen,
wir ewig suchen, mit uns zu vereinen.

tracing her maze of roads and shadow play,
facial expressions, their smallest details,
pressure of lips, twitching of skin,
titles she gave to raspy sounds, intended

to add insult to injury. it doesn't help to undress
the naked beauty that made cheap clothes
unfold the magic of precious silk.
what still affects me deeply, will always

make me abandon the words that i've found.
as i fix my gaze on colors, trace lines
in things that i believe belonged to her,

the scars heal on the figures that she cut.
who really gives a damn for the grand truths
we ever try to fathom. some find love.

10

wir ewig suchen, uns mit ihr zu einen,
die splitter, die ein ich zerstreut im leben,
die fäden, die zum ich wir erst verweben,
wenn, die verbanden uns, zu enden scheinen.

wie öd und leer wirken bekannte räume,
muss ich sie ohne ihre hand durchqueren.
misst sie nicht jeder winkel? mich verzehren
die kleinsten zeichen, die zu ihr ich säume.

noch tasten mund, natur nach ihrem wesen,
wie regelmässig waren ihre züge,
ikonen, wie jawlensky sie gelesen,

mundwinkel, durch die ich mich jetzt betrüge,
sie sei noch da. ich kann doch nur erblinden,
wenn sich im trennen lieben endlich finden.

we ever try to fathom why some find love,
and the splinters a self strews along its path,
the threads we weave to form a person
and those that have connected us expire.

familiar spaces now seem bleak and empty,
crossing them alone now, without her hand,
she is the measure of every nook and cranny.
the smallest signs of her eat at my heart.

mouth and hands, in search of her true nature,
the evenness that marked her face, its lines,
an icon jawlensky might have read in them.

the corners of her mouth make me believe
that she's still here. my mind and vision are
parting ways, our love became true, at last.

11

wenn sich im trennen lieben endlich binden,
soll mit granatäpfeln, all den symbolen,
die als figuren hatten ihr befohlen,
abstrakt zu werden, leinwand so zu schinden,

dass jedes glied sich rege, das gebunden
sein, was zu ihrem glanz als kranz ich flechte.
doch farblos bleibt, was ich ihr zeichnen möchte,
die wand, von ihr bemalt, pinsel geschunden,

sie wand gestalten in ihr linienspiel,
die bunt beleben, wogegen sie stritt,
und unverblümt sie, was ihr nicht gefiel,

zu blumen übermalte, was sie ritt,
fand seine frische form noch im verneinen,
auf sich zu setzen hilft im spielen keinen.

parting ways, our love became true, at last.
thus take pomegranates and all the symbols
who, as figures, called on her to become
more abstract, to haze the canvas, rattle

all the links in this chain—i will gather
and weave all she gave into a shining wreath.
while the picture i draw lacks her colors,
the walls she painted on, the brush she used,

her play of lines teemed with life that followed
a cause. she knew what she was fighting
but painted flowers over things she didn't like,

what drove her was cast into fresh new forms
even when she painted in the negative,
the card she played was one that she let go of.

12

auf sich zu setzen hilft im spielen keinen,
sie liess gesichter so mit sich verrinnen,
dass jeden zug, den sie gezogen innen,
entsprechen fand verwirkt im noch so kleinen

streich ihrer pinsel, kreiden. ausgezogen,
die bilder bloss zu stellen, auszukotzen
den irrsinn, nackt dem untergang zu trotzen,
war sie verheert, wie alle so belogen

von schönen, wie sie unterschied der farben
zu zeugen wusste. niemand kennt die zahl,
die glück bringt, jeder streich erzeugt die narben,

die ausgelegt im bild als freie wahl
zu sehen zwingen. wenn mich bilder binden,
was soll mir blau und gelb, rot, grün ergründen?

the card you play is one you're letting go of,
she let faces trickle off, into themselves,
and every line she drew to mark their features,
became a part of all the smallest strokes

of her brushes, chalk lines. she was out to
unmask pictures, fly them in the face of
lunacy. braving doom, defying fate,
she was devastated. beauty lied to

everyone. but she bore witness to the
difference between colors. no one knows
the lucky number, each stroke leaving scars,

spread around the picture, take one for free
but look and choose. haunted by images,
is it blue, red, or green i should have asked?

13

was soll mir schwarz und weiss, rot, grün ergründen,
wenn sie gedreht die kugel springen lassen
von zahl zu zahl. die formeln, die dies fassen,
können, was kommen wird, nur so verbinden,

dass zu stochastischen statisten machen
sie uns. wie ihre hand zuletzt noch sanft gewunken,
zu prüfen unser band, ist das versunken,
was sich mitteilte im geliebten lachen,

was sie mit schwung gezeichnet auf den wänden,
in stellungen und masken ausgedrückt,
die jetzt als ihr relikt das spiel beenden,

das sie mit allem, was sie war, bestückt.
wie sie im handel treiben es, verwildern,
geblieben wird nur sein den toten bildern.

is it blue, red, or green i should have asked
when they made the ball jump and roll from
number to number. the formulas for
all that is to come will be connected

to relegate us to stochastic extras.
one last time she gently waved her hand,
holding the strings of our bond, then i saw
her hand sink, with her smile, my love.

the flowing lines she painted onto walls,
what she expressed in these postures and masks,
is now a relic, her game has ended,

but still adds to her everything she was.
what would have been, the tricks still up her sleeve,
the images she left us with won't say.

14

geblieben wird nur sein den toten bildern,
gestalten, die versteckt sie, zu erwecken,
was barg sie, nicht mit nichts ins grab zu stecken,
sondern auf jede kurve zu erwidern,

was in ihr steckt. die stimme war schon schwach,
als sie mit jeder faser mich betörte,
jeden moment sich, als ob nichts sie störte,
gestalt und ausdruck gab. ob schlafend, wach

wusste sie ihrem zustand form zu geben,
zu der die zeichen, abgenutzt, nicht dringen.
im zwischen scheint, was sie ausmacht, zu schweben.

was brauchte dieses zeug, soll sie besingen,
ein licht entzünden zu fallenden lidern,
sie als vergangenes im jetzt zu schildern.

the images she left us with won't say,
we only wake the figures she disguised.
what did she leave us, not to lower it
into a grave but see to at every turn?

her voice had already become so weak
when she spoke to all my senses, moments
free of anything that could tip the balance
of figures, of expression. asleep, awake,

all that took shape translated into form
where jaded signs will never find their way.
it was the in-between where she could soar.

talk is cheap, of course, but song, and pictures
light up for falling eyelids, remembrances
they are the past but speak of her today.

15

am rad zu drehen, stellt es eher dar,
als sich auf seine speichen zu berufen,
die, schnellen sie hinauf zu hohen stufen,
die richtung wechseln, die vorher noch klar

gewesen, in lebendiges zu lenken
erinnerung, die jetzt erst im erstehen,
so wie gewesen vorher, die vergehen
sich im gewirr der wege, die zu denken

wir ewig suchen. wieso erst die einen,
wenn sich im trennen lieben endlich finden?
auf sich zu setzen hilft im spielen keinen!

was soll mir blau und gelb, rot, grün ergründen?
geblieben wird nur sein den toten bildern,
sie als vergangenes im jetzt zu schildern.

just call it a wheel that i'm turning round
don't point to its spokes and their movement,
the flying steps of their highest moment
that took them off their set course. outward bound,

lifewards, my mind is still looking that way,
and only now forming remembrances,
of time gone by, from growing distances,
tracing a maze of roads and shadow play

we ever try to fathom. some find love.
parted by fate we grew together, at last.
the card you play is one you're letting go of.

is it blue, red, or green i should have asked?
the images she left me with won't say
they are the past but speak of her today.

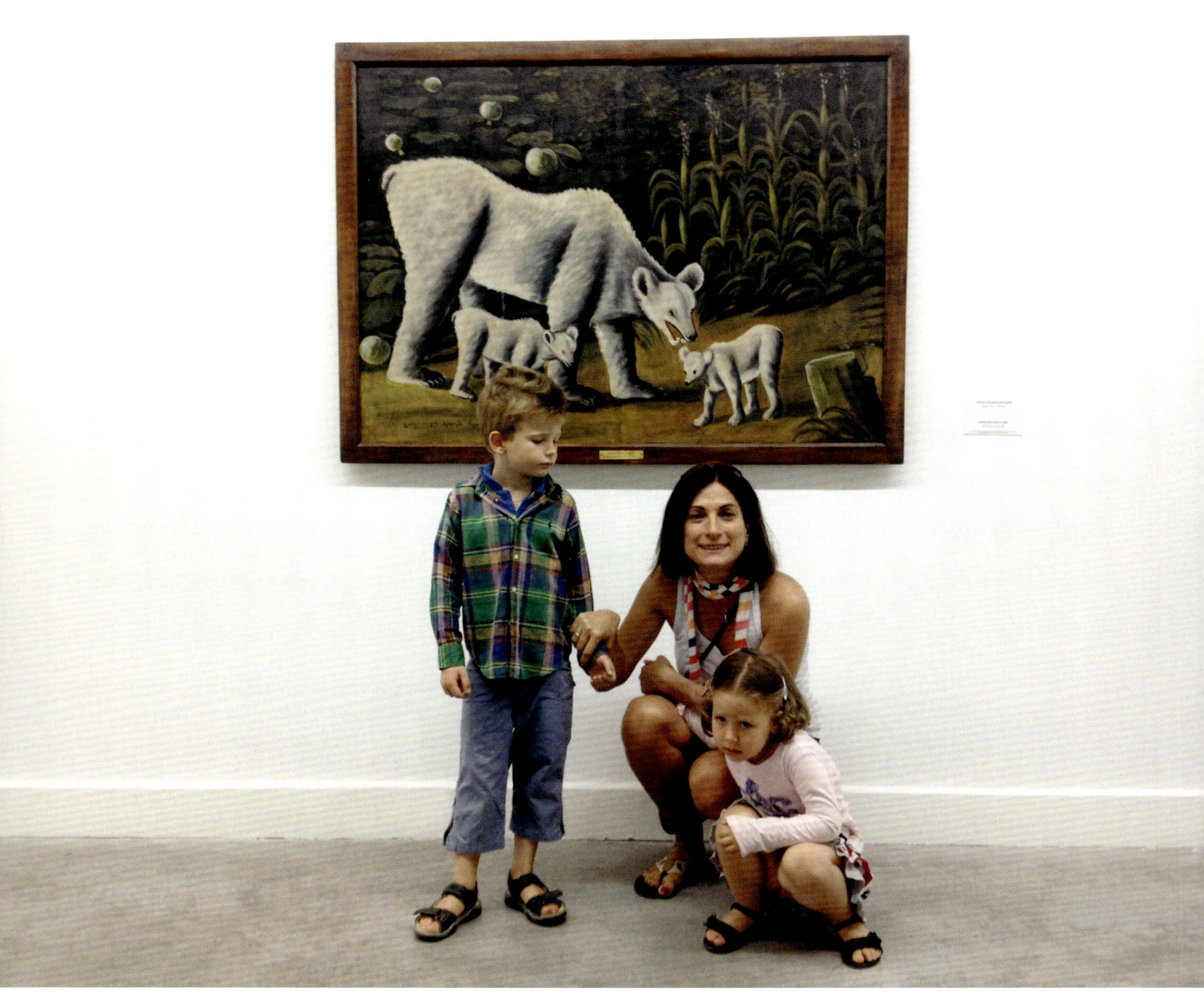

Tamuna Sirbiladze with her children, Lazare and Emily,
at the National Gallery, Tbilisi, 2013

Tamuna Sirbiladze (Tamar West)

02.12.1971—03.02.2016

Tamuna was born in Tbilisi, the capital of Georgia, on February 12, 1971, to Vakhtang Sirbildadze and Nunu Ghurchumelia. She started life together with her elder sister Keti. In nursery school on Lermontow Street she loved drawing and painting, and impressed her teacher so much that she organized an exhibition for the six-year-old.

In 1989, Tamuna graduated from high school on Rustaveli Avenue. From 1989 to 1994, she studied at the state academy of art in Tbilisi, where she gained a degree. After moving to Vienna in 1997, she studied until 2003 at the Academy of Fine Arts, where her teacher was Franz Graf. In 2003, she further extended her studies at the Slade School of Fine Art in London.

In the meantime, she had met the artist Franz West, whom she married in 2002 and with whom she collaborated on several art projects and works, until his death in 2012. Her children, Lazare and Emily, were born in 2008 and 2009. Her last years she lived together with Benedikt Ledebur.

Always very active, she was included in a group exhibition as soon as she moved to Vienna. Over the years she made a huge body of work, encompassing installations, videos, site-specific projects, and an enormous number of paintings. Her works have been featured in various exhibitions in galleries and museums all over Europe, including *Plakatentwürfe* at Galerie Gisela Capitain in Cologne (2001, a collaboration with Franz West), *Inconcurrence* (2007) at ColletPark in Paris, *Paintings and Elements* (2008) at Jonathan Viner Gallery in London, and *Laszive Lockungen* (2010) at Charim Ungar Contemporary in Berlin. In the last two years of her life she not only participated in the group show *Artists and Poets* at the Secession in Vienna, curated by the artist Ugo Rondinone, and in the group show *No Man's Land* at the Rubell Family Collection in Miami, she also received significant critical acclaim for two solo shows in New York, *Take it easy* at Bill Powers's Half Gallery and *"good enough" is never good enough* at James Fuentes gallery. Her show at Almine Rech Gallery in Brussels opened shortly before her death.

Exhibition history

Selected publications

artists and poets
Ugo Rondinone (ed.)
Secession, Vienna
2015

*NO MAN'S LAND: Women Artists
from the Rubell Family Collection*
Rubell Family Collection, Miami
2015

titles
onestar press, Paris
2014

Der Ficker No. 2
Benedikt Ledebur (ed.)
Schlebrügge, Vienna
2006

Selected exhibitions

Gnomons
group show with Lawrence Weiner,
Walter Robinson, Julie Ryan, Jason
Stopa, Carolyn Marks Blackwood,
Lazar Lyutakov, Doug Johnston,
and Karin Fauchard
Non-Objectif Sud, Tulette
2017

Amazing Girls / It's Complicated
Kevin Space, Vienna
2017

Tamuna Sirbiladze—Traces of Life
Galerie Eva Presenhuber,
Löwenbräu Areal, Zurich
2017

Franz West—ARTISTCLUB
21er Haus, Belvedere, Vienna
2016

*Tamuna Sirbiladze—Eve's apple—
in memory*
curated by Benedikt Ledebur
Charim Galerie, Vienna
2016

Two Projects—Tamuna Sirbiladze
Almine Rech Gallery, Brussels
2016

NO MAN'S LAND
Rubell Family Collection, Miami
2015

*Tamuna Sirbiladze—"good enough"
is never good enough*
James Fuentes, New York
2015

Tamuna Sirbiladze—Take it easy
Half Gallery, New York
2015

Artists and Poets
curated by Ugo Rondinone
Secession, Vienna
2015

Rade Petrasevic & Tamuna Sirbiladze
V.ARE, Parkhouse Cineplex, Vienna
2014

Siehe was dich sieht
21er Haus, Belvedere, Vienna
2014

Tamuna Sirbiladze—Damona
Charim Galerie, Vienna
2014

V Collection
Charim Galerie, Vienna
2013

39greatjones
curated by Ugo Rondinone
Galerie Eva Presenhuber, Zurich
2013

*Gaiety Is the Most Outstanding
Feature of the Soviet Union*
Saatchi Gallery, London
2012

Naked Ground
Galerie Lisa Ruyter, Vienna
2012

*Austria Davaj! Creative
Forces of Austria*
curated by Martina Kandeler-Fritsch
and Irina Korobina
Schusev State Museum of
Architecture, Moscow
2011

Das Dinghafte in der Kunst
Galerie Nikola Vujasin, Vienna
2010

Franz West—Double Squint
Almine Rech Gallery, Brussels
2010

Laszive Lockungen
Charim Ungar Contemporary, Berlin
2010

The Read Thread
Galerie Dana Charkasi, Vienna
2009

Until the End of the World
A.M.P., Athens
2009

About Premises and Promises
Galerie Andreas Huber, Vienna
2009

Pretty Ugly
Gavin Brown's Enterprise, New York
2008

Grazy
Werkstatt, Graz
2008

*Tamuna Sirbiladze—Paintings
and Elements*
Jonathan Viner Gallery, London
2008

Der Ficker
Jonathan Viner Gallery, London
2007

Inconcurrence
curated by Franz West
ColletPark, Paris
2007

Hamsterwheel
Arsenale, Venice
2007

*Sequence 1: Painting and Sculpture
from the François Pinault Collection*
Palazzo Grassi, Venice
2007

Der Ficker
Foundation de 11 Lijnen, Oudenburg
2006

Esperimento Illuminismo
Albertina Museum, Vienna
2006

Der Ficker—Haus Wittgenstein
Galerie Elisabeth and Klaus Thoman,
Vienna
2006

Seconda
Biennale internazionale d'arte
di Ferrara
2005

The Red Thread
Educational Alliance Gallery, New York
2005

Camere / Chambers
Rum, Rome
2005

Video Art Expo
curated by Luca Gurci
Bari
2004

Le Opere e i Giorni
Certosa Di San Lorenzo,
Padula, Salerno
2004

Update
curated by Hans Peter Wipplinger,
Museum of Modern Art, Passau
Künstlerhaus, Vienna
2004

Moon Light
collaboration with Franz West
Galerie Meyer Kainer, Vienna
2003

Franz West and Friends
curated by Anthony Auerbach
Austrian Cultural Forum, London
2003

La-Bas
curated by Stephan Schmidt-Wulffen
Nexus kunsthalle, Saalfelden
2003

Appartement Franz West
Deichtorhallen, Hamburg
2002

*Parlez Vous Francais,
English Dictionary*
Musée d'art contemporain, Marseille
2002

Plakatentwürfe
collaboration with Franz West
Galerie Gisela Capitain, Cologne
2001

Point of View
Künstlerhauspassage, Vienna
2001

Cultural Sidewalk—Gumpendorf2000
curated by Heidulf Gerngross
Vienna
2000

Aktuellestundentinnenarbeiten
curated by Kasper König
Semperdepot, Vienna
2000

Juana e Juanita
Galería Juana de Aizpuru, Madrid
2000

New Paintings
Museum of Modern Art, Tbilisi
1999

Auction show
Tea House Gallery, Tbilisi
1999

Graduate Group Show
State Academy of Arts, Tbilisi
1999

The Sun Will Rise
Old Gallery, Tbilisi
1999

Bricks and Kicks
Weather, Vienna
1998

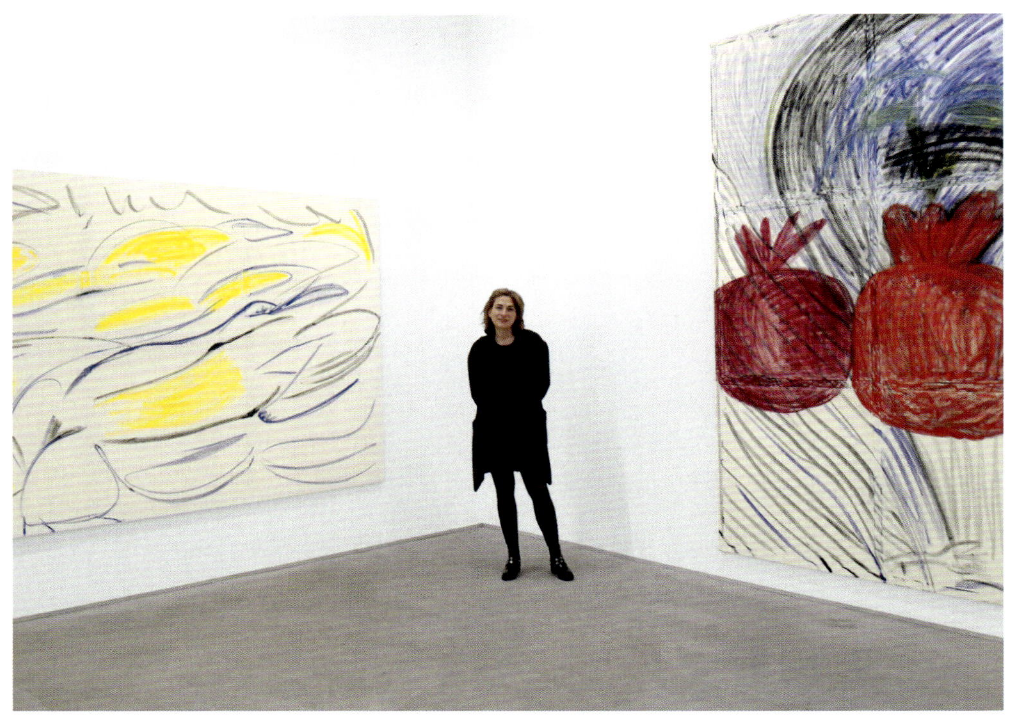

Sirbiladze at *"good enough" is never good enough*,
James Fuentes, New York, 2015

Acknowledgments

Benedikt Ledebur would like to thank David Zwirner
and Lucas Zwirner; Tamuna's parents, Vakhtang Sirbiladze
and Nunu Ghurchumelia; and her sister, Keti Sirbiladze.
For their help, thank you to gallerists Miryam Charim,
James Fuentes, Bill Powers, Eva Presenhuber, and Almine
Rech, and to artists Ugo Rondinone and Francis Ruyter,
who all supported Tamuna. For assistance throughout
this project thank you to Doro Globus, Deirdre O'Dwyer,
Sarah Schrauwen, Molly Stein, Jules Thomson, and
Anne Wehr.

Tamuna Sirbiladze

Published by
David Zwirner Books
529 West 20th Street, 2nd Floor
New York, New York 10011
+1 212 727 2070
davidzwirnerbooks.com

Editors
Benedikt Ledebur, Lucas Zwirner
Project Manager
Anne Wehr
Project Assistant
Molly Stein
Translator
Matthias Goldmann
Copy Editor
Deirdre O'Dwyer

Designer
Sarah Schrauwen
Production Manager
Jules Thomson
Color Separations
VeronaLibri, Verona
Printing
VeronaLibri, Verona

Typeface
Larsseit by Type Dynamic
Paper
GardaMatt Art, 170 gsm

Publication © 2017 David Zwirner Books
All texts © 2017 the authors
All artwork by Tamuna Sirbiladze © Estate of Tamuna Sirbiladze

ISBN 978-1-941701-80-5
LCCN 2017956272

Cover: *Breaking the Waves*, 2015 (detail)
p. 2: *Light Blue, Orange*, 2011 (detail)
p. 13: *Lotus*, 2015 (detail)
p. 49: *Moustage*, 2012 (detail)

Photography

Unless otherwise noted: photos by Nathan Murrell

p. 89: Whitney Museum of American Art, New York.
Purchased with funds from Frances and Sydney Lewis by
exchange, the Mrs. Percy Uris Purchase Fund and the Painting
and Sculpture Committee. Artwork © 2017 The Pollock-
Krasner Foundation / Artists Rights Society (ARS), New York
pp. 93, 135–137, 143: Courtesy Saatchi Gallery, London
pp. 94–102: Photos by Stefan Altenburger Photography,
courtesy Galerie Eva Presenhuber, Zurich
p. 105: 21er Haus, Belvedere, Vienna
pp. 106–117: Photos by Sven Laurent, courtesy Almine Rech
Gallery, Brussels
pp. 118–123: Courtesy James Fuentes, New York
pp. 124–131: Courtesy Half Gallery, New York
pp. 132–133: Photo by Jorit Aust, courtesy Secession, Vienna
pp. 138–141: Courtesy Almine Rech Gallery, Brussels
p. 142: Courtesy Benedikt Ledebur
p. 144: Photo by Lazare West
p. 154: Photo by Benedikt Ledebur
p. 158: Photo by Ingrid Dinter